ENDANGERED
PEOPLES
of Africa and the Middle East

ENDANGERED PEOPLES

of Africa and the Middle East

Struggles to Survive and Thrive

Edited by Robert K. Hitchcock
and Alan J. Osborn

The Greenwood Press
"Endangered Peoples of the World" Series
Barbara Rose Johnston, Series Editor

GREENWOOD PRESS
Westport, Connecticut • London

Library of Congress Cataloging-in-Publication Data

Endangered peoples of Africa and the Middle East : struggles to survive and thrive /
edited by Robert K. Hitchcock and Alan J. Osborn.
    p. cm.—(Greenwood Press "Endangered peoples of the world" series, ISSN 1525–
    1233)
    Includes bibliographical references and index.
    ISBN 0–313–30437–8 (alk. paper)
    1. Ethnology—Middle East. 2. Ethnology—Africa. 3. Minorities—Middle East. 4.
Minorities—Africa. 5. Acculturation. 6. Middle East—Ethnic relations. 7. Africa—
Ethnic relations. I. Hitchcock, Robert K. II. Osborn, Alan J. III. Series.
GN635.N42 E53 2002
305.8'00956—dc21   2001054712

British Library Cataloguing in Publication Data is available.

Library of Congress Catalog Card Number: 2001054712
ISBN: 0–313–30437–8
ISSN: 1525–1233

First published in 2002

Greenwood Press, 88 Post Road West, Westport, CT 06881
An imprint of Greenwood Publishing Group, Inc.
www.greenwood.com

Printed in the United States of America

The paper used in this book complies with the
Permanent Paper Standard issued by the National
Information Standards Organization (Z39.48–1984).

10 9 8 7 6 5 4 3 2 1

Copyright Acknowledgment

The editors and publisher gratefully acknowledge permission for the use of the following
material:

From an interview with Miria Matembe by Dee L. Aker, February 1999, Kampala, Uganda.
Used with permission of Ms. Matembe.

Every reasonable effort has been made to trace the owners of copyright materials in this book,
but in some instances this has proven impossible. The author and publisher will be glad to
receive information leading to more complete acknowledgments in subsequent printings of
the book, and in the meantime extend their apologies for any omissions.

Contents

Contents

Series Foreword

Barbara Rose Johnston

Two hundred thousand years ago our human ancestors gathered plants and hunted animals in the forests and savannas of Africa. By forty thousand years ago, *Homo sapiens sapiens* had developed ways to survive and thrive in every major ecosystem on this planet. Unlike other creatures, whose response to harsh or varied conditions prompted biological change, humans generally relied upon their ingenuity to survive. They fashioned clothing from skins and plant fiber rather than growing thick coats of protective hair. They created innovative ways to live and communicate and thus passed knowledge down to their children. This knowledge, by ten thousand years ago, included the means to cultivate and store food. The ability to provide for lean times allowed humans to settle in larger numbers in villages, towns, and cities where their ideas, values, ways of living, and language grew increasingly complicated and diverse.

This cultural diversity—the multitude of ways of living and communicating knowledge—gave humans an adaptive edge. Other creatures adjusted to change in their environment through biological adaptation (a process that requires thousands of life spans to generate and reproduce a mutation to the level of the population). Humans developed analytical tools to identify and assess change in their environment, to search out or devise new strategies, and to incorporate new strategies throughout their group. Sometimes these cultural adaptations worked; people transformed their way of life, and their population thrived. Other times, these changes produced further complications.

Intensive agricultural techniques, for example, often resulted in increased salts in the soil, decreased soil fertility, and declining crop yields. Food production declined, and people starved. Survivors often moved to new regions to begin again. Throughout human history, migration became the common strategy when innovations failed. Again, in these times, culture was essential to survival.

For the human species, culture is our primary adaptive mechanism. Cultural diversity presents us with opportunities to draw from and build upon a complicated array of views, ideas, and strategies. The Endangered Peoples of the World series celebrates the rich diversity of cultural groups living on our planet and explores how cultural diversity, like biological diversity, is threatened.

Five hundred years ago, as humans entered the age of colonial expansion, there were an estimated twelve to fourteen thousand cultural groups with distinct languages, values, and ways of life. Today, cultural diversity has been reduced by half (an estimated 6,000 to 7,000 groups). This marked decline is due in part to the fact that, historically, isolated peoples had minimal immunity to introduced diseases and little time to develop immunological defenses. Colonizers brought more than ideas, religion, and new economic ways of living. They brought a host of viruses and bacteria—measles, chicken pox, small pox, the common cold. These diseases swept through "new" worlds at epidemic levels and wiped out entire nations. Imperialist expansion and war further decimated original, or "indigenous," populations.

Today's cultural diversity is further threatened by the biodegenerative conditions of nature. Our biophysical world's deterioration is evidenced by growing deserts; decreasing forests; declining fisheries; poisoned food, water, and air; and climatic extremes and weather events such as floods, hurricanes, and droughts. These degenerative conditions challenge our survival skills, often rendering customary knowledge and traditions ineffective.

Cultural diversity is also threatened by unparalleled transformations in human relations. Isolation is no longer the norm. Small groups continually interact and are subsumed by larger cultural, political, and economic groups of national and global dimensions. The rapid pace of change in population, technology, and political economy leaves little time to develop sustainable responses and adjust to changing conditions.

Across the world cultural groups are struggling to maintain a sense of unique identity while interpreting and assimilating an overwhelming flow of new ideas, ways of living, economies, values, and languages. As suggested in some chapters in this series, cultural groups confront, embrace, adapt, and transform these external forces in ways that allow them to survive and thrive. However, in far too many cases, cultural groups lack the time and means to adjust and change. Rather, they struggle to retain the right to simply exist as other, more powerful peoples seize their land and resources and "cleanse" the countryside of their presence.

Efforts to gain control of land, labor, and resources of politically and/or geographically peripheral peoples are justified and legitimized by ethnocentric notions: the beliefs that the values, traditions, and behavior of your own cultural group are superior and that other groups are biologically, culturally, and socially inferior. These notions are produced and reproduced in conversation, curriculum, public speeches, articles, television coverage, and other communication forums. Ethnocentrism is reflected in a language of debasement that serves to dehumanize (the marginal peoples are considered sub-human: primitive, backward, ignorant people that "live like animals"). The pervasiveness of this discourse in the everyday language can eventually destroy the self-esteem and sense of worth of marginal groups and reduce their motivation to control their destiny.

Thus, vulnerability to threats from the biophysical and social realms is a factor of social relations. Human action and a history of social inequity leave some people more vulnerable than others. This vulnerability results in ethnocide (loss of a way of life), ecocide (destruction of the environment), and genocide (death of an entire group of people).

The Endangered Peoples of the World series samples cultural diversity in different regions of the world, examines the varied threats to cultural survival, and explores some of the ways people are adjusting and responding to threats of ethnocide, ecocide, and genocide. Each volume in the series covers the peoples, problems, and responses characteristic of a major region of the world: the Arctic, Europe, North America, Latin America, Africa and the Middle East, Central and South Asia, Southeast and East Asia, and Oceania. Each volume includes an introductory essay authored by the volume editor and fifteen or so chapters, each featuring a different cultural group whose customs, problems, and responses represent a sampling of conditions typical of the region. Chapter content is organized into five sections: Cultural Overview (people, setting, traditional subsistence strategies, social and political organization, religion and world view), Threats to Survival (demographic trends, current events and conditions, environmental crisis, sociocultural crisis), Response: Struggles to Survive Culturally (indicating the variety of efforts to respond to threats), Food for Thought (a brief summary of the issues raised by the case and some provocative questions that can be used to structure class discussion or organize a research paper), and a Resource Guide (major accessible published sources, films and videos, WWW sites, and organizations). Many chapters are authored or coauthored by members of the featured group, and all chapters include liberal use of a "local voice" to present the group's own views on its history, current problems, strategies, and thoughts of the future.

Collectively, the series contains some 120 case-specific examples of cultural groups struggling to survive and thrive in a culturally diverse world. Many of the chapters in this global sampling depict the experiences of indigenous peoples and ethnic minorities who, until recently, sustained their customary way of life in the isolated regions of the world. Threats to survival are often linked to external efforts to develop the natural resources of the previously isolated region. The development context is often one of co-optation of traditionally held lands and resources with little or no recognition of resident peoples' rights and little or no compensation for their subsequent environmental health problems. New ideas, values, technologies, economies, and languages accompany the development process and, over time, may even replace traditional ways of being.

Cultural survival, however, is not solely a concern of indigenous peoples. Indeed, in many parts of the world the term "indigenous" has little relevance, as all peoples are native to the region. Thus, in this series, we define cultural groups in the broadest of terms. We examine threats to survival and the variety of responses of ethnic minorities, as well as national cultures, whose traditions are challenged and undermined by global transformations.

The dominant theme that emerges from this sampling is that humans struggle with serious and life-threatening problems tied to larger global forces, and yet, despite huge differences in power levels between local communities and global institutions and structures, people are crafting and developing new ways of being. This series demonstrates that culture is not a static set of meanings, values, and behaviors; it is a flexible, resilient tool that has historically provided humans with the means to adapt, adjust, survive, and at times, thrive. Thus, we see "endangered" peoples confronting and responding to threats in ways that reshape and transform their values, relationships, and behavior.

Emerging from this transformative process are new forms of cultural identity, new strategies for living, and new means and opportunities to communicate. These changes represent new threats to cultural identity and autonomy but also new challenges to the forces that dominate and endanger lives.

Introduction

Robert K. Hitchcock and Alan J. Osborn

Endangered Peoples of Africa and the Middle East: Struggles to Survive and Thrive is about human populations residing in Africa and the Middle East, a diverse region that is connected geographically, culturally, and historically. The African continent is vast and covers 11.7 million square miles, or an area slightly larger than the combined area of the United States and South America (Table 1). Today, the African continent is home to some 771 million people distributed within fifty-four separate countries. Of the world's continents, Africa is by far the most diverse culturally. In Sudan, for example, there are over 200 ethnic groups speaking some 134 languages, while in Nigeria there are some 600 or more ethnic groups who speak as many as 505 different languages.

The Middle East, for purposes of this volume, is taken to include fifteen countries, ranging from Afghanistan in the east to Turkey and Syria in the west. Together, these countries cover a total of 2,704,730 square miles and support a population of 254,428,629 (Table 2). The Middle East includes large, petroleum-rich countries (e.g., Iraq, Iran, Saudi Arabia) and small countries such as Bahrain (an island monarchy) and a federation of seven small monarchies (the United Arab Emirates).

The Middle East is characterized by the predominance of the religion of Islam, and it is identified in part by the presence of Arabic-speaking peoples as well as non-Arab peoples (e.g., those in Iran, Turkey, and Israel). Some parts of the Middle East, like Africa, are coping with conflict, insecurity, and massive economic and political change. In the Middle East in the year 2001, there were a number of ongoing conflicts, including Turkey and Iraq versus the Kurds, the Iraqi government under Saddam Hussein versus the Shi'ite Muslim minority in southern Iraq, and Israel versus the Palestinians

Table 1
Country Size, Population, and Gross National Product Per Capita for Africa

Name of Country	Size (sq mi)	Population 2000 (millions)	Type of Government	Gross National Product Per Capita (US$; 1998)
Algeria	919,590	31.5	republic	4,595
Angola	481,351	12.9	nominally a multiparty democracy	999
Benin	43,483	6.1	republic under multiparty democratic rule	857
Botswana	231,803	1.6	parliamentary republic	5,796
Burkina Faso	105,869	11.9	parliamentary	866
Burundi	4,149	6.7	republic	561
Cameroon	183,568	15.1	unitary republic; multiparty presidential	1,395
Cape Verde	1,556	0.428	republic	3,192
Central African Republic	240,534	3.6	republic	1,395
Chad	495,755	7.7	republic	843
Comoros	838	0.694	independent republic	1,400
Congo	132,047	2.9	republic	846
Cote D'Ivoire	124,503	14.8	republic; multiparty presidential regime	1,484
Democratic Republic of Congo	905,568	51.7	dictatorship	733
Djibouti	8,494	0.638	republic	—
Egypt	386,662	68.5	republic	3,146
Eritrea	46,842	3.9	transitional government	984
Ethiopia	471,778	62.6	federal republic	566
Gabon	103,348	1.2	republic; multiparty presidential regime	5,615
The Gambia	4,363	1.30	republic under multiparty democratic rule	1,428
Ghana	92,101	20.2	constitutional democracy	1,735
Guinea	10,830	7.4	republic	1,722

2

Table 1 (*continued*)

Name of Country	Size (sq mi)	Population 2000 (millions)	Type of Government	Gross National Product Per Capita (US$; 1998)
Guinea-Bissau	13,946	1.2	republic, multiparty since mid-1991	573
Kenya	224,962	30.1	republic	964
Lesotho	11,718	2.2	parliamentary constitutional monarchy	2,194
Liberia	43,000	3.2	republic	—
Libyan Arab Jamahirya	679,362	5.6	republic	—
Madagascar	226,657	15.9	republic	741
Malawi	45,745	10.9	multiparty democracy	551
Maldives	116	0.286	republic	3,436
Mali	478,767	11.2	republic	673
Mauritania	397,955	2.7	republic	1,500
Mauritius	718	1.2	parliamentary democracy	8,236
Morocco	172,414	28.4	constitutional monarchy	3,188
Mozambique	309,496	19.7	republic	740
Namibia	318,260	1.7	republic	5,280
Niger	489,191	10.7	republic	729
Nigeria	356,670	111.5	republic transitioning from military to civilian	740
Reunion	969	0.699	overseas department of France	—
Rwanda	10,170	7.7	republic; presidential, multiparty system	—
Senegal	75,749	9.5	republic under multiparty democratic rule	1,297
Seychelles	67	0.082	republic	6,420
Sierra Leone	27,699	4.9	constitutional democracy	445
Somalia	246,202	10.1	parliamentary	—
South Africa	471,446	40.4	republic	8,296
Sudan	967,499	29.5	transitional—ruling military junta took power	1,240

Table 1 (*continued*)

Name of Country	Size (sq mi)	Population 2000 (millions)	Type of Government	Gross National Product Per Capita (US$; 1998)
Swaziland	6,702	1.008	monarchy; independent member of Commonwealth	4,195
Tanzania	364,901	33.5	republic	483
Togo	21,928	4.6	republic under transition to multiparty democratic rule	1,352
Tunisia	63,170	9.6	republic	5,169
Uganda	91,136	21.8	republic	1,072
Western Sahara	102,703	0.292	legal status of territory and question of sovereignty unresolved	—
Zambia	290,584	9.2	republic	678
Zimbabwe	150,804	11.7	parliamentary democracy	2,489

Source: Data from United Nations Population Fund 2000, www.unfpa.org/swp/2000; Population Reference Bureau, *www.prb.org/pubs/wpds2000*; CIA The World Fact Book 2001, www.odci.gov/cia/publications/factbook/.

in a conflict that began late in 2000 known as the Al-Aqsa Intifada. Conflicts within Afghanistan involving Soviet troops and U.S.-backed Mujahedeen (holy warriors) continued for ten years (1979–1989). Following the September 11, 2001 attacks upon the Pentagon in Washington, D.C., and World Trade buildings in New York City, the United States and allied forces bombed Taliban forces and sent in specially trained troops to search for Osama Bin Laden. At this time, this military action continues.

The Middle East's past also demonstrates evidence of major changes over time: humankind's first cities, some of them surrounded by fortifications to protect the inhabitants from opponents; the world's earliest systems of writing and record keeping; highly organized societies that were as sophisticated ritually as they were socially and politically; and complex and wide-ranging trading systems involving the exchange of minerals, food, wine, pottery, and other products. The boundaries on the map of the Middle East have been redrawn numerous times, and the domestic political landscape has been modified in subtle and not-so-subtle ways. The fifteen contemporary countries of the Middle East contain a diverse set of peoples, ranging from small-scale tribal societies such as the various Bedouin groups who occupy Saudi Arabia, Iraq, Israel, the West Bank, and the Sinai (now part of Egypt) to large-scale populations such as the Kurds who number

Table 2
Country Size, Population, and Gross National Product Per Capita for Middle East

Name of Country	Size (sq mi)	Population 2000 (millions)	Type of Government	Gross National Product Per Capita (US$; 1998)
Afghanistan	250,000	22.7	Theocratic republic	—
Bahrain	262	0.691	Monarchy	—
Iran	636,293	67.7	Theocratic republic	5,121
Iraq	167,924	23.1	Military regime	—
Israel	7,847	6.2	Parliamentary democracy	16,861
Palestinian Territory	2,426	3.1	Israeli-Palestinian Interim Agreement	1,560
Jordan	36,193	6.7	Constitutional monarchy	2,615
Kuwait	6,880	2.0	Constitutional monarchy	—
Lebanon	4,035	3.3	Parliamentary republic	4,144
Oman	82,031	2.5	Monarchy	—
Qatar	4,247	0.591	Monarchy	—
Saudi Arabia	900,004	21.6	Monarchy	10,498
Syrian Arab Republic	71,494	16.1	Military regime, republic	2,702
Turkey	301,384	66.6	Parliamentary republic	6,594
United Arab Emirates	32,000	2.4	Federation of small monarchies (7)	18,871
Yemen	203,850	18.1	Parliamentary republic	658

Source: Data from United Nations Population Fund 2000, www.unfpa.org/swp/2000; Population Reference Bureau, *www.prb.org/pubs/wpds2000*; CIA The World Fact Book 2001, www.odci.gov/cia/publications/factbook/.

some 20 million and are found in six countries and engaged in efforts to promote their cultural identity and gain greater control over decision making about their futures.

The Kurds and the Palestinians, among other Middle Eastern populations, consider themselves nations—groups who see themselves as "one people" on the basis of common ancestry, history, customs, language, institutions, territory, and religion.[1] In many ways, the Kurds and Palestinians lost out in the rush toward state formation in the Middle East in the twentieth century. This process also occurred in the cases of a number of minority populations in the region such as the Baluch in Iran and Afghanistan and the Alawis in Syria.

ETHNICITY AND IDENTITY

As this volume will demonstrate, cultures, societies, and ethnic groups appear, persist, and change as a consequence of local, regional, and global conditions. Various interrelated components of culture such as demography, economy, technology, political organization, and religion undergo numerous changes, some of them subtle, others dramatic, and still others massive and wrenching.

In order to understand the dramatic transformations that are happening in Africa and the Middle East, we need to examine briefly the variable nature of culture as a complex system that enables human populations to respond to a multitude of problems. These problems may involve our own biology (e.g., human diseases such as malaria, influenza, tuberculosis, and diabetes) or the natural environment (e.g., drought, floods, or deforestation, and competition or cooperation with other human populations).

Current world news seems to be filled with accounts of widespread conflict in Africa and the Middle East. It is very important, therefore, that we understand what ethnic groups are, how they form, and what their benefits and costs are for the peoples of Africa and the Middle East. For example, ethnic boundaries can be both inclusive and exclusive with respect to the accessibility of scarce or limited resources such as arable land, water, wildlife and livestock, jobs, or other forms of wealth. Although the news media usually makes passing reference to "age-old political and/or religious" disputes, many ethnic group conflicts throughout Africa and the Middle East result in part from human competition over scarce resources. Disputes and acts of aggression begin at these "fault lines" of economic disparity that are defined, in part, by ethnic distinctions. Anthropologists tell us that ethnic groups are collective groups of people who believe that they share a common ancestry. Membership in a common ethnic group frequently is defined on the basis of shared language, religion, dress (including body ornamentation), and food habits. Ethnic groups are often assumed to share cultural values, to be biologically self-perpetuating, and to define themselves (and to be defined by others) as a distinctive group.

Ethnic group members sometimes categorize themselves in terms of "we" versus "them." Members of such ethnic groups interact and communicate with one another by means of shared conventions, codes, symbols, and behavior patterns. In such instances, members of an ethnic group share actual genetic ties—they are differentially related to one another, depending on the total number of people included within the group.

Ethnic groups may also be defined from the "outside." Frequently, ethnic distinctions have been made by colonial governments. For bureaucratic purposes, colonizing states may arbitrarily split or lump indigenous populations into new groups. Such administrative and economic distinctions crosscut existing genetic, social, linguistic, religious, and cultural values in the newly conquered or incorporated lands. Frequently, ethnic affiliation is quite fluid. People certainly interact on both short-term and long-term bases across boundaries established by differences in physical appearance, genetic affiliation(s), food ways, cultural values, and/or religion(s). Members of some ethnic groups may be multilingual and are able to interact successfully across language boundaries. Ethnic groups may emphasize their "ethnicity" in order to maintain cooperative ties so that they can successfully compete in various economic and social situations. They may also manipulate their ethnic identities for their own purposes in seeking to achieve their various goals.

AFRICA AND THE MIDDLE EAST

For many people, Africa and the Middle East generate kaleidoscopic images of vast deserts, sinuous rivers, mist-shrouded mountains, rocky hills, and expansive grasslands. These spectacular, varied landscapes have captivated the imagination and interest of innumerable outsiders and insiders. For many people, Africa and the Middle East represent an alluring, yet dangerous, region—a set of places where the explorer, adventurer, fortune hunter, missionary, or colonist could quite easily become ill or die as the result of a thousand causes. For Africans and Middle Easterners themselves, the many challenges of the environments in which they reside pose risks, but they also present opportunities.

For the peoples of present-day Africa and the Middle East, the immense region represents a homeland that has sustained their ancestors and their families for millennia. The natural resources of this land continue to sustain the primary needs for many of the current generation. The people of Africa and the Middle East have relied heavily upon the support provided by their close and distant kin and upon assistance provided by governments, international agencies, churches, and nongovernment organizations. Approximately 36 percent of Africans live in cities, compared to a world average of 46 percent. In the Middle East, it is estimated that 60 percent of the population will be residing in cities by 2010.[2] A significant percentage of Africa's people are peasant farmers who live and work in rural areas and who supplement their income through various kinds of small-scale industries and income-generating activities. Middle Easterners, like Africans, often combine income-generating activities, engaging in trade and wage labor in addition to engaging, in many cases, in farming or herding.

Africa is the birthplace for humankind. Between 4 and 5 million years ago, an assortment of relatively large-brained, bipedal or upright hominids (humanlike creatures) began to expand their ranges along the margins of the grasslands and woodlands of eastern and southern Africa. For the next 4 million years, these early hominids would evolve biologically and culturally, and they would fill the entire continent and ultimately colonize the earth. As they did so, there were changes in the physical and cultural characteristics of the prehuman and human populations. It is believed by some that the ancestors of all modern humans, *Homo sapiens sapiens*, were found in Africa and that they gave rise to virtually all of the more than 6 billion people on the planet today. These were hunting and gathering populations who lived on the continent for millions of years and in some cases continue to do so in places such as the savannas of eastern and southern Africa and the rain forests of central Africa. Many of the continent's hunter-gatherers would shift to becoming settled villagers, domesticate a number of plants and animals, irrigate arid lands, develop iron metallurgy, travel and trade widely, and diversify their sociopolitical systems into numerous tribes, chiefdoms, states, and in some instances, empires.

The survival strategies of Africans and Middle Eastern peoples today are extremely variable, ranging from dryland and irrigated agriculture to livestock keeping (pastoralism) and from rural economic activities to wage labor in urban industries. Many people in the region combine work in what is known as the formal sector of the economy, in which people are provided wages in exchange for their services, with work in the informal sector, taking part, for example, in craft manufacture and the manufacture and sale of beer or palm wine to other people, as can be seen, for example, in some societies in West Africa. Some 50 million people in Africa and the Middle East, such as the Somali of the Horn of Africa and the Qashqa'i of Iran, as discussed in this volume, are herders of livestock and small stock (the latter category includes sheep and goats). Some 1.4 million Africans are foragers or part-time foragers who depend to a significant extent on wild plants and animals, as can be seen, for example, among the Okavango Delta peoples in northern Botswana (see Chapter 8). Foraging as a way of life may be rare, but a substantial number of people in Africa and the Middle East supplement their incomes through the collection of wild resources (e.g., medicinal plants and firewood).

The people of Africa speak more than 2,011—or 30 percent—of the world's 6,703 distinct languages.[3] A recent anthropological study of West African language diversity demonstrates that more people make use of a common language over larger areas in geographical regions characterized by greater resource risk. Ecological risks in West Africa are generated by limited, sporadic rainfall and resulting unpredictability of crop production.

African peoples within this region lessen the risks of food scarcity by involving themselves in larger and larger exchange or markets systems. Economic exchange is, then, mediated by means of a shared language.[4]

Many ethnic groups form extremely valuable economic ties that prove to be mutually beneficial. For example, the pastoral Fulani and their agricultural neighbors the Hausa in Nigeria, West Africa, have established such economic interdependence or symbiosis (mutual dependency). The Fulani and the Hausa speak different languages. The Fulani herd cattle and move about the savanna or grasslands in search of forage for their animals. Their lives are dictated primarily by the needs of their livestock. Between May and October, the Fulani follow the rains and resulting grasslands as they move northward toward the arid frontier near the Sahara Desert. They attempt to move their herds along the expanding front once the rains begin. Rains bring welcomed abundance of forage and drinking water for their cattle. The wet season, however, also brings tsetse flies (*Glossina* spp., carriers of human sleeping sickness and cattle-threatening trypanosomiasis), as well as mosquitoes (carriers of debilitating or life-threatening malaria). Once the rains cease and dry conditions return to the region, the Fulani and their cattle herds move southward.[5]

Seasonal movements of the Fulani and their cattle are responses to cyclical environmental changes. Their movements are also carefully coordinated with Hausa peoples who also inhabit this environment. Trade forms an important component of these interethnic relationships. The pastoral Fulani, then, trade milk, butter, and meat to the sedentary Hausa farmers for agricultural crops (bulrush millet, maize, peanuts, rice, sweet potatoes), salt, and metal tools. Furthermore, a very significant component of their symbiotic relationship involves Fulani livestock and Hausa farm fields. Fulani cattle fertilize Hausa fields as they graze on remnant crops following the harvest. In this case, we can see that the specialized economic roles of the Fulani and the Hausa are effectively combined into a multiethnic economic system that provides a relatively long-term, sustainable way of life for these people in western Africa.

In the recent past, Africa has experienced a number of devastating natural disasters including droughts, floods, and losses of wildlife and livestock. Droughts occur cyclically every three to five and six to eight years in northern Ethiopia and about every eight to ten years for the entire country. Scientists have learned that the El Niño Southern Oscillations (ENSO) and corresponding La Niña events (temperature changes in the Pacific Ocean that occur on a periodic basis) play a very central role in monsoonal rains and droughts that impact eastern and southern Africa. For example, between 70 and 85 percent of the floodwaters that have usually inundated Egypt's rich alluvial floodplains each year for the last six to seven millennia originate in the Ethiopian highlands. Rainfall in the highlands are, in turn, driven by the monsoons in the Indian Ocean to the east. Variations in water flow in the Nile at Aswan in Egypt are correlated with El Niño Southern Oscillations or warming trends in the ocean waters in the Pacific Ocean. Variation in the timing and the amount of flooding in the lower Nile Basin can now be predicted about one year in advance. Such important meteorological predictions will provide an extremely valuable tool for managing the critical water within the Nile Basin in eastern Africa and Egypt, a region that includes ten countries and covers a huge area—3,443,670 square miles.

At the other extreme, certain regions of Africa have experienced catastrophic floods. This was the case, for example, in areas along the Limpopo River in southern Mozambique in the January–March period 2000 and, more recently, in 2001 along the Zambezi River in central Mozambique. The 2000 Limpopo floods killed 929 people, displaced 733,000 others, and destroyed $1 billion in crops and property. More than 1,930 square miles of the coastal lowlands were covered with floodwaters, affecting biological productivity and farming potential. Floods, droughts, and other natural disasters have wreaked havoc in many parts of Africa, something that has led to initiatives to predict these kinds of problems.

Drought relief, rehabilitation, and labor-based development programs have helped in Africa and the Middle East after natural and human disasters. Morbidity (illness) rates among refugees and internally displaced people are declining in many areas as a result of better service provision by international agencies, governments, and nongovernmental organizations (NGOs). In the Republic of Botswana, not a single life was lost to starvation during the severe drought of the early 1990s, thanks to the effective nutritional and health surveillance and relief programs that were established there. Refugee and drought relief programs in central Africa and the Horn also served to save the lives of tens of thousands of people and to facilitate a process whereby at least some of them have been able to reestablish their economic systems, as can be seen, for example, in the cases of Eritrea and Ethiopia, as discussed in Chapter 4 by Lucia Ann McSpadden.

POPULATION ISSUES

Of the world's continents Africa has the highest rate of population growth. The rate of population increase equals 2.5 percent per year, which means that the total population of Africa will double by the year 2028. Forty-three percent of Africa's total population are under fifteen years of age, whereas the world average, according to the United Nations, is 31 percent. The percentage of the population below age fifteen in the Middle East is 40 percent.[6] In the 1960s, the Middle East had the world's highest population growth rate, but since about 1970, fertility levels have been declining. In a number of African and Middle Eastern countries, population expansion rates are outstripping food production. Competition between various kinds of land uses, such as agriculture and livestock keeping, is on the increase. Some people in Africa and the Middle East are moving into more marginal habitats in an effort to earn a living via agriculture and pastoralism, a process that is leading to higher rates of deforestation (the loss of forests) and desertification (the spread of deserts due to habitat losses as a result of overutilization by people and their animals and soil erosion, which leads to lower agricultural productivity). The losses of vegetation cover and soil erosion lead to higher soil temperatures, a process that, in turn, can lead to localized reductions in rainfall. These processes can contribute to a decline in the water table, thus making access to groundwater, crucial to the economic well-being of a substantial number of the region's people, more problematic.

In February 1994, journalist Robert Kaplan described what he saw as "the coming anarchy": overpopulation, scarcity, conflict, environmental degradation, and disease, which were, he argued, rapidly destroying the social fabric of our planet.[7] Nowhere were these factors more evident than on the continent of Africa. Lawlessness was far more significant in Africa, in Kaplan's estimation, than its experiments in democracy. The Food and Agriculture Organization (FAO) and the World Food Program (WFP) of the United Nations have pointed out that hunger is a major problem in Africa, with 1 person in 3 chronically undernourished and over 291 million people, more than the population of the United States in 2000, living on less than $1 a day. It is estimated that 22 percent of the population of Africa will be malnourished in 2015 unless steps are taken to alleviate hunger and poverty there.[8]

The United Nations International Conference on Population and Development (ICPD), held in Cairo, Egypt, in September 1994, explicitly linked population, environment, and development. For our purposes here, we will take *development* to mean the process whereby nations improve the well-being of their citizens. Africans and Middle Easterners see development and a healthy environment as basic human rights. Many people in the region also see population issues as crucial concerns of both individuals and communities. While they wish to retain the right to make their own choices about the numbers of children they have, they realize that large families may have as many costs as they do benefits. High rates of economic growth, while having positive impacts on standards of living, do pose risks for the environment. More and more efforts are being invested in the construction of large-scale urban, agricultural, and water development projects; hundreds of thousands of people in Africa and the Middle East (e.g., in Turkey) are being relocated to areas where they live in higher densities and place greater pressure on resources than they did before.

CONFLICTS AND THEIR CAUSES

The peoples of Africa and the Middle East have experienced substantial numbers of human conflicts, particularly since the colonial expansion of European states during the 1800s. Millions of African people were forcibly removed from their homes and sold into slavery in Brazil, the Caribbean, and the southeastern United States. Between 1700 and 1800, more than 5.5 million Africans were transported to the Western Hemisphere. Thirty-three percent of the slaves went to Brazil, 50 percent went to the Caribbean, and 6 percent were enslaved within what is now the United States.[9]

Africa and the Middle East served as staging grounds for many conflicts during both World War I and World War II, as well as the Cold War that involved the United States, the former Soviet Union, and their allies. The Cold War had a destabilizing and devastating effect upon many of the region's countries such as Angola, Somalia, and what is now the Democratic Republic of Congo (formerly Zaire). During this time, Africa and the Middle East constituted one of the most militarized regions of the world. Africa has experienced more than thirty wars in the past three decades. In 1996, for example, wars engulfed fourteen of Africa's fifty-four countries; these wars produced more than 8 million refugees. In 1999, wars ripped through more than twenty countries including Algeria, Angola, Chad, the Democratic Republic of Congo, Ethiopia, Eritrea, Namibia, Rwanda, Sudan, Uganda, and Zimbabwe. Many of these recent conflicts have specifically targeted civilian populations in the Great Lakes region of Africa in the early to mid-1990s, as well as in Sierra Leone and Sudan during the late 1990s and into the new millennium. Sudan, at the end of 1999, had 4 million people who were internally displaced, the largest internally displaced population in the world.[10]

In 1997, twenty-one of the world's poorest thirty countries were in Africa. Many of the valuable economic resources in Africa are controlled by the elite, as well as by foreign multinational corporations. The benefits of Africa's wealth are rarely enjoyed by the people themselves, especially by the poor. In the mid-1990s, Africa's combined external debt equaled U.S.$313 billion, a figure that represented 235 percent of its export income and 83 percent of its gross domestic product.[11] Africa also lacks any appreciable financial capital from countries outside the continent, though it does receive assistance from international organizations and multilateral development banks such as the United Nations, the World Bank, and the International Development Association (IDA).

The conflicts throughout Africa and the Middle East waste significant and vital economic resources. Some of the poorest countries in the region spend the most money on weapons purchases. In 1999 Eritrea expended more than 36 percent of its gross national product on weapons. Iraq spent an even greater percentage of its gross national product on weapons and the military.

African countries in general spent more than U.S.$8 billion in 1999.[12] Significant investments were made by some countries and rebel groups in antipersonnel weapons including land mines. Some countries in Africa, such as Angola, Mozambique, Ethiopia, and Somalia, have so many land mines scattered across them that it is difficult for their populations to work in the fields or even to walk on public roads without risk. Substantial sums of money have to be channeled into land mine clearance and into assisting people who have been injured and lost limbs from land mine explosions.

The African continent is essentially an ancient plateau composed primarily of low-grade iron. This landmass, however, is crosscut or punctuated by veins and volcanic pipes that are filled with various minerals (gold, copper, iron, mica, quartz, chrome, bauxite [aluminum ore], cobalt, zinc, and manganese), as well as precious gemstones (diamonds). Africa supplies 17 percent, 70 percent, and 80 percent of the world's copper, gold, and diamonds, respectively.

In addition, African oil has recently become more important on the world market, adding to the already substantial amount of oil coming out of Middle Eastern countries such as Saudi Arabia, Kuwait, Iraq, and Iran. Africa currently possesses roughly 7 percent of the world's proved reserves, or 75.4 billion barrels. A great deal of this oil is to be obtained from offshore deposits along Africa's western coasts that stretch from Nigeria to Angola. Forty-four major refineries in twenty-five countries produce 3,000 barrels per day, or 4 percent of the world's total daily oil product.[13] Wealth derived from such rich natural resources can potentially mean improved quality of life for many Africans. Equatorial Guinea, for example, earned $100 million in 1997 from crude oil production from Mobil Oil Corporation. Western nations including the United States, France, and Britain have worked very hard to establish and to maintain strong diplomatic, economic, and in some cases, military ties to African countries like Equatorial Guinea, Nigeria, Gabon, Cameroon, and Angola, as well as the Congo Republic. It is likely that the United States will grow to depend more and more heavily upon Angola and Nigeria for their oil. In 1998, Angola supplied roughly 10 percent of the U.S. demand for oil.[14]

More than three decades of oil production by Shell Oil in Nigeria have resulted in tremendous profits for both the oil companies (Shell, Mobil, Agipo, and Elf-Aquitaine) and Nigerian government officials. Nigeria produces nearly 2 million barrels of oil per day and remains one of the world's largest producers.[15] Nigeria's oil fields have probably generated several hundred billion (U.S.) dollars during the past thirty to forty years. Oil exploration, drilling, and spills have wreaked considerable environmental damage on the Niger Delta region of Nigeria and have exacerbated social tensions there, especially with the Ogoni, the indigenous people of the Niger Delta region, as described in Chapter 7 by A. Olu Oyinlade and Jeffrey M. Vincent. Farmlands have been despoiled, drinking water has been contaminated, and many fish populations have been decimated. In addition, oil-related development has led to increased landlessness, inflation, prostitution, and illegitimate children. In certain cases, the oil companies have been charged with destabilizing local communities through bribes and alleged killings of members of the opposition. Nigeria's tremendous oil wealth has only served to worsen the quality of life for its people.[16]

Oil is most probably now at the root of the eighteen-year-long civil war in Sudan. The government of Sudan and Canadian-based Talisman Energy have recently completed a 994-mile pipeline from Bentiu in the Sudd region of the south with Port Sudan on the Red Sea. Sudan's exportation of crude oil has recently increased very dramatically to more than 200,000 barrels per day. Annual oil revenues for the Sudanese government have now reached U.S.$1.8 billion and are expected to top U.S.$2 billion in 2001. Recent developments of Sudan's oil fields in the south of the country have been constructed and financed by American, Chinese, Malaysian, and Canadian companies.[17] There is little doubt that the Sudanese government has used oil revenues to finance genocidal activities that have been directed toward ethnic groups like the Nuba, Dinka, Nuer, and Shilluk in central and southern Sudan (for a discussion of the difficulties faced by people in Sudan, see Chapter 6 on the Nuba by Mona A. Mohamed and Margaret Fisher).

Recently, greater attention has been given to the international political significance of rich oil and gas reserves in the Caucasus region—particularly in the Caspian Basin (Azerbaijan, Kazakhstan, Turkmenistan, and Uzbekistan). Maximum estimates for this region equal 2000 billion barrels of oil and 565 to 665 trillion cubic feet (tcf) of natural gas.[18] Various countries and multinational energy and engineering companies from the United States, Britain, Russia, Turkey, Iran, Pakistan, and China are actively competing for controlling interests in a number of multibillion-dollar pipelines that will crisscross the Caucasus region.[19] There is reason to believe that the United States had already planned to establish a military presence in this region—especially within Afghanistan—prior to the attacks on New York City and Washington, D.C.[20] Afghanistan is not considered to be rich in oil and gas but it does provide a corridor for a 1,000-mile-long, 48-inch diameter pipeline that will carry more than 1 million barrels of oil per day. Interestingly, U.S.-based Unocal Corporation holds more than 46 percent of the interests in the international consortium of energy and engineering companies involved in planning this enormous pipeline system known as the Central Asian Oil Pipeline Project.[21] Once again, we find that access to, and control of, critical energy resources underlie many of the world's current conflicts.

Africa's wealth in diamonds has had even more devastating impacts on its people. Each year more than U.S.$50 billion is spent by the world's wealthy on diamond jewelry, and more than 65 percent of this figure is spent within the United States. Generally, only 5 to 10 percent of the world's diamonds are gem quality. Significantly, between 70 and 80 percent of the world's gem-quality diamonds are found in Angola.[22] Diamonds from Angola are sold to finance a decade-long, very complex war that has killed 500,000 people, mostly civilians. During the 1990s, this war involved fighting between a Socialist government and UNITA (Uniao National para a Independência Total de Angola). Many gem-quality diamonds from Angola are easily mined, and a great deal of the mining is carried out illegally. These "conflict diamonds" or "blood diamonds" are laundered through a number of neighboring countries, for example, Liberia, Sierra Leone, and Ivory Coast, en route to international diamond dealers in Israel, Belgium, Canada, and the United States. Many diamond companies throughout the world—including De Beers, Almazy Rossii-Sakha, Steinmetz, and Oderbrecht—have purchased gem-quality diamonds from Angolan Armed Forces (FAA) generals and through officials within the Empresa Nacional de Diamantes de Angola (ENDIMA) and UNITA, the guerrilla group contending for power in Angola that is led by Jonas Savimbi. The wealth represented by such sales amounted to U.S.$1 billion in 1996–1997 to the De Beers Company alone.

In 1999, it was believed that as much as U.S.$2 billion was obtained by government leaders and rebel forces in Sierra Leone from the sale of conflict diamonds. In Sierra Leone, rebel forces and their leaders armed with machetes have brutally maimed infants, children, and women; they have killed 75,000 civilians; and they have forced 460,000 people to flee into nearby countries. Conflict diamonds have provided a great deal of money for purchasing weapons and supplying rebel forces. Diamond industry officials estimate that 4 percent of the world's diamonds are blood diamonds—those sold on the market to raise funds to underwrite warfare and rebellion.[23] Efforts by the international community to prevent the sale of blood diamonds potentially could have impacts on the legal diamond trade, and such countries as Botswana, which are highly dependent on diamonds for their gross national product, could be affected negatively. The Republic of Botswana, for its part, uses a significant portion of its diamond revenues to finance an efficient health, education, and welfare system, some of which is aimed at combating HIV/AIDS, poverty, and other critical problems facing the country.

Given these examples, it would appear that one of the most horrific threats to people throughout the world may come from within and outside of one's culture simultaneously. In Sudan, the Democratic Republic of Congo, Nigeria, Angola, and Sierra Leone the atrocities of forced migration, ethnic cleansing, looting, torture, rape, starvation, and brutal murder are carried out against one's own people due to voracious human greed. These atrocities, in turn, are directly attributable to the profit motives of individuals, governments, and multinational companies that wish to sell death and to purchase precious resources such as oil, gold, diamonds, emeralds, and exotic timber.

According to representatives of some African and Middle Eastern groups who are at risk from the actions of governments and companies who have spoken at international forums such as the Human Rights Commission of the United Nations in Geneva, individuals and communities are having to cope with mass killings, arbitrary executions, torture, mental and physical mistreatment, arrests and detentions without trial, forced sterilization, involuntary relocation, destruction of their subsistence base, and the taking of children from their families. In some cases, these actions have been described as genocidal—the planned, systematic destruction of a people on the basis of who they are—much as occurred during the Holocaust in Europe in World War II. On the one hand, there is physical genocide, the destruction of indigenous peoples themselves; and on the other, there is cultural genocide or ethnocide, the destruction of a group's culture.

In Africa and the Middle East at the end of the second millennium, there were examples of both kinds of genocides being perpetrated. The terrible loss of life in the April–July 1994 period in Rwanda claimed between 500,000 and 800,000 victims, mainly Tutsi, moderate Hutu, and an unknown number of Twa (Pygmies), as described in Chapter 11 on the Rwandese by Clea Msindo Koff and Ralph J. Hartley. In Iraq in 1988, Saddam Hussein's military forces in Iraq unleashed chemical weapons on Kurdish villagers in a campaign known as Anfal, which led to the deaths of hundreds of people and the destruction of their communities.[24] Some 75,000 to 80,000 people have been killed since 1992 in struggles between members of Islamic fundamentalist groups and the government of Algeria. Tens of thousands of people were killed in the 1980s and 1990s in the struggle against Siad Barre and the faction fighting among clan groups in Somalia following Barre's fall in January 1991, as noted in Chapter 12, Virginia Luling's contribution on the Somali of the Horn of Africa.

These kinds of situations are by no means new in Africa and the Middle East. The Hereros of Southwest Africa (now Namibia) were treated brutally by the Germans in the early twentieth century (1904–1907). Those who were not killed in direct action were driven into the Kalahari Desert, where thousands of people died of thirst and starvation. This kind of process is seen today, as well, notably in the Sudan. Internally displaced people and refugees, caught in the crossfire between warring states, often are at tremendous risk. This was the case with refugees in the Eritrea-Ethiopia border war of 1998–2000, as discussed by Lucia Ann McSpadden in Chapter 4, and in the Nuba Mountains of Sudan.

There are several types of genocide involving African and Middle Eastern peoples. The first of these is genocide in the context of a struggle between a state and an indigenous group or collectivity of several collaborating groups who are resisting the actions of the state. Few, if any, nations have willingly given up their land and resources, and some of them have sought actively to assert their autonomy, as seen in the case of the Mali and Niger with respect to the Tuareg, as described by Susan Rasmussen in Chapter 13, or the Kurds in Turkey and Iraq, as discussed by Laurel Erickson in Chapter 5. Often defined by governments as insurgents, separatists, or terrorists, resisting nations tend to consider themselves freedom fighters or people seeking self-determination. Many of these groups are numerically outnumbered and outgunned by the state, so they resort to guerrilla tactics or civil disobedience. Some states have conscripted members of indigenous or minority groups into their armed forces, sometimes at gunpoint. This was the case, for example, in southern Africa, where the South African Defense Force (SADF) drafted members of !Kung, Khwe, and Vasakela San (Bushmen) groups in the war against the South West Africa People's Organization (SWAPO) in Angola and Namibia in the 1970s and 1980s. In fact, the San were characterized by some researchers as "the most militarized ethnic group in the world."[25]

Another major context in which genocides and massive human rights violations against indigenous peoples occur is where efforts are made to promote social and economic development, often characterized as being "in the national interest." Sometimes called developmental genocides, these kinds of actions occur when states, agencies, companies, or transnational corporations oppress local peoples during the course of implementing various kinds of development projects. Some analysts see the destruction of indigenous groups as a "necessary by-product" of economic development. One of the defenses offered by government officials to charges of genocide is that the killings of indigenous people cannot be defined as genocide if they are done for "economic" reasons.

The harming of local peoples by multinational corporations is occurring in a number of parts of Africa and the Middle East. The establishment of oil exploitation programs in west and central Africa and the Sudan, the cutting of timber in central Africa, and the extraction of minerals in western, central, and southern Africa have all had serious negative consequences for local peoples. The implementation of large-scale hydroelectric projects, many of them now funded by consortiums of private banks rather than the World Bank or other international finance institutions (IFIs), has resulted in the displacement of literally millions of people, many of them indigenous or minority groups, as seen, for example, in the case of people along the upper Euphrates River in Turkey and along parts of the Nile River in northeastern Africa. All too frequently, local people have been forced out of development project areas with little or no compensation provided to them either in the form of alternative land or cash for lost assets. Involuntary resettlement and loss of land access have had the effect of increasing internal social tensions, some of which are exhibited in higher rates of spouse and child abuse, divorce, and suicide among local people.[26]

Ecocide, the destruction of ecosystems by states, agencies, or corporate entities, is a problem facing people in several parts of Africa and the Middle East. This can be seen, for example, in the case of Ogoniland in Nigeria, where Shell Oil has failed to deal with the pollution caused by their petroleum extraction activities (Chapter 7). Genocidal actions sometimes occur where there is also purposeful environmental destruction. For example, herbicides such as Agent Orange were allegedly used to clear forests so that counterinsurgency actions could proceed in Zimbabwe during the 1965–1980 liberation struggle. In southern Iraq in the period following the Gulf War, using herbicides Saddam Hussein's military forces destroyed the land and resource base of Shi'ites in the swamps at the mouths of the Tigris and Euphrates Rivers.

Another context in which human rights violations occur is one that is not normally recognized in the human rights and environmental justice communities—conservation-related violations. Although it is extremely important to protect endangered animals and plants, in many parts of the world, national parks, game reserves, and other kinds of protection areas have been established, often at significant cost to local communities, many of whom have been dispossessed as a result. Forced relocation out of conservation areas has all too often exacerbated problems of poverty, environmental degradation, and social conflict. In the course of state efforts to promote conservation, legal restrictions have been placed on hunting and fishing through national legislation. Such legislation has not only reduced the access of indigenous peoples to natural resources, but it has also resulted in individuals and sometimes whole communities being arrested, jailed, and in some cases, killed, as is noted in Chapter 3 by Stuart Marks on the Bisa of Zambia.

Even more disturbing than the high rates of arrest are the charges that people have been mistreated by game scouts and other officials. There have been a number of incidents in Africa where people claimed that they were tortured or received inhumane or degrading punishment when suspected of poaching or when being questioned about other people who might be engaged in illegal hunting. There have been cases where people have died of injuries inflicted upon them by game scouts, as occurred at !Xade in the Central Kalahari Game Reserve, Botswana, in August 1993, when a forty-year-old man died after being questioned by game scouts. Community leaders in the central Kalahari argued that authorities stepped over the line from antipoaching to persecution. Human rights organizations such as Amnesty International and Survival International took note of these allegations, as did the United States in its *Country Reports on Human Rights* for 1993.[27]

Some indigenous groups are taking matters into their own hands, blockading company roads into forest areas and stopping tourists from entering tourist areas and national parks. Such an event occurred in Namibia in 1997, when a group of Hai//om blockaded the entrance to Etosha National

Park. Police arrested seventy-three Hai//om for this action, although they eventually let them go. Others are using less confrontational tactics, appearing before the United Nations and congressional subcommittees in the United States and holding teach-ins and training sessions on how to write letters to boards of directors of companies. The San of Botswana, for example, had a representative body, the First People of the Kalahari, attend the meetings of the Human Rights Commission in Geneva in March 1996, where a presentation was made about the plight of the San people and the need for recognition of their basic human rights. San and other indigenous peoples from various parts of Africa have attended the meetings of the Working Group of Indigenous Populations of the United Nations in Geneva for the past two decades.

Those areas of Africa and the Middle East where population densities are high and where there is intense competition for resources tend to have significant environmental, social, and economic problems. It must be stressed that innovative efforts are being made to address these problems in the region. Community-based natural resource management programs (CBNRMPs) in southern and eastern Africa (e.g., in Zambia) and parts of the Middle East (e.g., in the Sinai region of Egypt, as noted in Chapter 2 by David Homa) are helping to reduce wildlife losses and to provide incomes to local communities. The San of Botswana, the Pygmies (TWA) of central Africa, the Tuareg of the Sahara, the Somali of the Horn of Africa, and the Mzeina Bedouins of Egypt have been called conservationists par excellence for their abilities to sustain themselves without doing irreparable harm to their habitats. They apply their wide-ranging environmental knowledge in the utilization and protection of resources and the areas in which they are found. Balancing population and environment is not easy, but it is possible.

THE THREATS OF DISEASE

Africa and the Middle East are facing major health issues, ranging from HIV/AIDS to newly emerging diseases such as Ebola, an extremely lethal virus from the tropics, or, as one journalist described it, "the hot zone." Virulent strains of malaria and dengue fever, spread by mosquitoes, are on the increase. On the other hand, river blindness—onchocerciasis, a disease carried by black flies—has been reduced significantly, owing to a multinational spraying and health education effort carried out with support from the United Nations, the U.S. Agency for International Development (USAID), and other agencies in the Senegal River Basin and surrounding areas.

Africa is the global epicenter of HIV/AIDS in the new millennium. HIV/AIDS represents a substantial threat to human health, and it ranks as one of the most important diseases facing humankind in the twenty-first century. Since its initial clinical identification and description some two decades ago, AIDS has resulted in over 16 million deaths worldwide. The United Nations Program on HIV/AIDS (UNAIDS) estimates that there are 36.1 million people worldwide who are either HIV positive or living with AIDS. Of these 25.3 million are in Sub-Saharan Africa. HIV/AIDS is also on the increase in the Middle East.[28]

Nearly 6,000 Africans die each day from HIV/AIDS. Twenty-one countries on the African continent exhibit the highest rates of HIV infection in the world. During 1999, approximately 3.8 million Africans contracted an HIV virus, and nearly 11 million children lost their parents to this epidemic.[29] Orphans, who currently number some 12 to 14 million in Sub-Saharan Africa, are placing a tremendous burden on families and communities who are attempting to assist them. Rates of infection have increased significantly in southern and eastern Africa during the 1990s, particularly in regions where adult males leave their homes and families to seek work elsewhere and are more apt to have sexual relations with prostitutes. In more economically depressed areas, these prostitutes tend to have increased numbers of clients, and increased promiscuity appears to ultimately produce even more virulent strains of HIV viruses. There are several countries in southern Africa, including Botswana and Zimbabwe, where rates of HIV infection now exceed 25 percent of the adult population. The HIV/AIDS epidemic has had a tremendously devastating impact upon African population structure, the labor force, and the economy. These costs have canceled out much of the per capita growth that African countries have experienced during the past several decades.

Most people in the developing world, including Africa, do not have access to antiretroviral therapies and drugs due to cost, availability, and the lack of health programs and facilities. In spite of the constraints, tremendous efforts are being made to curb the spread of the disease. Health education programs, including AIDS education, are on the increase in many parts of Africa, and it appears that in some parts of the continent, such as Uganda, Rwanda, and Botswana, as noted in this volume, the programs are having positive impacts.

Recently, veterinary authorities throughout Africa and the Middle East have recognized a range of animal diseases that involve wildlife, livestock, and in some instances, human populations. Livestock diseases are not new to the African continent. During the late 1800s, the rinderpest virus was introduced to eastern and southern Africa, where it decimated up to 95 percent of the cattle owned by highly mobile, pastoral peoples including the Maasai of Kenya and Tanzania as well as countless wild antelopes such as buffalo and wildebeest.

A number of livestock diseases are carried by insects including the tsetse fly (*Glossina* spp.) that spreads blood parasites (*Trypanosoma* spp.) to herds of wild ungulates as well as domesticated animals. These parasites cause sleeping sickness in both humans and animals. Cattle herders like the

Fulani of Nigeria move their herds frequently in advance of the rains and the spread of the tsetse flies.

Other livestock diseases such as foot and mouth disease (FMD) and Rift Valley fever (RVF) are caused by viruses. Lungsickness (contagious bovine pleuropneumonia [CBPP] and brucellosis are caused by bacteria. During the early 1990s, hundreds of thousands of cattle were killed by government personnel to control a major outbreak of CBPP in northern Botswana, a process that had major impacts on the social and economic well-being of thousands of people who were dependent in part upon cattle for their subsistence and income (see Chapter 8). During September and October 2000, Rift Valley fever (RVF) spread from cattle in eastern Africa to herds in Saudi Arabia and Yemen.[30] Rift Valley fever is a viral hemorrhagic fever that causes flulike symptoms or encephalitis and ultimately death. Such outbreaks and the threats of the spread of diseases across international borders have devastating economic impacts given the importance of livestock sales. Exports of meat and other livestock products have been banned recently throughout Africa and the Middle East including Kenya, Uganda, Eritrea, Ethiopia, Sudan, Nigeria, and Yemen.

ENVIRONMENTAL DEGRADATION

Africa and the Middle East in general lack large areas of arable land except in some of the fertile river valleys. Soils in many parts of the region are poor for agriculture due to their deficiencies in phosphorus, organic material, and moisture absorption capacities. Africa and the Middle East have experienced substantial soil losses through erosion that has been caused by deforestation and desertification. Considerable areas of forest and shrub lands have been cleared for farming, timber, and fuel wood. Firewood is the major source of fuel for cooking, heating, and other domestic tasks for 80 percent of Africa's population. Africa's demand for fuel wood to cook meals exceeds 22 billion cubic feet per year.[31] In areas of greater scarcity, people have altered their diets, reduced the number of meals, and developed more efficient stoves.

Africa and the Middle East are also experiencing water shortages due to population growth, rapid urbanization, and climate change. Africa and the Middle East's water and their people are not distributed evenly across the region. In Africa, thirteen countries supply 80 percent of the freshwater. Consequently, competition for freshwater is increasing, and a number of cooperative transboundary water management plans and treaties like the Nile Basin Initiative have been implemented.

We have all seen television news broadcasts of violent clashes between Israeli soldiers and Palestinian civilians (usually young, rock-throwing men) in communities on the West Bank and the Gaza Strip. These acts of aggression and violence are said to be the result of long-term enmity between

Jews and Arabs. Political scientist Thomas Homer-Dixon, the director of the Peace and Conflict Studies Program at the University of Toronto, has argued that recent conflicts have arisen in this region of the Middle East, in part, because of the scarcity of freshwater. He has pointed out that Israel now uses more fresh water each year than they "earn" or receive from rainfall and rivers that flow through their lands. In fact, Israel, Jordon, and Gaza currently use 113 billion cubic feet of water per year, yet renewable water supplies equal only 85 billion cubic feet per year.[32] This annual deficit results from the fact that deep wells (drilled by the Israelis) "overpump" the aquifers or underground sources of freshwater.

Forty percent of Israel's fresh water is derived, then, from beneath the West Bank territory where many Palestinians live. During the past several decades the Israeli government has imposed very stringent restrictions upon water use and water allocation within the West Bank. As Homer-Dixon has pointed out, there is a very marked disparity between the Israeli and Palestinian residents of the West Bank with respect to water access and use. Israeli settlers have greater access to expensive well drilling equipment and pumps than do the Palestinians. Lema Bashir in Chapter 9 on the Palestinians describes this situation in more detail.

Israeli wells have been drilled deeper than the Palestinian wells. As a consequence, water levels have been depressed deeper and deeper. Salt water has been drawn into these "vacuums" and has contaminated freshwater supplies that remain closer to the surface. Palestinians have traditionally made use of pumped water in order to irrigate their fields. The area of their irrigated farmlands has declined nearly 85 percent during the 1990s. In addition, some of this farmland has been confiscated by the Israelis. Polluted drinking water and reduced food supplies have served to worsen health conditions among the Palestinians—particularly among the children. Homer-Dixon concluded that increased economic disparities and environmental degradation have caused or, at least, exacerbated ethnic conflict between Jewish and Arab people within this region of the Middle East.

A major issue facing Africa and the Middle East is the presence of "environmental refugees"—people who have had to leave their homes and move elsewhere because of environmental change, drought, and the loss of resources caused by climatic or human-induced events (e.g., overutilization of forest resources for firewood). Environmental degradation, famine, and conflict all too often are tied together, resulting in large numbers of people being on the move both within their own countries and across borders. Some of these people can be considered "economic refugees"—people who move in order to obtain jobs and earn income. A fairly sizable proportion of economic refugees are urban migrants, people who relocate from rural to urban areas in the hopes of finding new opportunities and a better lifestyle.

Many of the problems facing African and Middle Eastern peoples today are the result of global processes, specifically colonization and expansion of mercantile trade and development, which have deprived them of their lands and lifestyles. These processes are ongoing, not least in the form of resource exploitation. Today, another global process—the development of international laws recognizing indigenous and minorities and women's rights—has the potential of redressing past injustices and ameliorating present circumstances. For African and Middle Eastern peoples, it is crucial to identify and define the best combination of international, regional, national, and local policies and governance to promote their welfare and enhance their standards of living.

From the perspective of peoples in Africa and the Middle East, colonization was essentially "Europeanization," involving the imposition of European concepts of sovereignty, religion, and civilization. One effect, perhaps the crucial one, was the drastic reduction of local peoples' land bases and their restriction to progressively smaller areas. In South Africa, for example, "homelands" were created by the Native Land Act in 1913 and Africans surrendered 87 percent of their land to white settlers and companies.[33] In Botswana, much of the most productive land was set aside as freehold land and given to white farmers. When their lands were lost, local peoples also lost livelihoods, graves and other sacred sites, history (for history was written on the landscape), and much of their religions. Europeans and their colonial offshoots offered in return their form of civilization, based on Christianity, individualism, and private property ownership. In virtually every area of the world where colonization took place, local peoples were subjected to intensive pressures to assimilate, to become European, and therefore to disappear. In this way the "indigenous problem" or "native problem" would be solved without a more overt strain of genocide. Local peoples, however, did not disappear but have endured. Their identities, however, often were fractured by the pressure of assimilation efforts.

These identities have been fortified in recent years as local peoples have reasserted their rights to traditional homelands and challenged the assumptions and mechanisms that resulted in their dispossession. In doing so, they have extracted concessions from the still-colonizing powers that govern them. In South Africa, for example, /Khomani San have been able to claim rights over a portion of the land surrounding the Kalahari Gemsbok Transfrontier Park, the first transboundary park in southern Africa, which is shared between South Africa and Botswana. In parts of the Sinai, Bedouin populations, as noted by David Homa (Chapter 2), have been able to obtain comanagement rights over national parks and reserves. Similar efforts can be seen in other parts of Africa and the Middle East, including Kenya, Tanzania, Zambia, Cameroon, Mali, Iran, Jordan, Oman, Saudi Arabia, and Turkey.

Conservation and development programs cost a great deal of money. In order to undertake conservation and development projects, most countries, including many of those in the developing world, must borrow funds. They do this by seeking assistance from multilateral development banks and from private banks (e.g., the Bank of America, Chase Manhattan Bank). Some countries have also turned to environmental nongovernment organizations willing to help pay off debts in exchange for their setting aside conservation areas in a strategy known as debt-for-nature swaps. Others have sought to generate their own funds through community-based natural resources management programs, tourism projects, and rural industries, as seen, for example, in the Okavango Delta region of Botswana, as discussed in Chapter 8 by John Bock and Sara E. Johnson.

Global wealth flows have changed enormously over the past fifty years since the International Monetary Fund (IMF), the World Bank, and the United Nations were founded. What has *not* changed is the domination of these flows by wealthy institutions, agencies, and individuals. Over a quarter of the world's population is below the poverty datum line, the line below which it is impossible for an individual to sustain herself or himself. Poor people in the developing world argue vociferously that they have literally been pushed into poverty by both international institution and government efforts to deal with the debt problem. Debt is causing difficulties in a number of African and Middle East countries, where prices have risen at much faster rates than economies have grown. The proportion of malnutrition among children has increased in many of the countries that have undertaken economic reforms. Infant mortality rates have also risen in some areas. Workers' wages have fallen in some of these same countries, resulting in lower buying power at the local level, hurting regional economies.

RESPONSE: STRUGGLES TO SURVIVE CULTURALLY

African and Middle Eastern communities and groups have begun to organize among themselves and to collaborate with a variety of support organizations in an effort to oppose negative policies and promote human rights. How successful these efforts will be depends very much on whether or not private companies, intergovernmental organizations, states, and nongovernment organizations are willing (1) to come up with strict internationally recognized human rights and environmental standards, (2) to monitor development and conservation activities as they are implemented, and (3) to enforce those standards. What this means, in effect, is that private companies will have to be held to the same standards as governments, and they must be liable to prosecution for genocidal actions and human rights violations.

The international community needs to take further steps to develop a code of business and social ethics that protects the rights of people in areas where businesses are operating. Governments and companies must live up to their obligation to protect local peoples and not compromise their rights under the weight of "progress," economic growth, or free trade. All institutions, whether they are multinational corporations (MNCs), governments of nation-states, nongovernment organizations, or community-based organizations, need to work together to promote the rights not just of endangered peoples but of all human beings.

In recent years, recommendations have been made by indigenous and minority groups and their supporters that the goals of these peoples can best be achieved (1) if they are allowed to participate fully in needs assessments, development planning, and project implementation, (2) if they are provided information on which to base decisions, and (3) if they have the right to determine their own futures. "Participatory development" has become a catchphrase for the kind of approach that many indigenous and minority peoples and the organizations with whom they work are advocating. Various means of bringing about local participation have been suggested, including allowing local people to take part in all phases of the development process and assuring that local people have control over their own land and natural resources.

The concept of participation is one that is not easy to define. It can mean the right to make decisions about development action. Participation can also mean the process whereby local communities and individuals take part in defining their own needs and coming up with solutions to meet those needs. In addition, participation can refer to situations in which local communities and individuals share in the benefits from development projects and are fully involved in generating those benefits. As Robert Chambers notes, "Rural development can be redefined to include enabling poor rural women and men to demand and control more of the benefits of development."[34] Participation can thus be said to mean simply putting people first. Efforts have been made to promote strategies of community consultation, mobilization, and organization as a means of overcoming development constraints among local peoples.

There is much debate among local communities and their leaders about the goals and objectives of their struggles. Virtually all want a greater say in decisions that affect them, and they would all like to see their standards of living enhanced. Some peoples want autonomy, which they see as the right to make their own decisions. They argue that autonomy means the right to be different and to be able to preserve, protect, and promote customs, values, and ideals that they hold dear. Autonomy and sovereignty imply protection from discrimination and preservation of cultural, linguistic, and spiritual values from assault by the dominant majority. Indigenous and minority peoples in Africa and the Middle East want the right to practice their own cultures, to teach their children mother tongue languages, and to be able to take part in their own customary activities without interference, as is noted in a number of chapters in this book (e.g., Chapter 5 on the Kurds, Chapter 8 on the Okavango peoples of Botswana, Chapter 10 on the Qashqa'i of Iran, and Chapter 13 on the Tuareg).

Toward the end of the twentieth century and in the new millennium there has been a widespread set of social movements of indigenous and minority peoples who are seeking fair and just treatment and protection of their civil, political, social, economic, and cultural rights.[35] These movements are aimed in part at gaining access to information and seeking rights to participate in decision making concerning the plans and programs of international agencies, governments, and private companies that might affect local peoples. The organizations formed by these groups engage in numerous activities, from taking cases to court to participating in demonstrations, and from holding workshops and training sessions to carrying out research and disseminating reports. They host meetings to which representatives of local groups are invited. These organizations also sometimes serve as liaisons between members of local groups and other agencies (e.g., state bodies devoted to indigenous or minority affairs or private companies).

The building of capacity for local decision making has been done in a number of ways, as noted in a number of chapters in this volume. It has been facilitated through the holding of workshops or community discussion sessions in which ideas about democratic processes of public policy formation have been addressed. It has also been promoted through training of various kinds (e.g., in how to form committees, draw up constitutions, and run meetings). In addition, capacity building has been facilitated through a number of innovative nonformal educational means, including doing problem-solving exercises, drawing up case studies, and performing role-plays about situations in which communities find themselves. A number of communities have drawn up their own materials and curricula for schools that address social, cultural, and ideological issues of importance to their cultures. These kinds of strategies have been very effective in helping to establish community-based organizations and strengthening cultural identities.

Today, there are literally thousands of grassroots organizations and institutions seeking to enhance their livelihoods and gain greater control over their areas. Many of these organizations are engaged in sustainable development activities. They are carrying out innovative agricultural projects, social forestry programs, and soil and water conservation activities. They are lobbying international agencies, including the United Nations, the World Bank, and the European Union, to be more responsive to their concerns.

By doing local, national, regional, and international networking and by increasing their involvement in civil society, African and Middle Eastern peoples have taken some important steps toward gaining recognition of their social, economic, and cultural rights. It is hoped that the lessons learned from the diverse strategies they have employed will enable them to survive and prosper over the long term.

ACKNOWLEDGMENTS

We wish to thank Greenwood Press Acquisitions Editor Wendi Schnaufer, Series Editor Barbara Rose Johnston, and the staff of Greenwood Press for their enormous contributions to this volume. We would also like to thank Laurel Erickson of the Refugee Resettlement Program of Catholic Social Services in Lincoln, Nebraska, for her extensive efforts in helping to bring this book to completion. And last but by no means least, we wish to express our deepest gratitude to the authors who contributed their time and ideas to this volume.

NOTES

1. This definition of "nation" is derived from Bernard Nietschmann, "The Fourth World: Nations versus States," in *Reordering the World: Geopolitical Perspectives on the Twenty-first Century*, ed. George Demko and William B. Wood (Boulder: Westview Press, 1994), 226.

2. United Nations Population Fund (20 November 2001), www.unfpa.org/swp/2000/english/indicators/indicators2.html.

3. See Barbara F. Grimes, ed., *Ethnologue, Volume 1: Languages of the World*, 14th ed. (Dallas, TX: SIL International, 1996), 151–440; Daniel Nettle, *Linguistic Diversity* (Oxford: Oxford University Press, 1999), 116–117.

4. Daniel Nettle, "Language Diversity in West Africa: An Ecological Approach," *Journal of Anthropological Archaeology* 15 (1996): 403–438.

5. Derrick J. Stenning, "The Pastoral Fulani of Northern Nigeria," in *Peoples of Africa*, ed. James L. Gibbs, Jr. (New York: Holt, Rinehart and Winston, 1965), 361–402.

6. Population Reference Bureau (1999), *www.prb.org/pubs/wpds99/wpds99_africa.htm*.

7. Robert Kaplan, "The Coming Anarchy," *The Atlantic Monthly* (February 1994): 44–76.

8. U.S. Department of State, "Conference: Partnership to Cut Hunger in Africa" (June 19, 2001), http://www.aec.msu.edu/agecon/fs2/africanhunger/framework_plan_eng.pdf.

9. Paul Bohannan and Philip Curtin, *Africa & Africans* (Prospect Heights, IL: Waveland Press, 1995), 185.

10. U.S. Committee for Refugees, *World Refugee Survey 2000* (Washington, DC: Author, 2000), 117.

11. United Nations Environment Programme, Global State of the Environment Report, 1997, *http://www.grid2.cr.usgs.gov/geo1/ch/ch2_4.htm*.

12. Ibid.

13. Mbendi—Information for Africa, Africa: Oil and Gas Industry, July 12, 2000, http://www.mbendi.co.za/.

14. Howard French, "Competition Heats Up for West Africa's Oil," *New York Times*, March 7, 1998.

15. Ibid.

16. African Commission on Human Rights and Peoples Rights, Appendix F, April 2000, http://160.94.193.60/hreduseries/ripple/app/appendixf.html; Africa Policy Information Center (APIC), "Crimes of Shell," *www.africapolicy.org/docs97/shel9705.2htm.*

17. Africa On Line, "Sudan: Oil Companies Linked with Counterinsurgency," *http://www.africaonline.com/site/Articles/1,3,42197.jsp.*

18. Michael T. Klare, *Resource Wars: The New Landscape of Global Conflict* (New York: Henry Holt and Company, 2001), 72.

19. Richard Norton-Taylor, "The New Great Game," *Guardian Unlimited*, March 5, 2001.

20. George Arney, "US" Planned Attack on Taleban," *BBC News*, 18 September 2001, *http://news.bbc.co.uk/hi/english/world/south_asia/newsid_1550000/1550366.stm.*

21. Jon Flanders, "Oil War II, the Sequel: The Empire Strikes Back in the Caspian," 13 November 2001, *http://www.indymedia.org/front.php3?article_id=70755&group*; Energy Information Administration, "Afghanistan," September 2001, *www.eia.doe.gov.*

22. Global Witness, "A Rough Trade: The Role of Companies and Governments in Angolan Conflicts," 1998, *www.oneworld.org/globalwitness/.*

23. Ibid.

24. Middle East Watch and Physicians for Human Rights, *The Anfal Campaign in Iraqi Kurdistan: The Destruction of Koreme* (New York: Human Rights Watch, Boston: Physicians for Human Rights, 1993).

25. Robert G. Gordon, University of Vermont, personal communication to Robert Hitchcock, 1985.

26. See World Commission on Dams, *Dams and Development: A New Framework for Decision-Making. The Report of the World Commission on Dams* (London: Earthscan Publications, 2000).

27. U.S. Department of State, *Country Reports on Human Rights* (Washington, DC: Author, 1993), 13–14.

28. Joint United Nations Programme on HIV/AIDS (2001), *www.unaids.org/epidemic_update.*

29. Ibid.

30. Food and Agriculture Organization of the United Nations, "Pastoralists in Eastern Africa Hard Hit by Rift Valley Fever and Other Diseases," (February 17, 1998), *www.fao.org/NEWS/1998/980203-e.htm.*

31. Samir Amous, Food and Agriculture Organization of the United Nations, "The Role of Wood Energy in Africa" (2001) *http://www.fao.org/docrep/X2740e.*

32. Thomas F. Homer-Dixon, "Environmental Scarcities and Violent Conflict," *International Security* 19, no. 1 (1994): 5–40; and Thomas F. Homer-Dixon, *Environment, Scarcity, and Violence* (Princeton, NJ: Princeton University Press, 1999).

33. "History," South African Yearbook, 2000/2001, *http://www.gov.za/yearbook/history.htm.*

34. Robert Chambers, *Rural Development: Putting the Last First* (London: Longman, 1983), 140.

35. Franke Wilmer, *The Indigenous Voice in World Politics: Since Time Immemorial* (Newbury Park, CA: Sage Publications, 1993); S. James Anaya, *Indigenous Peoples in International Law* (New York: Oxford University Press, 1996); Minority Rights Group International, *World Directory of Minorities* (London: Author, 1997); Thomas D. Musgrave, *Self-Determination and National Minorities* (Oxford: Clarendon Press, 1997); John H. Bodley, *Victims of Progress* (Mountain View, CA: Mayfield, 1999).

Chapter 1

The Afghans

M. Catherine Daly

CULTURAL OVERVIEW

The People

Afghanistan has an ethnically and linguistically mixed population, but the residents are often referred to collectively as Afghans. The historic founders of the country are Pushtuns, who today make up approximately 38 percent of the country's total population. Major ethnic groups continue to inhabit geographically single-ethnic villages clustered together around more mixed towns. There are some twenty-one documented ethnic groups in Afghanistan. The major groups in the country besides the Pushtuns are the Tajiks (25 percent), followed by Hazaras (19 percent), Uzbeks (6 percent), and other minor ethnic groups (12 percent, including Turkmens, Baluchis, and Aimaq).[1]

Because of this ethnic diversity, many languages are spoken in Afghanistan. Officially, two languages are acknowledged: Pashto and Dari. Pashto is an Indo-Iranian language influenced by Arabic and Persian origins, while Dari is an Afghan variant of Persian. The ethnic majority of Pushtuns speak Pashto, and the remaining groups incorporate Dari with local ethnic variations. This tendency toward national bilingualism is enhanced with Arabic, the language of Islam. Islam is the dominant religion in Afghanistan used in religious schools called *madrassas* and during the five daily calls to prayer (*azam*). Most of the country's people are Sunni Muslim but a Shi'ite minority exists.

The peoples of Afghanistan derive from a strong nomadic tradition that is centuries old and linked to both the Arab Middle East and the Indian subcontinent. Owing to seasonal changes, the geographic austerity of the environment and the agricultural cycle are linked. Historically, Afghans have been characterized as a migratory or a nonsedentary population moving from one region to another.

A significant percentage of Afghanistan's population left the country during the conflicts following a coup in April 1978 and the invasion by Soviet troops in December 1979. The unofficial estimated population of Afghanistan ranges somewhere between 13 and 18 million. Population figures are difficult to establish because of the large Afghan refugee population and internally displaced population within Afghanistan. According to United Nations High Commissioner for Refugees (UNHCR) figures, Afghans are the largest single caseload refugee population in the world, numbering over 2.6 million people.[2] In 1998, the total population of Afghans living in areas contiguous to Afghanistan was approximately 3 million. Some 1 million Afghans live in permanent camp settlements in Pakistan. There are approximately 4 million Afghan people who are currently dependent upon outside humanitarian assistance (as of December 2001). These figures do not include refugees living in regional noncamp urban centers of Pakistan (2 million), Iran (1.5 million), Turkmenistan (1,500), Uzbekistan (8,800), and Tajikistan (15,400). In 2001, over 600,0000 refugees left Afghanistan due to continued civil war, drought, famine, and homelessness. Recently, more than 200,00 Afghans fled into neighboring Pakistan following the initiation of the U.S.-directed bombing raids in November and December 2001. According to UNHCR statistics in early December 2001, more than 3.6 million Afghans remain outside Afghanistan and more than 1 million have been internally displaced.[3]

The Setting

Afghanistan's geography, approximately 245,000 square miles in size, features a wide variety of habitats and terrain. It is situated along old trade routes between the Middle East and Asia. It is a landlocked country bordered by China, Iran, Pakistan, Tajikistan, Turkmenistan, and Uzbekistan. One of the distinctive geographic characteristics of Afghanistan is the Hindu Kush, "roof of the world," the foothills of the Himalayas, which nearly divides the country from the Pamir mountain range of Tajikistan in the northwest to the southeastern area bordering Pakistan. Nowshak, the second highest mountain range in the world, lies within Afghanistan. These mountain ranges of Afghanistan offer impressive landscapes because of the rugged and barren terrain and inhospitable character.

In contrast to the treacherous mountainous areas, deserts are interspersed with isolated fertile valleys, river basins, and oases throughout Afghanistan. The Dasht-I-Margo desert and the Registan arid and semidesert areas provide another relatively inhospitable environment in which to exist. For centuries the mountainous and desert terrain have provided a challenge to those traveling the old silk routes between Chinese and Mediterranean civilizations. The most notorious route, the Khyber Pass, is a rocky narrow passage on the border of Afghanistan and Pakistan.

The river systems of the Amu Darya in the north, the Arghandab in the south, and the Kabul in the east balance the mountainous and desert regions of Afghanistan. These rivers provide the necessary irrigation for Afghanistan's 15 percent agricultural landscape.

During 2001, over half the population was affected by the worst drought in over thirty years. Grain production has fallen by more than half the national requirements due to recent droughts in 2001. Nearly 1 million Afghans faced starvation during the late 1990s. Prior to the recent deliveries of emergency food, blankets, tents, and medical supplies during late 2001, many Afghan people faced suffering and, in many cases, death.[4] The result is that in addition to the large refugee population a migratory internally displaced population has returned in search of scarce resources.

Traditional Subsistence Strategies

Afghanistan's economy is closely linked to its geography and agriculture. Historically, economic control through exploitation of these resources has been the province of local village leaders and ethnic groups in power. Prior to the 1980s, economic and educational reforms instituted by the government initiated the development of rural and urban economies. However, in the twentieth and early twenty-first centuries, the Afghan economy reverted to its agricultural base. Continued tensions among ethnic groups and regional and international interests have evolved with the intensified exploitation of water, oil, and gas reserves.

Currently because of the Taliban Islamic Movement of Afghanistan or Taliban restrictions on development, economic advancement has been limited. Development activities that take place are a result of a variety of government and nongovernment organizations. In the rural areas of Afghanistan, the economy is based almost exclusively on subsistence agriculture. There is a division of labor that is gender based, with males and females engaging in different types of agricultural activities as well as alongside one another. Farmers and herdsmen comprise approximately 90 percent of the population.[5] Wheat and barley are the primary agricultural crops, but there are also regional crop specializations of cotton, fruits, and vegetables, some of which have commercial potential.

Afghanistan's involvement in the cultivation, production, and transportation of drugs, especially opium, provides much higher economic returns than does the raising of food and production of textiles. Afghanistan produces the majority of the world's supply of opium, its largest cash crop. In 2000, Afghanistan produced 75 percent of the world's opium—nearly

3,500 tons.[6] Drug trafficking, along with the arms trade supported by the Taliban, provides a strong smuggling network of drugs in exchange for money, material resources, and weapons. Although opium was once a banned crop before the Taliban controlled the cities and provinces, the new government subsequently coerced farmers to harvest the opium that today supports the purchase of high-tech weaponry and the underwriting of governmental activities. In response to opium production the international community has enforced economic restrictions on Afghanistan and the Taliban-controlled government.

For the last twenty years a well-developed network of local and international nongovernment organizations has assisted in economic development and humanitarian aid that have helped Afghan communities increase their degree of economic self-sufficiency. Many of these programs have a gender dimension and attempt to cater to the traditional division of labor in Afghan society, where women govern the domestic sphere and men the public. The majority of successful women's programs focus on textile craft economies and agricultural activities suitable within the circumscribed domestic environment. Men's programs emphasize, in some instances, similar kinds of activities but provided in public settings of workshops and cooperatives. For example, women may weave rugs in the confines of the family residence, whereas men weave in a refugee camp workshop.

For a period of time during the 1960s and 1970s, there was an increase in nonagriculturally based employment in urban areas. The majority of women continued to work primarily in the home environment, but women who worked outside the family worked primarily in industry, education, health care, and civil service positions. But since 1996 Taliban rule has forbidden women to work outside the home. They no longer work with development workers or in hospital or educational settings, and even home-based enterprises are affected. Afghan men have continued to retain their public personae but now as shopkeepers and in civil service and administrative positions.

In recent years economic development has taken on a global significance; there is competition among Western countries and foreign businesses vying for control of water rights and the rich oil and gas reserves supplied by the Middle East and Central Asia to Western and Asian markets. The development of irrigation systems and the gas and oil infrastructure (such as pipelines) are linked to ethnic politics and religious fundamentalism.

Social and Political Organization

Social and political organization in Afghanistan are interrelated. Beginning at the family level, political organization is kinship based along ethnic ties in rural areas that are acknowledged in the urban areas. Afghanistan is ruled by cultural and religious prescriptions or codes of conduct that are both ethnic and Islamic in nature. The Pushtun majority predominates and consistently invokes their Pushtunwali codes of conduct. Loyalty and honor, hospitality, and chivalry are part of a code of tribal conduct that begins with the family and extends to the village or tribe and to the ethnic group. The Taliban, which is composed of a Pushtun majority, has institutionalized these codes, which along with Islamic religious values are governing Afghanistan with more strict civil rules.

The extended family serves as the major economic and social unit in Afghanistan. Traditionally, Afghan social structure is based on family kinship patterns that reflect a male bias generalized as patriarchal in character. Men's and women's roles are clearly defined according to cultural and religious norms and prescriptions for behavior. Roles are gendered and differentiated between the domestic/female and public/male spheres of everyday life. There are rural and urban differences, and it is not uncommon for women in rural settings to contribute to agricultural pursuits. Though some flexibility in employment and education evolved during reforms periods of Afghanistan's history, the Taliban now strictly enforces the expectations of gender specialization. Women provide for the family in the home environment, and they are physically restricted to this environment. This is especially the case in urban centers. Men, on the other hand, support their families in economic pursuits that extend beyond the confines of the family. According to the Taliban, women who do not follow the prescribed gender roles presumably offend not only Afghan society but the religion of Islam.

Based on gendered roles and traditional life patterns, Afghan women are thought to be homogeneous. Their familial roles are circumscribed by ethnic and religious as well as rural and urban environments. However, prescribed variations do exist across geographic areas and from one ethnic group to another. The factor that varies most is the participation of women in economic production within the agricultural and pastoral economy and the manufacturing industries.

Ideally, the home reflects a nuclear and/or extended family structure that predominates in rural villages and is extended to urban areas. This pattern today is questionable as countless families live in both Afghanistan and in camp and noncamp settings of regional and international diaspora communities. Disrupted families are the norm. Despite changes in family structures, the cultural and religious prescriptions for male/female behavior requires that family honor and loyalty are still safeguarded values that continue, reminiscent and in defense of gendered roles and family values.

Population statistics and demographics do not represent the complexity of internal and external Afghan history nor of the geopolitics of the region, both of which have contributed to the legacy of Afghanistan. It is possible to outline six historical time periods of Afghanistan: the Pre-Islamic period; the Medieval and Late Medieval Islamic period; the period of Afghan

Empire; the "Great Game" or European Imperial period; the period of the Independent Monarchy; and the current political environment.

Afghan leaders during these periods vacillated between issues supporting status quo cultural and religious values and introducing reforms that provided a progressive atmosphere for women in particular to work and live. Some of these issues included abolition of child and forced marriages, the levirate (the custom whereby a man is obliged to marry his dead brother's widow), and exorbitant bride prices and marriage gifts. There was also support for widowed and divorced women's rights, female education, removal of the women's full body head covering (*chaadaree*), and the end of female seclusion (*purdah*). The rights of women has been a contentious topic in recent years in Afghanistan, as the Taliban has sought to restrict the activities of women, including the imposition of a ban on women's work outside the home and the requirement that women who are out in public be accompanied by a *mahram* (a close male relative such as a brother, father, or husband).

Afghanistan's recent social and political history is marked by three important dates: the 1978 Afghan coup, the 1979 Soviet invasion, and the 1996 Taliban rule. These three dates are significant because they mark the end of modernization and civil life in Afghanistan. They also emphasize the regional familial and ethnic boundaries that confounded new political alliances of special interests related to economic and environmental interests. Two noteworthy Afghan groups that have endured and affected Afghanistan are the Mujahideen and the Taliban. Since both groups claim a Pushtun majority and an Islamic legitimacy to their efforts, it is difficult to separate ethnicity, religion, and politics in Afghanistan. The popular belief is that the Mujahideen, or Afghan freedom fighters, considered themselves involved in a *jihad*, or holy war, against the Soviet invasion of Afghanistan in the late 1970s. The Mujahideen was essentially a coalition government made up of seven different political parties that had in the past formed the Afghan Interim Government. In practical terms, the Mujahideen initially operated at the village level to defend Afghan citizens against military intervention and other atrocities.

In contrast to the Mujahideen, the Taliban evolved as a group of religiously oriented students who were deeply disturbed by the behavior of the leaders of the Mujahideen, who were, in their opinion, involved in corrupt practices. Unlike the Mujahideen, the members of the Taliban, led by self-proclaimed leader Mullah Mohammed Omar, had relatively little formal education or government experience, but, like the Mujahideen, their focus is a military one, aimed at controlling the Afghan population. Taliban policies are enforced through an entity known as the Department for the Promotion of Virtue and the Prevention of Vice.

Afghanistan's history for centuries can best be described as contentious as a result of environmental and political pressures and the internal and

Veiled women in Afghanistan.

external conflict for economic control of these resources in the region. The conflict extends from the level of family-, tribe-, ethnic-, and religious-based struggles for control of the population and use of scarce environmental and material resources to economic assistance and military support and intervention in Afghanistan. The contradiction is that because of ethnic and religious loyalties Afghanistan has never been a politically united or unified country with a national identity; at the same time, ethnic and religious loyalties have never allowed Afghanistan to succumb to outside military or political forces.

Religion and World View

The dominant religion in Afghanistan is Islam. Eighty percent of the population is Sunni Islam, and 20 percent is a Shi'ite Islam minority. Although both Sunni and Shi'ite Muslims observe the "Five Pillars of Islam," the Sunni believe that Islamic leaders should adhere to the wishes of the community. The Shi'ite believe that the community should be controlled by the religious-political authorities. Although not necessarily ethnic based, the Pushtun majority are Sunni, while the minority populations, Hazara and Ismaili Muslims, are Shi'ite. Corresponding tensions exist between Sunni and Shi'ite Muslims and the ethnic groups they represent to the extent that there are documented cases of Shi'ite genocide. The paradox is that the religion of Islam is potentially one of the major, if not the exclusive, unifying factors in Afghanistan. Cultural as well as religious codes of conduct govern the everyday life and behavior of both Afghan men and women. The cultural or traditional codes are those of the dominant ethnic group, the Pushtun's Pushtanwali. Pushtunwali is acknowledged throughout Afghanistan as a system of rights and obligations that honors the sanctity of the family and ethnic group. A recurring issue among Afghan social behavior is the ultimate determining factor of family status in any Afghan community: female virtue and honor. An Afghan woman's virtue and honor reside in her conduct, visibility or lack thereof, and her appearance in the community.

The Taliban interprets the perceived restrictive rules and obligations of the Qur'an (the holy book of Islam), and of Islamic or Sharia Law regarding women's behavior and appearance. The religion of Islam is the strongest cultural link to the Middle East, and it is the strongest unifying variable among Afghans, but it is finessed by the Taliban to control Afghans in general and women in particular. Both Pushtanwali and Islamic codes of conduct are invoked to govern male and female behavior. But in a social structure that favors male patriarchy and male superiority, women's rights as documented throughout Afghanistan's political history are a recurring theme in the country's struggle for regional and international recognition.

THREATS TO SURVIVAL

Civil war, terrorist activity, drug production, human rights abuses, drought, and the effects of globalization have caused tremendous hardships among Afghans and have threatened their well-being. Some of the most seriously affected members of the Afghan population have been women, children, and the elderly. Today the nonsedentary nature has been seemingly coopted by a more sedentary pattern that tends to reflect either residence in a rural agricultural community and/or in a nearby urban center.

Afghanistan has suffered extreme economic hardships brought on by centuries of shifting political alliances and conflict. Contentious ethnic and religious groups within Afghanistan, followed by contiguous regional peoples of the Middle East and Asia, and finally British, former Soviet, and U.S. colonial and imperial imposition, have contributed to changing residential and economic patterns.

Those few fertile areas of Afghanistan are threatened by chemical fertilizers and pesticides used by its neighbors in bordering riverine areas. In addition, depletion of these natural resources, along with deforestation caused by rural and urban populations seeking local fuel sources, is significant. Thus, the harsh physical environment, combined with resource degradation problems, has affected the Afghan population, who in many ways are isolated from the region and the international community.

Since Taliban rule began in 1996, organizations such as The Feminist Majority Foundation, Physicians for Human Rights, and the Revolutionary Association for the Women of Afghanistan have responded to and criticized specific human rights issues of Afghan women. The most visible sign and symbol of human rights abuse by the Taliban is the mandatory enforcement of the full body covering, the *chaadaree*. Criticisms offered by these groups include threats to the survival of Afghan women, human rights concerns delineated in 1948 in the UN's Universal Declaration of Human Rights:

Restricted movement of all females between private/public domains a violation of Article 13, "the right to freedom of movement";

Suspension of formal primary/advanced education for females, which violates Article 26, "the right to education";

Denial of health care for women, especially when provided by men, a violation of Article 25, "the right to standard living adequate health";

Forbidding of female employment outside the home environment, which violates Article 23, "the right to work"; and

Mandatory regulations on female appearance, a violation of Article 27, "the right to freely participate in the cultural life."[7]

However, these criticisms are not without social costs to Afghans. Many men, formerly heads of households and extended family networks, have been either killed or disabled. As a consequence, programs have targeted vulnerable women as wives, mothers, and children who are the remaining employable people in disrupted nuclear and extended families. In a patriarchal society that honors male superiority and family honor, these programs strain the disparity between male/female relationships and ethnic and religious codes of conduct. Whether employed within or outside the home, women seek economic independence for their family at the same time their honor and male relatives stand to lose respectability in the community.

Current Events and Conditions

Current practical questions related to Afghan women's human rights have coalesced in the symbol of women's oppression, their appearance. Practices associated with appearance attributed to Islamic affiliation have tended to be socially critiqued by "outsiders" as a form of gender apartheid, female oppression, an ethnic stereotype, and a kind of religious orthodoxy.

The Taliban's Ministry for Propagation of Virtue and Prevention of Vice announced that its decrees regarding Afghan women's appearance safeguarded the honor and virtue that are essential values of Afghan culture. To ignore these edicts, according to the Taliban, is un-Islamic and punishable by Islamic Sharia Law. Women had to be covered when leaving the home environment; covering meant wearing the *chaadaree*, or full body covering, over the customary ensemble of dress worn by Afghan women. In addition to wearing the *chaadaree*, specific items of dress were forbidden in public because they allegedly evoked male sexual interest. More specific rules governing dress were related to the feet: wearing white socks, sandals, high heel shoes, and ankle bracelets. Other sensory experiences were controlled, and in some instances, gendered garments and the origin of their manufacture are unacceptable. There were repercussions for women who chose to contradict Taliban policy, ranging from verbal abuse to physical assault, and, in some instances, execution.

Since the attack upon the United States on September 11, 2001, and the U.S.-led invasion of Afghanistan a number of weeks later, a number of Afghan women and members of the Revolutionary Association of the Women of Afghanistan (RAWA) met with the U.S. Congress. They requested that future aid to their country be strongly linked to improvements in the lives of Afghan women.[8]

These rules are presumed to be derived from ethnic or tribal codes of conduct and Islamic Sharia Law. The assumption is that Afghan women gain honor by seclusion and invisibility. What is clear from these policies is that Afghan women's lack of appearance in public assures them of inadequate health care for themselves and their children, illiteracy and loss of education, unemployment, and economic dependence for generations.

Cultural preservation issues also loom large in Afghanistan. A recent development in Afghanistan is the destruction by Taliban soldiers of statues and other cultural monuments in the country, some of which are Buddhist. During twenty days in March 2001, Taliban soldiers completely destroyed two gigantic carved stone figures of the Buddha about 150 miles from the capital of Kabul. These two monumental sculptures measured 125 feet and 175 feet tall, respectively. The supreme Taliban leader Mullah Mohammed Omar had them destroyed because they represented non-Islamic "graven images."[9] Cultural preservation is clearly a sensitive issue at the international, national, and local levels.

The political relationship between Afghanistan, the United States, and most of the world has changed in a most dramatic and profound way since the tragedies of September 11, 2001. This chapter was written prior to the George W. Bush Administration's marked change in foreign policy with respect to Fundamentalist Islamic–directed terrorist actions. Journalists had tended to characterize the Bush Administration's foreign policy as one of isolationism. They had asked a number of questions regarding how Bush might then prioritize the major challenges posed in the international arena. Following the attacks upon the United States, Osama Bin Laden, Mullah Mohammed Omar, and the al-Qaeda organization quickly defined the course of U.S. foreign policy, as well as the actions and concerns of many other nations throughout the world. As the U.S.-directed bombing campaign began in October, November, and December 2001, humanitarian assistance in the form of food packets, medical supplies, blankets, and tents was simultaneously infused into the region. Once again, the lives and culture(s) of the Afghan people would be changed in many very significant ways.

RESPONSE: STRUGGLES TO SURVIVE CULTURALLY

Afghanistan is examined here because some of its people claim Arab heritage and a close relationship with Iran. Its people and culture(s) have recently been threatened and placed at great risk by external governments, warfare, human rights abuses, drought, and hunger. As mentioned, nearly 4 million Afghans (approximately 15 percent of the total population) have fled their country and now reside outside in neighboring countries. Afghanistan has experienced twenty-five years of nearly continuous armed conflict and during that time a number of countries and nongovernment organizations have attempted to provide much needed assistance.

Since the Afghan coup of 1979, numerous UN organizations and government and nongovernment aid agencies have worked diligently to provide health care, food, education, and economic projects for internally displaced Afghans and Afghan refugees. The UN role working with Afghans is significant but fraught with politics. The most prominent UN program is the UNHCR, the United Nations High Commissioner for Refugees. Because Afghans are, by UN definition, an internally displaced people (IDP), they cannot be assisted automatically by the UNHCR. Only people who flee across an international border qualify for the agency's help according to international standards involving people seeking protection from oppression in their home countries. So Afghans receive assistance if they live in the refugee camps, and consequently Afghans fare better if they leave their homeland.

There are many foreign governments that provide assistance to Afghan refugees. The United States provides the largest funds to Afghanistan. This year it will contribute approximately $150 million. However, this figure is approximately one-third less than previous monies. In some cases, the projects have achieved a degree of success, and people are better off than they were before. In other cases, Afghan refugees face arduous conditions. Many of these programs have targeted vulnerable members of the population, particularly women, children, and the elderly. For example, the U.S. Agency for International Development (USAID) has contributed thousands of tents, blankets, and medical supplies to Herat, Afghanistan, and Peshawar, Pakistan. In addition to various U.S. government agencies, there are other foreign governments committed to aid and assistance to Afghanistan. These include but are not limited to Denmark, Iran, Japan, Pakistan, Saudi Arabia, Pakistan, and Sweden.

The role of nongovernment organizations (NGOs) in Afghanistan and Pakistan is significant. The majority of the humanitarian assistance, education, and economic development, health care, and general social services are provided by NGOs. ACBAR, the Association and Coordinating Body of Afghan Relief, provides an accounting of all registered NGOs as well as an educational research center for development workers and researchers. Each NGO specializes in a service sector and may even work collaboratively with other government organizations and NGOs. For example, PARSA, Physiotherapy and Rehabilitation Support for Afghanistan, is a small NGO that receives small grants from USAID to work directly with widows of Kabul. One such project is a wool-spinning cooperative. In the refugee camps, small-scale microcredit schemes have been established in which individuals and small groups are able to obtain small loans that they repay over time. The credit that they have received has facilitated their involvement in textile craft economies including carpet and clothing production.

The need to debate Afghan people's role and identity in each new political era is strongly linked to Afghanistan's internal struggle to individuate and consolidate a multiethnic identity that contrasts with an autonomous Afghan national identity. This identity struggle extends from internal ethnic rivalry for access to scarce resources within Afghanistan to the Afghan national identity struggles against colonial and imperial contenders for regional control of their natural resources. Though Afghans in general are an endangered people and culture, by ignoring the UN Universal Declaration of Human Rights, the current politics of the ruling Taliban further threatens the survival of Afghan women in particular and consequently the future of Afghanistan.

FOOD FOR THOUGHT

When Afghans are thinking and talking about their immediate concerns, their everyday struggle is to maintain their roles in the familial context of an extended family network as fathers, brothers, sons, mothers, wives, daughters-in-law, and sisters and to provide for the health, education, and economic well-being of their families. Ultimately, the inability of Afghans to be proactive facilitators in this process jeopardizes and endangers the survival of the Afghan family and the country of Afghanistan.

A major question to be addressed about Afghanistan is, How is it possible for other countries and the public at large to deal with a government and a society that chooses to impose restrictions on the behavior of its citizens in such a way that those restrictions have negative implications for the well-being of many or most of the country's population? The efforts of agencies such as the UNHCR and nongovernment organizations have gone some way toward helping segments of the Afghan population. The issue to be faced now is how to ensure that all stakeholders, including the ruling governmental body, are willing to participate in a process that brings about peace, social justice, and human rights.

Questions

1. In what way has the physical environment contributed to the isolation and independence of the Afghan people?

2. Which customs and internal and external social and political views have affected the well-being of Afghanistan's population?

3. What types of traditional and religious codes of conduct have been used to control Afghan women's behavior and appearance and consequently their human rights?

4. How might codes of conduct either facilitate or inhibit Afghan women's gender, ethnic, and religious identity?

5. Is it appropriate for the Taliban government to destroy cultural monuments and sites? If not, what kinds of pressures can be brought to bear on Afghanistan to stop the destruction of the country's cultural heritage?

NOTES

1. CIA—The World Factbook 2001, *www.cia.gov/cia/publications/factbook/geos/af.html.*

2. United Nations High Commissioner for Refugees (UNHCR), "Crisis in Afghanistan" (2001), *www.unchr.ch/cgi-bin/texis/vtx/afghan.*

3. Ibid.

4. Ibid.

5. Louis Dupree, *Afghanistan* (Princeton: Princeton University Press, 1980), 18–19.

6. Preston Mendenhall, "Afghanistan's Cash Crop Wilts" MSNBC, (2001), *www.msnbc.com/news/564809.asp?cp1=1.*

7. United Nations, *Universal Declaration of Human Rights, 1948–1998* (2001), *www.un.org/Overview/rights.html.*

8. Sue Pleming, "Afghan Women Push for End to Gender Apartheid," Reuters (Asia), December 11, 2001, *http://asia.reuters.com/news . . . CFEYKEEATGIWD?type.*

9. William L. Rathje, "Why the Taliban Are Destroying Buddhas," *USA Today,* August 13, 2001, *www.usatoday.com/new . . . archaeology/2001–03–2-afghan-buddhas.htm.*

RESOURCE GUIDE

Published Literature

Christensen, Asger. *Aiding Afghanistan: The Background and Prospects for Reconstruction in a Fragmented Society.* Copenhagen: Nordic Institute of Asian Studies, 1995.

Gauhari, Farooka. *Searching for Saleem: An Afghan Woman's Odyssey.* Lincoln: University of Nebraska Press, 1996.

Griffin, Michael. *Reaping the Whirlwind: The Taleban Movement in Afghanistan.* London: Pluto Press, 2001.

Human Rights Watch. *Afghanistan: New War Puts Women's Rights in Peril.* Human Rights Watch Publication. Available at www.hrw.org/press/2001/10/afghanistan.htm.

———. *Humanity Denied: Systematic Violations of Women's Rights in Afghanistan.* Human Rights Watch Publication. Available at www.hrw.org/reports/2001/afghan3/.

Kaplan, Robert. "The Lawless Frontier." *The Atlantic Monthly* (September 2000): 66–72, 74–78, 80.

Magnus, Ralph H.H., and Eden Naby. *Afghanistan: Mullah, Marx, and Mujahid.* Boulder, CO: Westview Press, 1998.

Maley, William, ed. *Fundamentalism Reborn? Afghanistan and the Taleban.* New York: New York University Press, 1998.

Marsden, Peter. *Afghanistan: Minorities, Conflict, and the Search for Peace.* London: Minority Rights Group International, 2001.

Rashid, Ahmed. *Taleban: Militant Islam, Oil and Fundamentalism in Central Asia.* New Haven, CT: Yale University Press, 2000.

U.S. Department of State. *The Taliban's War Against Women*. Washington, DC: Bureau of Democracy, Human Rights, and Labor, U.S. Department of State.

Films and Videos

Afghan Exodus. 1980. Disappearing World Series, Films Incorporated Video.
Afghanistan: Exporting the Taleban Revolution. 1999. Films for the Humanities and Social Sciences. http://www.films.com/.
Afghan Women. 1994. Documentary Educational Resources, Watertown, MA.
CBS Reports: The Battle for Afghanistan. 1997. 60 Minutes, CBS Inc., New York, NY.
The Kirghiz of Afghanistan. 1975. Disappearing World Series, Films Incorporated Video.
The Pushtun: A Tough People in a Hard Land. 1996. Procia-Media Productions.
Shroud of Silence. 1998. Feminist Majority Foundation.

WWW Sites

The Afghanistan Foundation
http://afghanistanfoundation.org/

Afghanistan Online
http://www.afghan-web.com

Afghan Women and Education
www.erols.com/kabultic

The Afghan Women's Mission
http://www.afghanwomensmission.org

Dacaar
http://www.dacaar.org/

Feminist Majority Foundation Online
http://www.feminist.org/

"Help Afghan Women" Campaign, The Feminist Foundation
www.feminist.org

Ockenden International
http://www.ockenden.org.uk/

PARSA
http://www.parsa-afghanistan.org/

Physicians for Human Rights
http://phrusa.org/

Revolutionary Association of the Women of Afghanistan
http://www.rawa.org/

United Nations High Commissioner for Refugees
http://www.unhcr.ch/statist/98oview/ch1.htm

Organizations

Afghanistan Peace Association (APA)
P.O. Box 540926
Flushing, NY 11354–0926
Telephone: (718) 461–6799
Fax: (718) 866–8616
Email: AfghanPeaceA@hotmail.com

Afghan Refugees Weaver's Project
Cultural Survival, Inc.
221 Prospect Street
Cambridge, MA 02139
Email: cisnc@cs.org

Association for Peace and Democracy for Afghanistan (APDA)
6300-A Springfield Plaza
PMB 525
Springfield, VA 22152
Telephone: (703) 941–1589
Fax: (713) 823–9037
Email: info@apdaghanistan.org

Center for Afghan Studies
University of Nebraska at Omaha
Omaha, NE 68182–0006
Telephone: (402) 554–2376
Email:world@unomaha.edu

Revolutionary Association of Women of Afghanistan (RAWA)
209 Pennsylvania Avenue, SE, Suite 700
Washington, DC 20003
Telephone: (202) 543–1177
Fax: (202) 534–7931
and
P.O. Box 374
Quetta, Pakistan,
Email: rawa@rawa.org

Women's Alliance for Peace and Human Rights in Afghanistan
P.O. Box 77057
Washington, DC 20013–7057
Telephone:
Email: info@wapha.org

Chapter 2

The Bedouin of the South Sinai, Egypt
David Homa

CULTURAL OVERVIEW

The People

The Bedouin of the South Sinai, though not indigenous peoples of the region, are the first permanent inhabitants of the Sinai Peninsula. They are largely a nomadic people. The Sinai Peninsula is part of the Arab Republic of Egypt. The Sinai is often split both politically and geographically between the south and north. The Sinai Bedouin living in the southern half of the Sinai migrated to the region over a 1,500-year period. Physical and social boundaries were created as each tribe entered the South Sinai.

Currently there are ten different tribes living in the southern half of Sinai, Egypt. Each tribe has its own ancestral origin and time of arrival; however, all tribes are now facing similar challenges. The tribes of the South Sinai include the Jabaliyyah, Huweitat, Aleigat, Bani Wasil, Hamada, Mzeina, Awlad Sa'id, Gararsha, Sawalha, and Ahali et-Tur. An eleventh tribe, the Taraabiin, is considered by some to be part of the South Sinai, whereas others place it in the central Sinai. Tribal names are often traced to a founding male member. Family and tribal affiliation help cement the political structure of the South Sinai.

Nomadic Bedouin, sharing similar lifestyles and speaking numerous dialects of Arabic, make up an estimated 10 percent of the population of the Middle East. Nonetheless, the cultures and societies of each Bedouin tribe vary, depending on the tribe's location, history, and interactions with other groups and the state. Sinai Bedouin are primarily descendants of Bedouin who migrated from the Arabian Peninsula during the late fourteenth and

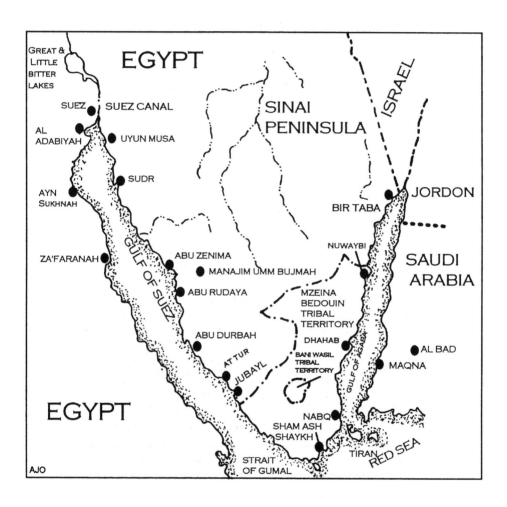

early fifteenth centuries, though there are exceptions as to when certain tribes arrived in the Sinai. Jabaliyyah Bedouin are said to be descendants from a small group of soldiers brought sometime in the sixth century to defend the monks of Saint Katherine's Monastery. Mzeina Bedouin did not arrive until the seventeenth century from the Arabian Peninsula, and most recently, Huweitat Bedouin arrived from the Arabian Peninsula in the early twentieth century.

Due to the fact the northern Sinai is the only land connection between Asia and Africa, Bedouin of the northern Sinai have dealt with outsiders for millennia. Conversely, South Sinai Bedouin have lived in relative isolation, apart from the multitude of travelers visiting Mount Sinai over the past several hundred years. As the differing Bedouin tribes have entered the South Sinai, physical and political boundary adjustments have been made following differing levels of disputes caused by the incoming tribes. Over time, each tribe settled into its own rhythm with other tribes and the environment. The past century, however, has brought major changes regarding how Bedouin interact with their environment and the increasing number of outsiders coming into the South Sinai.

The Setting

Covering approximately 24,897 square miles, the Sinai Peninsula is located between Africa and Eurasia. The Sinai Peninsula is bounded by the Mediterranean Sea to the north and the Red Sea to the south. The Red Sea splits into the Gulf of Suez on the west side of the peninsula and the Gulf of Aqaba on the east side. Egypt's mainland is to the northwest, and Israel borders the northeast side of the Sinai. The southern Sinai occupies approximately 6,500 square miles between the Gulf of Aqaba to the east, the Gulf of Suez to the west, and the Tih Plateau to the north. These geographical boundaries coincide very closely to the traditional and current governing body of the South Sinai called the Sina al-Janubiyya.

There are several key geographic features that influence the lives of Sinai Bedouin in the southern region. The main land features include the *wadi* (dry riverbed), *jabal* (mountain), the *naqb* (pass between mountains), and the *ras* (headland). The Gulfs of Aqaba and Suez are unique in that no natural rivers flow into them. With nearly year-round sun the Gulf water supports a diverse array of saltwater fish and an extensive network of coral reef. In some locations, the coral reef runs uninterrupted for scores of miles along the coast.

The Sinai's climate is influenced by its latitudinal position around thirty degrees north latitude. The Sinai, a desert of both rock and sand, receives less than an average of four inches of rain per year. Temperatures range from 32°F in January around Saint Katherine's (a historically significant monastery) to 86°F to 92°F in July along both the southern coast and the north end of the Gulf of Aqaba.

The climate and topography support a large variety of plants and a limited number of animals in the Sinai. The range of plants (trees, shrubs, and grasses of various types) in the Sinai includes from 900 to 1,200 different species. Over time, wild plants in the Sinai have developed several means of adapting to limited precipitation; one example can be seen in the deep root systems of trees and shrubs. Another strategy is the growth cycles of Sinai grasses, which grow only after rain has passed through the area in which the grasses hibernate.

The main animal species of the Sinai include lizards, rodents, and birds as well as a minimal number of ibex (wild mountain goats) and gazelles, which are the only larger animals commonly found in the Sinai. Wolves, hyenas, and possibly leopards have reportedly been seen in limited areas of the Sinai. Domesticated camels, goats, and sheep play an important role in a Bedouin home. Camels are employed primarily for transportation, whereas goats and sheep are valued for their by-products including milk and its derivatives, wool, and occasionally meat. Both plant and animal populations of the Sinai are affected by climate and increasingly by humans. Human impact comes by way of visitors to the Sinai and Bedouin who are living there.

Traditional Subsistence Strategies

The Sinai environment shapes subsistence strategies for Bedouin. South Sinai Bedouin historically have been defined as pastoral nomads. They are considered pastoral due to the animal herds they keep and their nomadic practices, moving from place to place in order to gain access to grazing and water and to interact with other groups. One exception is the Jabaliyyah Bedouin who have been relatively sedentary over the centuries with their connection to Saint Katherine's Monastery. In the past, Bedouin followed a seasonal migration pattern, or *rihla*. Camels, goats, and sheep were herded from grazing area to grazing area. Fall and winter were spent in a lower altitude *wadi* due to cooler weather and lack of grazing areas in the higher elevations. Spring and summer were spent in grazing pastures higher in the mountains.

Today few South Sinai Bedouin follow the traditional *rihla* for several reasons. The Egyptian government has been strongly encouraging Bedouin to settle. Also, loss of traditional grazing lands has forced Bedouin men to seek wage labor employment beyond their tribal territory and sometimes beyond the Sinai itself. Finally, the Egyptian government began a major Sinai development plan in 1994 that will continue until 2017. This project has, and will, continue to affect the areas in which Bedouin have access. This does not mean Bedouin no longer look to the desert for resources;

nonetheless, Bedouin rely far less on the desert for their daily needs than they did in the past.

Bedouin diet is dependent to some extent on where the tribe is residing. Those tribes living near the sea will take advantage of seafood that is readily available. Bedouin living inland depend on plant and animal resources found in the Sinai. In addition, goat's milk and milk by-products such as yogurt are found in nearly all Bedouin diets. Camel's milk can be used if needed and in certain circumstances. Women often make bread products such as pita bread each morning. Today pita is mass-produced in towns but is still made by individual families both in villages and those living in and traveling through the Sinai. Other foods important to a Bedouin diet include eggs, dates, figs, garden vegetables, and meat. The latter, however, is usually eaten only on special occasions including weddings and holidays. As Bedouin settle in towns, their diet has been changing with the introduction of processed foods bought from a local grocer. Nonetheless, traditional styles of cooking are not being made completely obsolete with the introduction of new food sources.

Social and Political Organization

Family ties and tribal relationships are significant components of Bedouin life. The family, both nuclear and extended, is the most important relationship for a Bedouin. Descent is traced patrilineally (descent through the male line) including blood and marriage ties. While a Bedouin family unit is made up of a father, mother, and their children, the family home may be inhabited by the father's other relatives such as his grandparents, parents, or a brother and his family. A very small number of men have more than one wife. Though having more than one wife is technically legal, the economic resources needed for this practice make it unattainable except for only the wealthiest of Bedouin men. Today a growing number of adult males have wage labor jobs. Men have been known to travel far distances within the Sinai to find work, even venturing to foreign countries for employment.

Politically, the South Sinai is split among ten tribes residing in the region. The main political organization is the Towara Alliance. The Towara (mountaineers) tribal alliance of the South Sinai is divided into two groups. The first group includes the Aleigat, Bani Wasil, Hamada, and Mzeina tribes. The second group includes the Awlad Sa'id, the Gararsha, and the Sawalha tribes. Three tribes, the Jabaliyyah, the Ahali et-Tur, and the Heweitat, are not members of the Towara Alliance. Today the Towara Alliance exists only under the greater control placed on it by the Egyptian government. The political entities that have ruled the Sinai have, until very recently, given little consideration to the will or desire of the Sinai Bedouin. Often events are beyond the control of Sinai Bedouin, for example, the political upheaval created by the conflict between Egypt and Israel, particularly in the past fifty years.

Each tribe controls certain territorial areas. Territorial borders may be crossed and land in another tribe's territory can be used under certain circumstances, animal grazing being a common example. This behavior is known as a policy of "open grazing territories." Kindness shown to another tribe may be returned at a later date. Each tribe has its own territory that is recognized by the other tribes and by the Egyptian government as well. However, the Egyptian government does not hold tribal territories above the greater good of Egypt as a whole.

Under Israeli rule, the Sinai was primarily considered militarily important. The Bedouin were generally left alone during Israel's rule of the Sinai. The Israeli government did set up "Bedouin centers" in the early 1970s. These centers provided basic services such as medical clinics and elementary schools.

Today, Bedouin have only minimal representation in the Egyptian government. Sheikhs from the Sinai act as representatives for their tribes, reporting to and having dialogues with officials in the Egyptian government. However, any real power rests in the hands of the government officials like South Sinai governor Major General Mustafa Afifi.

Religion and World View

Bedouin are Muslim people who follow the religion of Islam. In the midseventh century Muslims believed that Allah (God) imparted his teachings through the angel Gabriel to the prophet Mohammed. Allah's teachings were set down in the Quran (Islam's holy book), the main Islamic text by which all Muslims live. Though religion has always played a central role in Bedouin life, over time South Sinai Bedouin have gone through differing levels of religious piety. One example of an Islamic revival came about following the return of the Sinai to Egypt in the early 1980s. A continuing impetus for focusing on Islam has come by way of the increasing number of tourists visiting the Sinai. Visitors have brought with them lifestyles and beliefs that run counter to the teachings found in the Quran. Females in various manners of undress on the beach along with male and female interaction were deemed inappropriate.

Bedouin place great importance on celebrations and religious rites centered on Islam. Marriage is one example of a celebration that brings together large numbers of people, particularly if two people are marrying from different tribes. Marriage within a group is common among Sinai Bedouin. Marriage to a first cousin will help keep both political and economic stability between and among a tribe or subtribe. Men and women are expected to follow the laws of the Quran and accept their role in society based on the Quran's teachings.

THREATS TO SURVIVAL

Demographic Trends

The Sinai has a population of approximately 300,000 people, of which 50,000 are Bedouin (16 percent).[1] The South Sinai is home to a population ranging from 7,000 to 13,000 Bedouin, depending on the source. Egyptian government officials and Bedouin tribes both dispute the exact number, as each side strives for control of resources in the Sinai, and the larger the population numbers, the greater the degree of resource control. Not long after the return of the Sinai to Egyptian control in 1982, tens of thousands of Egyptians, who had previously lived in the Sinai, came back to their former homes in the Sinai. The Egyptian government is implementing plans to increase the population of the Sinai to over 3 million people by 2020, with the intent of easing population pressures found elsewhere in Egypt along the Nile River. The current population aim for the South Sinai alone is 3 million people by the year 2020.[2]

Ninety-eight percent of Egypt's population is located in less than 5 percent of Egypt's land.[3] Over 60 million people occupy the Nile Basin in Egypt. By the first decade of the third millennium, more than 20 percent of the country's population will live in Cairo, and population densities will possibly exceed 349,650 people per square mile, some of the highest densities in the world. The government is being forced to look for development alternatives beyond the Nile Valley and the Nile Delta in order to lessen population pressures. Areas once considered marginal such as the Sinai are now considered logical and necessary places to turn to for their development potential. From the perspective of the Egyptian government, it was necessary to develop a major plan to make the Sinai a viable option for population relocation. As development plans took shape, Sinai Bedouin generally were not consulted about the potential impact on their life and livelihood including access to water, grazing land, and other critical resources. The influx of Egyptians only exacerbated an already tenuous relationship between the Egyptian and Bedouin populations that has existed for centuries.

Current Events and Conditions

Bedouin throughout Egypt and specifically in the South Sinai are facing two major threats: population increase and land development. Both threats will place a strain on already limited resources. The first threat comes from the need for Egypt to lessen population pressures, particularly along the Nile River Basin. Egyptian government officials implemented a plan starting in 1994 to help relieve population pressure throughout the Nile valley. The main focus of this plan is massive development to the infrastructure (e.g.,

53

construction of canals, pumping stations, tunnels, and roads) in the Sinai to support the growing number of people moving to the Sinai.

The second threat, related directly to the population increase, is land development to support the incoming population. Developments will lessen the land available for Bedouin use, and they will increase the consumption of and dispute over already limited available resources in the Sinai. Some of these land developments include the establishment of new communities and the construction of roads and other kinds of infrastructure.

Sinai Bedouin have dealt with various occupying forces of the Sinai for centuries. The Ottoman Empire, the British, the Egyptians, and the Israelis have all controlled the Sinai at different times in history. The Sinai has changed hands five times in the past fifty years just between Egypt and Israel. Real authority over the Bedouin did not begin until recent decades, as the Sinai has become more economically useful and a viable option for population relief. Current rule by the Egyptian government is not total, as various alliances and tribal groups still retain a certain degree of power at the local level. Tribal leaders handle local disputes and internal problems such as using another person's well for water without permission. This minimal power may soon disappear as the population increases and the Egyptian government takes greater control of the Sinai for development purposes.

One impact of population pressure is coming from the growing number of tourists to the Sinai. Tourists usually are only short-term visitors to the Sinai. The problem is coming from the large number of people needed to take care of and run tourist facilities. A few sites in the South Sinai have witnessed particularly strong growth. One example is the town of Dahab, one of the largest settlements of the South Sinai. Dahab lies 84 miles south of the Egyptian-Israeli border and 62 miles north of Sharm al-Sheikh at the tip of the Sinai Peninsula. The town of Dahab has a population of over 5,000 people. The town can be broken down into three different areas: the main administrative center; Asala, where Mzeina Bedouin live; and the *masbat* (cove) where the majority of tourists reside. Mzeina are the main Bedouin group living in the Dahab area.

A growing number of Egyptians and foreigners have been moving into Dahab since the mid-1980s to take advantage of the increase in tourism. Social pressure from the rapidly changing environment of Dahab is making the task of cultural survival and retention a far more difficult one, especially for young Bedouin. The growing numbers of tourists bring with them monetary and social influence. Bedouin youth living near tourist destinations are more vulnerable to these influences as they come into contact with vastly different lifestyles and beliefs. Some Bedouin youths are opting to deal with tourists instead of attending school.

A rapidly increasing population puts a strain on the limited resources of the Sinai in general and on the Bedouin in particular. Even in the desert

Three Bedouin girls take a break from selling bracelets to tourists in Dahab, Egypt. (Courtesy David Homa)

environment of the Sinai, water plays a central role for Bedouin existence. Water has always been a scarce resource in the Sinai. Measures are being taken to lessen the coming population explosion. In 1999 the 150-mile-long Al-Salam irrigation canal began to bring water from the Nile to the Sinai. Even with the Al-Salam canal, continuing population increase along with rapid tourism development will result in additional stresses on the Bedouin's habitat and resources.

Like many Bedouin groups in the Middle East, the Sinai Bedouin are facing what many consider to be policies of assimilation, the process whereby their cultures are changed through the implementation of national education, development, and language policies by the government.

A major shift over time in the Sinai has been a reduction in the mobility of Bedouin groups, in part through active efforts of the government to encourage Bedouins to settle down and reside in single locations year-round. No longer nomadic, most Bedouins are now living in stationary villages and are facing all of the problems of long-term residence: pollution, crowding, and limited access to water and energy.

The Bedouin, who once were remote from the centers of Egyptian power, are now increasingly integrated into the Egyptian state. This integration comes at some cost: They lose some of their cultural traditions; they no longer teach their mother tongue languages to their children, and they interact extensively with the Egyptian state. Some Sinai Bedouin join the Egyptian army. Others work in Cairo and other cities in a variety of jobs. Some of them are even investing in beach-side resorts in the Sinai.

Sinai Development

Social and economic development—the efforts to improve the well-being of the citizens of Egypt—is affecting Bedouin and others throughout the Sinai. To take one example, the Jabaliyyah Bedouin are a small tribe of 1,500 people who live near the Saint Katherine Monastery in the mountains of the South Sinai. The mountainous region where Saint Katherine is located once supported a wide variety of wild plants and animals as well as people and their livestock. Bedouin such as the Jabaliyya and Mzeina have long been aware of the need to protect the environment, and one way to do that, they realize, is to establish community-based conservation projects.

Several factors have negatively affected the environment. First, as the need for wage labor employment for Bedouin has increased, the importance placed on protecting their environment has decreased. Second, as increased numbers of tourists have come into the Saint Katherine area during the past several decades, the environment has begun to suffer the fate of misuse and overuse by tourists and Bedouin alike. The Jabaliyyah and Bedouin tribes in the Sinai can no longer ignore what is happening to their environment. Egyptian plans for major developments in the Sinai are potentially the greatest threat to cultural survival for Sinai Bedouin.

The history of the Sinai and Bedouin has changed over time and through countless political shifts. The formation of Israel in 1948 made the Sinai a vital military location for both Israel and Egypt. Though the land was politically important, both governments paid little attention to the Sinai Bedouin. Initially, development came slowly to the Sinai. Completion of a black-top road around the coast of the Sinai in 1972 was the first major hardtop roadway to connect the southern part of the Sinai to Egypt proper. The new road increased the number of people visiting the Sinai and the potential for industrial development. The next change came with the return of the Sinai to Egypt in 1982 following completion of the Camp David Accord. Most recently, in 1994 the Egyptian government implemented the

National Project for the Development of the Sinai. Since then the rate and number of changes have increased substantially.

The project aims at increasing agricultural lands and production, tourism, and industrial activity. Food production is a priority for the Egyptian government. Egypt produces 100 percent of its agricultural crops on irrigated lands, and a significant proportion of its population derives its livelihood from these areas. Currently, Egypt uses less than 5 percent of its land to feed and house more than 90 percent of its people. In the past, areas such as the Sinai have been marginal in terms of agricultural production, though it has supported populations engaged in minimal mixed production systems (agriculture, small-scale rural industries, pastoralism, and wage labor). The Egyptian government plans to increase agricultural production by nearly doubling cultivated land from over 3 million feddans (1 feddan = 1.038 acres) to nearly 8 million feddans by 2017.

Industrial activity will include increased oil production off the southern Sinai coast along with resettling industrial projects from Egypt proper. An example of industrial change is that of quarry operations in the Sinai. One of the main materials quarried, in the past often illegally, is granite. The number of illegal granite quarry operations is slowly decreasing. Problems still exist, though, with the remaining quarries. Rock quarries require vast amounts of water, an already scare resource in the Sinai. They also produce dust that has effects on the health of people living nearby. There is a growing sense of resentment on the part of Bedouin and others in the Sinai toward the kinds of development activities that are taking place.

RESPONSE: STRUGGLES TO SURVIVE CULTURALLY

Cultural survival for Sinai Bedouin will come through adaptation to a complex political, economic, and environmental set of situations over which they will have relatively little control. Each tribe and individual will have to recognize the need to adapt to the various changes, but the manner by which this will be accomplished is still to be determined. Bedouin tribes have had very little, if any, voice in development plans for the Sinai since the ultimate say concerning current and future Sinai development rests in the hands of the Egyptian government. Changes in the Sinai are yielding different results and consequences, but nearly all the changes affect the Bedouin directly or indirectly.

Two ways that Sinai Bedouin are attempting to promote their well-being and enhance their cultural survival are through grassroots mobilization to preserve their culture, traditions, and languages and through resource management, some of it related to cultural tourism. Bedouin are responding to these changes by working on local-level cultural programs in which they are obtaining information on their history, languages, and customs. They are then using this information in the development of school curricula and materials used by schoolchildren and Bedouin community-based cultural organizations.

The Bedouins have made some small gains in the area of tourism, marketing their culture and selling Bedouin crafts. Ironically, tourism has in some ways actually enhanced cultural diversity among Sinai Bedouin. The Sinai has very limited natural resources. Nonetheless, nature has provided numerous distinct areas that contain rare species of plants and animals. Bedouin tribes living in the Sinai have for centuries learned about and passed down the knowledge of the land on which they live. Significant abuse of the land by Bedouin tribes has been rare. At first the Egyptian government paid little attention to the hidden resources of the Sinai. Protected areas have slowly begun to take shape.

There are four protected areas in the Sinai: Ras Mohammad National Park, the Nabq Managed Resource Protected Area, the Abu Galum Managed Resource Protected Area, and the Saint Katherine Protected Area. Approximately 4,426 square miles in the South Sinai are under state protection. Bedouin have had a limited role in the creation of the protected areas despite having lived in the Sinai for centuries. One exception is the Saint Katherine Protected Area of the South Sinai. Bedouin tribes living in or near the protected area were given the opportunity to participate in the creation of the protected area and today participate in its management.

Bedouin representatives from different tribes in the region worked with the Egyptian Environmental Affairs Agency (EEAA) to develop what has become the St. Katherine Natural Protectorate, a park covering 1,679 square miles. Jabaliyyah Bedouin continue to play an active, though limited, role in the park. Over twenty members of the tribe act as *haris al-biyah*, or "nature guards," helping with the park development and upkeep. The park is home to a large variety of animals and nearly thirty-five species of plants found only in the park. Saint Katherine Park is a good example of where the local community can take part in its own future.

Another example of Bedouins helping to manage their environment is through the need to deal with increasing problems of garbage and pollution. The rising numbers of visitors, new residents, and recent industrial developments in the Sinai are generating problematic quantities of waste and refuse. In late 1998 near the town of Nuweiba, an environmental nongovernmental organization (NGO) called Hemeida began operation of a garbage recycling plant.[4] It was a small center initially employing only ten people. Benefits to local Bedouin, such as employment, were limited at the beginning of the project. The center is beginning to incorporate Bedouin into the business. Recently, local Bedouin trucks were being rented to help with garbage collection. Bedouin, along with others living in the Sinai, can potentially benefit from the development of environmentally friendly businesses such as garbage-processing centers.

Today, nearly all Bedouin tribes must confront the tourist industry, each in their own way. One strategy initially developed in the 1970s by Mzeina in the town of Dahab was the creation of a beach resort for travelers coming to the area. Small huts sprang up along the beach for backpacking travelers. At the time, income from tourism was increasing the standard of living for a small number of the Mzeina. Following Israel's return of the Sinai to Egypt in 1982, the potential for tourism development continued to expand. Egyptians saw the potential for development in the Sinai and decided to take advantage of the sun and sea, while Mzeina and other Bedouin tribes were pushed to the periphery.

In Dahab, Mzeina have not been allowed to directly own businesses that cater to tourists. This rule is not necessarily legal but rather a social rule placed on Mzeina people by the Egyptians. There was a fear among a few officials that Bedouin would benefit from the tourist market before Egyptians. The situation is changing as Mzeina have very recently entered into partnerships with Egyptians. Non-Bedouin people have gained the upper hand in controlling the tourist market. Mzeina do have the option to rent their land on which an Egyptian wants to build. A small number of Mzeina families receive rent for the use of their land along the water's edge. The money they receive is a minimal percentage of total revenue Egyptians take in from tourists.

The Egyptian government has ultimate control of tourist developments in the Sinai. In the summer of 1999, an example of government control occurred near the town of Nuweiba.[5] Two Bedouin men and their families had developed a small tourist site along the beach. The men said they had gone through all the necessary legal procedures for building a tourist camp. The needed paperwork never seemed to be processed, and the men were continuously told to come back for several years.

In 1982, the Egyptian government declared that all land outside of town limits in the Sinai would be owned by the government. Bedouin did not want to accept this decision but could do nothing to change it. The government legally owned the land that the two Bedouin men had built on. However, the men believed the land belonged to their family by right of living there for many years. The Egyptian government sold the land to an Egyptian developer who was once the chairman of the Egyptian Tourist Authority (ETA). In July 1999, three truckloads of soldiers, two bulldozers, and a number of other vehicles arrived at the Bedouin tourist camp. By sundown, the men's camp along with numerous other "illegal" camps had been destroyed.

The Tourist Development Authority (TDA) said the Bedouin had illegally developed the site. And the Egyptian government has the final say about landownership and land development. Ultimately, the future of Bedouin will be affected heavily by government policies such as this one, but the Bedouin are learning to challenge the system, organizing themselves into grassroots groups and pressuring their leaders to talk to the government on their behalf. Some Bedouin groups, including the Mzeina, are turning to the World Wide Web and the Internet and are communicating with other peoples, some of them indigenous, around the world. Some of the Sinai Bedouin are in direct communication with Bedouin in the Gaza Strip and Israel and are seeking means to resolve conflicts and promote peace among Bedouin, their neighbors, and the states in which they reside.

According to the Mzeina, Bedouin culture is slowly coming into its own as a source of pride and income. Project activities such as the Bedouin Support Program allow women to incorporate cultural styles and designs into their work, which is then sold to tourists visiting the South Sinai. The Saint Katherine Visitor Center is another example of Bedouin being given the opportunity to display their work and culture for visiting tourists who may hopefully gain a better understanding of the people who have lived in the Sinai for centuries.

FOOD FOR THOUGHT

How can the Bedouin be part of the future of the Sinai without losing their own identity? One way is to make sure their culture does not change substantially or disappear as the Egyptian government develops the Sinai. While this task will not be easy, being part of the process is their best hope for survival both as individuals and as a tribal culture. One illustration of Bedouin helping with cultural survival is seen in national protectorates such as the Saint Katherine Protected Area. Another example is the effort of some Sinai Bedouin to teach their own languages and cultural traditions in the schools. It is inevitable, according to many Bedouin, that they will need to give up certain aspects of their traditions, such as the nomadic life, in return for the preservation of their culture as a whole.

Bedouin have their own ideas concerning what should happen to the Sinai. The Egyptian government also has grand plans for the Sinai, many of which conflict with those of the Bedouin. It appears the Egyptian government's plan will ultimately win due to their power and control of nearly all aspects of the Sinai's land, resources, and infrastructure. The Bedouin will need to deal carefully with the coming transformations to preserve their culture.

Questions

1. What role has history played in how Bedouin have lived their lives?
2. Who has control of preserving traditional ways of customs, languages, and beliefs of Sinai Bedouin? If it is the Bedouin themselves, how can cultural preservation effort be enhanced? If it is the Egyptian government, how might the Bedouin influence government policies and practices?

3. In what ways can Bedouin be given a greater voice in and control over the rapidly expanding tourism industry in the Sinai?

4. What could be done to allow Sinai Bedouin to continue their traditional lifestyles while allowing development projects to go forward in the Sinai?

5. In what ways has tourism affected the cultures of Africa and the Middle East as a whole? How can tourism activities be improved to ensure the well-being of people and the habitats in which they live?

NOTES

1. SinaiNet, "Discover Sinai," 2001, *http://www.sinainet.com.eg/discover.html.*

2. Egypt State Information Service, "The National Project for the Development of Sinai: Objectives, Mainstays, and Potentials," 2001, *http://www.sis.gov.eg/public/html/text02.htm.*

3. International Rivers Network, "Massive Nile River Diversions Planned," 1997, *http://www.irn.org/pubs/wrr/9706/nile.html.*

4. "Bedouin Camp Demolished," *Cairo Times,* 3, no. 1 (July 22–August 6, 1999).

5. Ibid.

RESOURCE GUIDE

Published Literature

Greenwood, Ned. *The Sinai: A Physical Geography.* Austin: University of Texas Press, 1997.

Hobbs, Joseph J. *Bedouin Life in the Egyptian Wilderness.* Austin: University of Texas Press, 1989.

Homa, David. "Interaction between Travelers to Dahab, Egypt and Bedouin Youth." Master's thesis, Department of Anthropology, University of Nebraska, Lincoln, 1997.

Lavie, Smadar. *The Poetics of Military Occupation: Mzeina Allegories of Bedouin Identity under Israeli and Egyptian Rule.* Berkeley: University of California Press, 1990.

Lavie, Smadar, and William C. Young. "Bedouin in Limbo: Egyptian and Israeli Development Policies in Southern Sinai." *Antipode* 16, no. 2 (1984): 33–34.

Perevolotsky, Avi. "Territoriality and Resource Sharing among the Bedouin of Southern Sinai: A Socio-Ecological Interpretation." *Journal of Arid Environments* 13 (1987): 153–61.

Smith, Valene L., ed. *Hosts and Guests: The Anthropology of Tourism.* Philadelphia: University of Pennsylvania Press, 1977.

Films and Videos

Bisha—The Awesome Fire Test. 1995. Produced by Elia Sides and Nira Sherman-Sides. Filmmakers Library, 124 East 40th Street, New York, NY 10016.

Telephone: (212) 808–4980. This video centers around the *bisha* ceremony that is part of a system of law and order called *Haj El Orfi*—The Law of Knowledge. The film looks at other parts of Bedouin culture and the law of the Bedouin.

WWW sites

Egyptian Organization for Human Rights (EOHR). EOHR was founded in 1985 to work for the support and defense of human rights in Egypt.
http://www.eohr.org.eg/

Egypt State Information System. The site provides important information on Egypt's National Project for the Development of the Sinai.
http://www.sis.gov.eg/

Egypt WWW Index. This site offers a wide variety of links to Egypt and the Sinai. Information on history, health, and environment issues and numerous newspapers can be accessed from this site.
http://ce.eng.usf.edu/pharos/

Infomate, Department of Natural Protectorates, Egyptian Environmental Affairs Agency. This site gives a generous overview of the environmental issues of the Sinai. The site includes information on protected areas in the Sinai, the Bedouin populations, human impact, and environmental and development concerns.
http://www.sinaiparks.gov.eg/

Union of International Associations. This is an excellent source for locating NGOs throughout the world. A helpful site for locating NGOs working in the Sinai.
http://www.uia.org/

Organizations

Afro-Asian Peoples' Solidarity Organization
89 Abdel Aziz Al Saoud Street
Manial El-Roda, Cairo, Egypt
Telephone: 20–2-363–6081
Fax:20–2-363–7361
Email: aapso@idsc.gov.eg

Arab Organization for Human Rights
91 Al-Marghany Street
Heliopolis, Cairo, Egypt
Telephone: 20–2-418–1396
Fax: 20–2-418–5346
Email: aohr@link.com.eg
Web site: http://www.aohr.org,

Center for Bedouin Studies and Development
Ben-Gurion University

Sede Boqer, Israel 84990
Email: Bedouin@bgumail.bgu.ac.il
Web site: http://www.bgu.ac.il/bedouin/

Community and Institutional Development (CID)
11 El Gabalaya Street, 3rd Floor, Suite 9
Zamalek, 11211
Cairo, Egypt
Telephone: 20-2-322-0832
Fax: 20-2-340-2660
Email: cid@intouch.com

Egyptian Organization for Human Rights (EOHR)
8/10 Matahaf El-Manyal, Floor 10
Manyal El Roda
Cairo, Egypt
Telephone: 20-2-363-6811
Fax: 20-2-362-1613
Email: eohr@link.com.eg

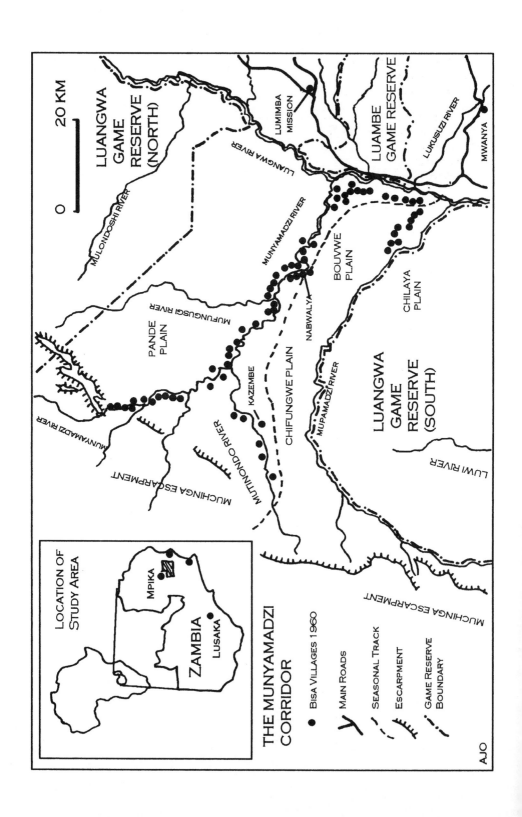

THE MUNYAMADZI CORRIDOR

- BISA VILLAGES 1960
⋏ MAIN ROADS
SEASONAL TRACK
ESCARPMENT
GAME RESERVE BOUNDARY

LOCATION OF STUDY AREA

ZAMBIA

MPIKA

LUSAKA

0   20 KM

LUANGWA GAME RESERVE (NORTH)

LUANGWA GAME RESERVE (SOUTH)

LUAMBE GAME RESERVE

MULONDOSHI RIVER

LUANGWA RIVER

LUMIMBA MISSION

LUKUSUZI RIVER

MWANYA

MUNYAMADZI RIVER

MUFUNGUSHI RIVER

PANDE PLAIN

BOUVWE PLAIN

CHILAYA PLAIN

NABWALYA

KAZEMBE

CHIFUNGWE PLAIN

MUTINONDO RIVER

MUPAMADZI RIVER

MUCHINGA ESCARPMENT

MUNYAMADZI RIVER

LUWI RIVER

MUCHINGA ESCARPMENT

AJO

Chapter 3

The Bisa of Zambia

Stuart A. Marks

CULTURAL OVERVIEW

The People

The Bisa of the Luangwa Valley of Zambia in southern Africa are a population of 7,000 to 8,000 agriculturalists who inhabit a strip of land known as the Munyamadzi Corridor, between the South and North Luangwa National Parks. Most Bisa live in scattered homesteads close to their fields along perennial streams in the area. The Bisa are known for their hunting abilities.

Like the other ethnic groups currently inhabiting northern Zambia, the Bisa had their origins centuries ago in an earlier empire formerly situated in southeastern Zaire (now the Democratic Republic of Congo). The Bisa say that it was from this former state that their ancestors came and that disputes arising from land scarcity led to their immigration (estimated as around A.D. 1600). During these migrations, certain smaller groups emerged as leaders and subordinated the other groups in their vicinities. Thus the Bisa separated from the Bemba (who became eventually an important and more powerful rival on the central African plateau), and among the Bisa, the Mushroom clan (Ngona) became the dominant political group and the lineage from which their chiefs were selected. Initially, the Bisa settled on the plateau around the Bangweulu Swamps and eastward to the Muchinga Escarpment, while the Bemba settled further north on the plateau.

From atop the Muchingas, the Bisa knew the adjacent Luangwa Valley as a hunting territory as groups from the plateau made seasonal forays there in search of wild game and for trade with other groups further east. More permanent residence in the valley came probably in the seventeenth and eighteenth centuries as Bisa settlements were noticed there by the Portuguese and later by other European explorers, including David Livingstone in 1866. During the nineteenth century, skirmishes with the Bemba on the plateau forced many Bisa to take refuge within the escarpment and in the valley. At the same time, the arrival and settlement on the eastern plateau by the Ngoni (part of the Zulu diaspora) caused considerable movements and exchanges among valley residents. The Valley Bisa were participants in both slave and ivory trades and were expanding their spheres of influence eastward across the Luangwa River when the British South Africa Company began its pacification of the region around 1890.

Although the Bisa currently living within the Luangwa Valley came from those now living on the plateau, those in the valley have come to differ in significant ways from those on the plateau. These differences include environment, basic food staples, history, language, and more recently, educational and economic opportunities. Their current lifestyles are similar to neighboring groups from slightly differing ethnic backgrounds and histories whose plight they also share. Today, many "Valley Bisa" are also living under different chieftaincies.

Agents of the British South Africa Company cared not for learning local history, customs, and language, yet their strong sense of and belief in their "civilizing mission" caused them to become ruthless in establishing control and in reshaping local institutions into their own molds. They established an administrative post among the Valley Bisa and manned it with a European officer, a contingent of troops, and staff from 1899 until 1908. After this outpost (*boma*) was abandoned for health reasons, the site served as a medical facility for researching the causes and extent of human sleeping sickness and other tropical diseases.

Written records became the memory and basis for decisions, with British values the source of new laws and institutions. Administrators (or native commissioners) established their own political hierarchy among chiefly lineages, supporting some with salary and authority while dismissing others. They conscripted local labor to build roads and to work for European enterprises elsewhere (such as building railroads, mines, towns, and carrying supplies). They assessed a head or hut tax that was to be paid in currency, thus forcing local men to work for Europeans. They sought to change the ways people lived. People were forced to abandon their stockades and scattering of huts (which had provided security earlier) and to live in orderly villages where the houses were all in a line. They aspired to change agriculture from a "wasteful" slash and burn to using the same plot of ground every year. This imposition did not last long as there was no substitute fertilizer for the ash of burned vegetation, and the few European commissioners were faced with a rebellion unless they retracted this requirement. Europeans also enforced game laws that made most local ways of taking wildlife illegal and restricted access to the larger forms of game such as elephants, hippos, and rhinos.

The 1930s saw sweeping changes in colonial policies. Under the principles of indirect rule, more authority was restored to the sanctioned chiefs, who were expected to rule at local courts, to toe the colonial line, and to control local movements and behavior. About 1940, the Luangwa Valley Game Reserves were established to the north and south of the perennial streams along which most Valley Bisa lived. Individuals and groups living within these declared game reserves were encouraged to move elsewhere; some took up residence under other ethnic chiefs. These new boundaries placed restrictions on Valley Bisa movements and on their uses of widely dispersed resources and stretched their abilities to cope within an environment that was often marginal for agriculture. Subsequently, the Valley Bisa have been restricted to the narrow neck of land known as the Munyamadzi Corridor.

The Setting

The Luangwa River, and its drainage basin, is an important geographic and geologic feature in northeast and eastern Zambia. This river extends for some 450 miles northeast from its confluence with the larger Zambezi River where Zambia shares borders with Zimbabwe and Mozambique. In physical appearance, the Luangwa Valley is a flat-bottomed trough bounded by an abrupt escarpment in its west and a more gradual incline in the east. The Muchinga Escarpment that forms its western border rises in places upward of 3,000 feet and more above the valley. These topographical features, together with more recent history and the shift in commercial trade routes from east-west to a north-south direction, have contributed to the isolation of and the declining welfare of most of the valley's remote human residents during the twentieth century.

The valley is a hot place with a mean annual temperature of around 80°F. The hottest month is October, just before the annual rains begin; the coolest occurs in June when frost sometimes occurs. The valley receives most of its rainfall during a five-month period between November and May. For the people living in the center of the valley, rainfall is usually sufficient to grow their food staples. Yet this rain falls in highly variable and irregular patterns, and droughts are not infrequent. In addition, heavy rainfall on the western plateau may cause water to cascade over the escarpment, causing devastating flooding in the valley below. These flash floods are particularly damaging to settlements and fields along tributaries of the Luangwa River. June to October are the dry season months when the landscape becomes parched, and most vegetation is consumed by fires.

The tsetse fly (*Glossina morsitans*), the carrier of sleeping sickness to humans and to their domestic stock, occurs through most of the Luangwa Valley. The occurrence of this intermediate host precludes the keeping of livestock; yet wildlife, which is immune to the pathogen, abound.

Today, four national parks cover a large portion of the valley floor. These parks contain substantial numbers of elephant, buffalo, hippopotami, warthog, zebra, wildebeest, together with smaller numbers of other antelopes and carnivores. Large numbers of these mammals also are found in the Game Management Areas where people such as the Valley Bisa, Chewa, Senga, and Kunda reside.

Traditional Subsistence Strategies

Throughout the Luangwa Valley, the principal mode of subsistence is a shifting agriculture typical of many places in east and central Africa. These shifting cultivation systems are responsive to local conditions and are continually changing in response to variable circumstances. Cleared fields are abandoned generally once the site shows signs of diminishing crop productivity and if too many wild mammals (elephants or mice) and other pests are attracted to the site.

The main staples in valley agriculture are sorghum and maize. Varieties of pumpkins and cucumbers are usually planted with these staples, along with a number of other plants including groundnuts (peanuts), sugar cane, cowpeas, beans, and cassava. Fruit trees, sweet potatoes, and ground nuts became common when the larger mammals such as elephants and hippos, together with the baboons, decreased in numbers in the late 1970s. Still, these fruit trees and crops must be planted within or adjacent to settlements to guard against depredations by wild mammals.

The agricultural work cycle mirrors the rainy season, with clearing fields and planting crops taking place immediately prior to the expected rains in October. Weeding is continuous during the rains with protection of the grains and harvesting at the end of the rains in May or June. Success of a planting depends on the timing and duration of the rains. Crop failure has become more frequent in recent years as drought periods have increased. Too much rain can be just as damaging as too little, as when the swollen rivers overflow their banks and pour into adjacent fields. Crops are placed strategically close to settlement houses, often in a protective format surrounded by houses, to guard against night depredations by elephants and other wild mammals. Considerable loss after harvest occurs from insects and rodents within the storage bins.

Most of the food comes from cultivated plants. People also depend on products of wild plants, not only for food but for building materials for their houses and bins, for firewood, and for medicines. Lacking domestic stock because of the tsetse fly, the Valley Bisa largely depend on wild animals and fish as sources of animal protein. They also keep domestic fowl,

A school is let out for the day so the students can help butcher and carry the meat from a buffalo killed for their teacher (with back to camera) by a local hunter. The salaried teacher, who paid the hunter a minimum amount for his skills, will smoke the meat for sale on the plateau to supplement his salary. (Courtesy Stuart Marks)

but these are generally sold to outsiders for cash to obtain other essential goods. Hunting continues as an important career route for some men who gain a local reputation among their kin by protecting crops against wildlife depredations and by providing relatives meat when an animal is killed.

Social and Political Organization

Among the Valley Bisa, the main descent and residential groupings are matrilineal—often an extended cluster of men, women, and children who trace their descent from a named female ancestress. Identification with and loyalty to this descent group is the dominant affiliation with numerous cultural traits such as names, behaviors, rituals, and food preparations to distinguish its members from neighboring groups. Each residential group holds sacred the memories and names of its expired ancestors and solicits their aid in decision making and in maintaining the integrity of this group through time.

Each matrilineage (a kin group whose members trace descent through known links in the female line from a common female ancestor) is exogenous, although there is a preference for marrying cross-cousins. Polygyny (the marriage of one man to more than one woman at a time) is not uncommon; neither is divorce. A man's relatives make a small, token payment to the bride's family (a custom known as bride price), and initially the couple resides in her village where he engages in bride-service (working for the wife's family) for a short period. Individuals also belong to larger spatial groups such as clans, who may be called upon for hospitality away from their home village. Clans are sets of kin who believe themselves to be descended from a common ancestor but who cannot specify the links back to that founding ancestor.

Each residential group has its own recognized leader. These leaders help settle local disputes and serve as spiritual intermediaries between the living and dead members of the matrilineage. Larger residential units of villages have their headmen who are recognized formally by the chief and the state.

The chief and his matrilineage are recognized as "owners of the land." In a physical, moral, and spiritual sense the welfare of his subjects are said to be reflected in his health and wealth. The chief is recognized by the state, receives a salary and paid staff to assist in his duties, and holds council with representatives from the major matrilineages.

Religion and World View

Religion and world view among the Valley Bisa vary considerably among individuals, depending upon experience and contact with the outside world. Some are Catholics and are closely affiliated with the Catholic mission and hospital atop the adjacent plateau. Others belong to charismatic Protestant groups. Most Bisa retain elements of "traditional" religion. This belief system has five main components: (1) belief in the existence of a supreme being, Muzili Mfumu; (2) belief in the existence of ancestral spirits, who possess the power to withhold or bestow upon their living descendants the desirable things in life, as well as a host of other spiritual beings; (3) belief in certain supernatural impersonal and unrelenting forces that afflict an individual or an innocent person, should an individual vary from prescribed patterns of behavior at specific times; (4) belief in the power of certain plant and animal substances that when properly prepared can be used for good or harm; (5) belief in the antisocial and destructive powers of sorcery.

THREATS TO SURVIVAL

The Valley Bisa have faced many challenges to their survival and ways of life. Yet the challenges of the last decades have been the most severe, as demonstrated by their demographic trends.

Demographic Trends

The earliest population figures for the Valley Bisa were taken in 1910 by agents of the British South Africa Company. Their recorded numbers were 2,124 adults and 1,420 children. Counts by the colonial authorities showed a slowly increasing population, with between 50 and 70 percent of adult men working elsewhere in southern Africa. The last colonial census in 1963 showed an adult population of 2,224 adults (with only 38 percent men in residence) and 3,559 children.[1] Subsequent government reports have assumed a gradually increasing population reaching some 7,000 to 8,000 residents in the 1980s, but these figures may be inflated. The most recent government census of 1990 places the total population of the Valley Bisa in the Munyamadzi Corridor at 4,827.[2] Clearly, Bisa population numbers and densities are rising. The demographic structure of the Bisa population is in many ways reflective of that of Zambia and of southern Africa as a whole: high fertility (births), large numbers of young people age fifteen or below, and high mortality; some of the deaths are due to HIV/AIDS and to tuberculosis and malaria.

The more recent droughts, alternating with flash flooding of fields and settlements, together with disease outbreaks exacerbated by the slowness and frequent difficulties of governmental assistance, have caused many households to leave the corridor and settle elsewhere. The magnitudes of these shifts are difficult to assess because ethnic labels, tribal affiliations, and individual identifications have always been more flexible in local minds than is suggested by their formalization in administrative minds and on their maps. This fluidity among the Valley Bisa and neighboring groups continues today with shifts to the plateau or across the Luangwa River.

Current Events and Conditions

Under the British colonial administration, large chunks of the Bisa's valley land were designated as game reserves. Additional territory, the Chifungwe Plain, considered as essential elephant habitat, was taken from the Valley Bisa in 1973 when the game reserves were redesignated as national parks. The enforcement of these boundaries has increasingly narrowed the environmental and resource options for the Valley Bisa. Not only are they prohibited from benefiting from the land, water, wildlife, and vegetative resources within the national parks, but within the corridor itself, their settlements and land uses are restricted by regulations whose objective is to enhance wildlife populations for others who legally can afford the high license prices established by government. Until recently, human settlements were constrained to a comparatively few sites where water and fertile soils (two limiting factors) occurred along the banks of the corridor's two perennial streams. The digging of water wells away from the river, projects sponsored and paid for through foreign aid, has recently opened up new areas for settlement.

Since wildlife is an important earner of foreign exchange through safari hunting and tourism, the Zambian government has sought to increase wildlife populations by legally restricting and criminalizing local off-takes of wildlife. The valley residents find this particularly vexing and troublesome, for they have not been given new opportunities to compensate for their losses or to make their customary livelihoods more sustainable. Since the late 1980s, wildlife protection has increasingly depended on the employment of local scouts, who with their local knowledge of activities and people have driven local wildlife activities underground and into secrecy. If caught hunting, trapping, or with wildlife meat, local people may be beaten, fined, imprisoned, and even killed, depending on circumstances. Such harsh penalties without compensation for local loss or costs, referred to as "coercive conservation," extend beyond the apprehended individual and may put his relatives at risk as well. This criminalization of local hunters of wildlife has not turned the Valley Bisa and others into conservationists, for they continue to take wildlife as circumstances permit, with secrecy providing a cloak for these activities.[3]

During the 1960s and 1970s, local hunters' kills of game were widely distributed among households. Currently, comparatively few households manage to supply themselves with meat while refusing to distribute it to others. Within the local idiom, this refusal to share denies their relationships with others. Such ruptures in cultural expectations when coupled with local explanations for why some prosper while others suffer contributes to considerable local strife and disharmony. These suspicions surface in accusations of sorcery against a few who become the victims in attempts to explain the misfortunes of others.[4]

Environmental Crisis

Restrictions imposed on land uses and the denial of all resources within the neighboring national parks and on settlements and certain activities within the corridor have increased the effects of environmental crisis within recent years. During the 1990s, droughts became increasingly prolonged and severe. Even when the rains have been adequate, flash flooding caused by heavy rainfall on the plateau and local food failures caused by depredations by mammals and by birds (Quelas—sparrowlike birds) have increased local hardships. Under these stressful conditions, diseases such as cholera, smallpox, tuberculosis, and malaria break out and take their toll on all segments of the human population. Given the isolation and difficulties of communication and transport, government aid is often late in responding to these crises.

Living among abundant wildlife while being denied customary traditions for protecting one's life and livelihood has not been easy. Supposedly, the wildlife scouts are armed and are legally tasked to kill dangerous mammals and to respond to emergencies involving wild animals. Yet they are often without ammunition, without proper authority, or too far away to deal in time with such critical situations. Within a very short time period (an hour), elephants can devastate a field that has taken months of work to bring to yield. With regional elephant populations increasing again in the 1990s and into the new millennium, their confrontations with humans may be tragic. In 1997, elephants killed three people, including a pregnant woman, who were trying to protect their crops.[5]

There are other hazards of living among wildlife as well. During the early 1990s, fifteen Valley Bisa were reported killed or maimed by crocodiles. These reptiles are particularly dangerous for women and young girls whose domestic tasks require that they spend hours each day at the river washing clothes, dishes, and grains and ferrying water back to their households. The digging of wells to tap into groundwater supplies away from the rivers since 1997 has lessened attacks by crocodiles. Deadly encounters with lions, hyenas, buffaloes, and other mammals occur less frequently.

Sociocultural Crisis

As with many rural populations, the Valley Bisa have had to cope recently with an intergenerational breakdown in shared customs and expectations. In particular, young boys who have attended boarding schools and have been tutored by teachers rather than parents and the kin group find little in their parents' activities, material possessions, and culture that interests them. This discontinuity expresses itself in the conversations of the elderly, when youngsters appear and act independently and refuse to respond to their expectations. Young men are mobile and when they find

73

employment, they usually spend their earnings on clothes and on themselves rather than sharing their money and possessions with their kin—as their elders expect. The breakdown of villages into smaller settlements enables the young to keep their distance from the scrutiny of their elders.

RESPONSE: STRUGGLES TO SURVIVE CULTURALLY

Although land alienation has been contentious and a cultural issue for some time, the Valley Bisa and their chief were able recently to stop another assault on their estate. In his enthusiasm for reconstructing "merrie old Africa" (creating conditions favorable for elephants with 100-pound tusks and bringing back the rhino), an American entrepreneur in 1992 offered a newly elected Zambian government what seemed like a great deal: The entrepreneur would accept wildlife enforcement activities in the corridor and pay millions of dollars in return for a long-term lease. Whereas nearly every official in the new government seemed in favor of the deal, the newly appointed chief refused to approve this deal.[6] In conjunction with his allies elsewhere, including those in the party that had lost the recent election, the chief's decision stood despite the entrepreneur's attempt to make the deal more attractive locally by airlifting tons of grain into the corridor to avert a developing famine.

The plights of many Valley Bisa households and their precarious existence and reliance on wildlife in times of uncertainty and harsh circumstances are reflected in the words of a village headman, who also hunted for his kin:

My [maternal] uncle taught me to take wildlife with a gun and with snares just in case the situation changed as it has today with so many game guards. Their presence, which (is to) prevent us from pursuing game, is contrary to the wishes of our ancestral spirits. This is a very bad situation. Our ancestors settled this country of wild animals, killed, and fed upon them. Yet in their killing, these animals have never decreased in numbers. Outside people say, "You have finished the animals." Now I ask you, how can a muzzle loading gun finish animals when it fires only once in comparison with semi-automatic weapons? Rather it is those people who come from the plateau (and beyond) to kill for business who are the ones who have diminished our animals.[7]

Another hunter said the following:

As the situation is now, numerous game guards and scouts have produced a meat shortage that is now the talk of the village. I have thought of ways to solve this problem. The demand to hunt wild animals continues to ring in my head. I am forced [causative tense] to snare to continue to live up to my social expectations and obligations. Guns do make noise and attract scouts. Ancestral spirits are impressed by their descendants enjoying a good life and eating well [with relishes of meat] in many ways. There are many ways to supply meat for one's relatives.[8]

Despite these adversities, the Valley Bisa have received some benefits that some groups are using to strengthen their security in an uncertain world. ADMADE (Administrative Management Design), a community-based natural resource management program established in Zambia in 1989 provides some tangible returns from sport hunting by outside groups.[9] The funds that have been generated have been used to construct houses for teachers, schools, and clinics and to build water wells. The program has also provided food during chronic droughts. This support has provided a basis for at least some individuals to secure employment elsewhere. Their remittances (cash and goods) assist their relatives back in the valley. Others have contacts in government who may assist in times of crises, such as backing the refusal of the chief to lease his domain to an outsider. Still others, realizing the political, economic, and cultural importance of "their" wildlife, increasingly discuss it with reference to their own identity and survival.

FOOD FOR THOUGHT

The livelihood and identity of the Valley Bisa and other minority groups elsewhere are still based on biological resources. Some American Indian groups in the U.S. Northwest who depend on salmon, wildlife, and crops face similar circumstances. This is also the case for the Inuit of the Arctic regions of Canada, the United States, Greenland, and Siberia. All of these groups are facing problems as a result of competition for resources and efforts on the part of international organizations, multinational corporations, and agencies to restrict the hunting, gathering, and other resource exploitation activities of local people. Local peoples are responding in a variety of ways, seeking to promote their rights to subsistence and economic well-being as part of their identities. They are doing this in part through participating in community-based resource management programs (CBRMPs), overseeing their resources, and taking part in the development of a wildlife management regime. They also make their own use of wildlife and other natural resources, using wildlife and other goods for food and for purposes of exchange. At the same time, they are striving to conserve their resource base and to engage in activities that are sustainable over the long term. Only in this way, say the Bisa, can they, like other African populations, strike a positive balance between conservation and development, honor their ancestors, and make a better world for their descendants.

Questions

1. If you are employed as a consultant, what strategies could you suggest to the Valley Bisa to increase their autonomy and survival?

2. In many parts of the world, great differences in power and wealth exist between various groups that have interests in wildlife. Often, the influences on government are directly proportional to the distance from an area (i.e., those groups living further from an area have the greatest wealth and influence). Although people benefit from the use of wildlife as good, they must also deal with wild animals that destroy their gardens, kill their livestock, and—on occasion—attack them. How would you devise a management scheme that allocates wildlife to each group according to its needs? How would you structure an equitable resource management system?

3. What are the conflicting value systems of the Bisa and conservationists regarding wildlife?

4. In what ways can societies like the Bisa build on their traditional systems of knowledge about resource management to ensure the long-term survival of both people and wildlife?

5. In what ways might it be possible for an indigenous people to cooperate with the private sector (in this case, the safari industry) to enhance incomes and employment while at the same time helping the country as a whole?

NOTES

1. Stuart A. Marks, *Large Mammals and a Brave People: Subsistence Hunters in Zambia* (Seattle: University of Washington Press, 1976); *The Imperial Lion: Human Dimensions of Wildlife Management in Central Africa* (Boulder, CO: Westview Press, 1984).

2. Republic of Zambia, *Census of Population, Housing, and Agriculture: Preliminary Report* (Lusaka, Zambia: Central Statistical Office, 1990).

3. Marks, *The Imperial Lion.*

4. Ibid.

5. Barbara Ludman, "The Menace of Bullish Elephants," *Daily Mail & Guardian*, March 15, 1999, *www.mg/news/99mar2/15mar-elephants.html.*

6. Bisa elder in the Luangwa Valley, personal communication to Stuart Marks, 1992.

7. Ibid.

8. Bisa hunter in the Manyamadzi Corridor, personal communication to Stuart Marks, 1990.

9. David Shepherd Conservation Foundation, "The Long War: Zambia's Fight for Wildlife," *http://www.dscf.demon.co.uk/project7.htm.*

RESOURCE GUIDE

Published Literature

Bonner, Raymond. *At the Hand of Man: Peril and Hope for Africa's Wildlife.* New York: Alfred A. Knopf, 1993.

Burdette, Marcia M. *Zambia: Between Two Worlds.* Boulder, CO: Westview Press, 1988.

Freehling, Joel, and Stuart A. Marks. "A Century of Change in the Central Luangwa Valley of Zambia." In *Conservation of Biological Resources*, ed. E.J.
Milner-Gulland and Ruth Mace. Oxford: Blackwell Science, 1998. 261–78.

Gibson, Clark C. *Politicians and Poachers: The Political Economy of Wildlife Policy in Africa*. Cambridge: Cambridge University Press, 1989.

Gibson, Clark C., and Stuart A. Marks. "Transforming Rural Hunters into Conservationists: An Assessment of Community-Based Wildlife Management
Programs in Africa." *World Development* 23, no. 6 (1995): 941–957.

Marks, Stuart A. *The Imperial Lion: Human Dimensions of Wildlife Management
in Central Africa*. Boulder, CO: Westview Press, 1984.

———. *Large Mammals and a Brave People: Subsistence Hunters in Zambia*. Seattle: University of Washington Press, 1976.

Owens, Delia, and Mark Owens. *The Eye of the Elephant*. Boston: Houghton Mif-
flin, 1992.

Western, David, and R. Michael Wright, eds. With Shirley C. Strum. *Natural Connections: Perspectives in Community-Based Conservation*. Covelo, CA: Island Press, 1994.

Films and Videos

"Deadly Game." March 30, 1996. ABC Television, *Turning Point*, New York, NY.

The Debt Crisis: An African Dilemma. 1988. First Run/Icarus Films, 32 Court
Street, 21st Floor, Brooklyn, NY 11201.

A Zambian Safari. 1990. Anubis Production International, Department N., P.O.
Box 50859, Tucson, AZ 85703.

WWW Sites

Africa South of the Sahara—Select Internet Sites: Zambia
http://www-sul.stanford.edu/depts/ssrg/africa/zambia.html

Owens Foundation for Wildlife Conservation (see North Luangwa Conservation
Project)
http://www.owens-foundation.org/

The Southern African Development Community (SADC) Natural Resources Management Programme (community-based natural resource management in southern African countries)
http://www.cbnrm-sadc.co.za

Zamnet Communications Systems, Ltd.
http://www.zamnet.zm/

Organizations

Africa Resources Trust (ART)
Box A860
Avondale, Harare, Zimbabwe

Telephone: (263) 4–732254
Fax: (263) 4–731719

Africa Wildlife Foundation
1400 Sixteenth Street, NW, Suite 120
Washington, DC 20036
Telephone: (202) 939–3333
Fax: (202) 939–3332
Email: africanwildlife@awf.org
Web site: www.awf.org

Nyamaluma Institute for Community-Based Natural Resource Management
Nyamaluma Research and Education Camp
P.O. Box 82
Mfuwe, Zambia

World Conservation Union (IUCN/Zambia)
Email: iucn@zamnet.zm

World Wildlife Fund (U.S.)
1250 Twenty Fourth Street, NW
Washington, DC 20037
Telephone: (202) 293–4800
Fax: (202) 293–9211

Zambia Indigenous Peoples Cultures and Languages Association
Lusaka, Zambia
Email: zamclass@cbnow.com

Chapter 4

The Eritreans and Ethiopians

Lucia Ann McSpadden

CULTURAL OVERVIEW

Almost 14 million Africans had been forced to flee their homes by the end of 1999.[1] Of these, more than 3 million were refugees—about 200,000 more than the previous year. Approximately 10.6 million were displaced within their own countries and became what are known as internally displaced persons (IDPs). The refugee situation in the Horn of Africa,[2] located in the northeast corner of Africa, continues to be one of the world's largest, most intractable, and most complex human tragedies, one in which millions of persons are endangered and their very existence threatened.

The countries of the Horn—Djibouti, Eritrea, Ethiopia, Somalia, and Sudan—continue to produce a breathtakingly large number of refugees. Although these countries have different political issues, different ethnic and religious characteristics, and different colonial backgrounds, they are all linked. The causes of the mass population movements in the Horn of Africa include war, religious conflicts, secessionist movements, ethnic rivalries, human rights abuses, political repression, drought, and environmental degradation. For example, the border war between Eritrea and Ethiopia, which began in 1998 and continued through May 2000, displaced over 1 million Eritreans—one-third of the Eritrean population—and over 400,000 Ethiopians. The war was a savage one, with tens of thousands of combatants killed on each side, some in situations eerily reminiscent of the trench warfare of World War I in Europe.

The two countries that have contributed the majority of refugees and that have experienced protracted conflict, drought, and large-scale changes in their political and economic systems are Eritrea and Ethiopia.

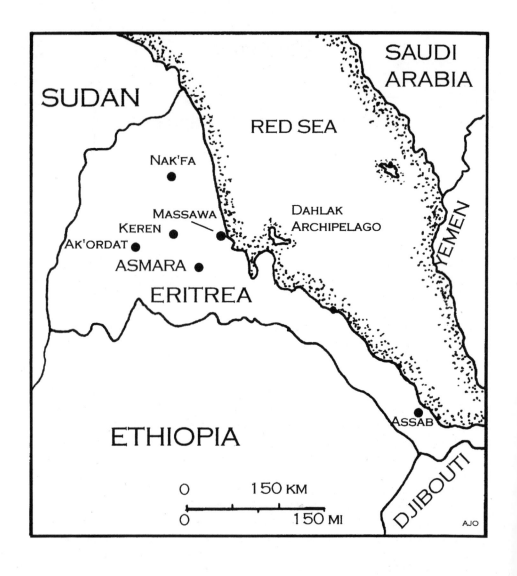

The People

Eritrea became an independent nation–state on May 25, 1993, when its status was recognized by the United Nations and other countries. Eritrea came about as a result of the longest-standing conflict in Africa—a thirty-year struggle with Ethiopia. Although Eritrea is a small country—containing approximately 3 million people—it exhibits considerable ethnic diversity.[3] There are eight official languages: Afar, Arabic, Blean,[4] Hadareb, Kunama, Saho, Tigre, and Tigrinya. Tigrinya and Arabic are two of the most widely used languages.

Ethiopia has a population of 58,730,000 and is quite diverse with respect to ethnicity and religion. There are an estimated 70 to 80 ethnic groups scattered across the extremely variable landscape of Ethiopia. Oromo form the largest group (40 percent); others include the Amhara (25 percent), Sidamo (9 percent), Somali (6 percent), and the Tigreans (5 percent). The Oromo live primarily in the southern and eastern regions. The Amhara have traditionally occupied and dominated the fertile highlands. The Tigre live primarily in the northwestern region. Amharic, Tigrinya, Oromo, Sidamo, Somali, English, and Arabic are the most common of the eighty-two languages that are spoken in Ethiopia. In contrast to Eritrea, there is only one official language, Amharic. The ethnic groups that reside in northern Ethiopia within the Blue Nile Basin include the Gumuz, Mao, Koma, and Bertha. The people of Ethiopia who are in the Nile Basin tend to be agropastoral populations who raise a variety of crops and keep livestock, small stock, and poultry.

The Setting

Ethiopia and Eritrea are marked by a huge mountain plateau rising abruptly from the extremely hot, arid plains and coastal areas to a mean height of between 7,000 and 8,500 feet. The fertile highlands extend from Asmara, the capital of Eritrea, in the north to Addis Ababa, the capital of Ethiopia, in the south. This mountain plateau is crosscut by the Great Rift Valley running from the Red Sea in the northeast to Kenya in the southwest. The eastern portion of the plateau is inhabited predominantly by the Oromo, Somali, and nomadic pastoralists. It drains into the Indian Ocean. The Amhara, Tigre, and agropastoralists occupy the western portion. This area drains into the valley of the Nile in Sudan.

Temperatures in the highlands range from 50°F to 84°F and regularly reach 100°F in the lowlands. Less than twenty inches of rain fall annually in the lowlands, while the highlands may receive thirty to forty inches. Both Eritrea and Ethiopia are located in the easternmost part of the Sahel, the grassland or savanna that extends across the southern part of the Sahara and experiences periodic drought and occasional heavy downpours.

Erosion and deforestation are serious problems in the highlands. At the beginning of the twentieth century, approximately 40 percent of Ethiopia was covered with climax forest. By 1950, forest cover was reduced to 16 percent and in 1990 forest cover was reduced to 2.8 percent of the country's area.[5] Eritrea faces similar deforestation and environmental degradation.

Traditional Subsistence Strategies

Traditional subsistence patterns in this part of northeastern Africa vary with the geography. In the highlands, peasant farmers—90 percent of the population—live in sedentary, agricultural, Ethiopian (Coptic) Christian communities of extended families that are the focal point of all cultural, social, and political life. The Copts were the Christian descendants of the ancient Egyptians. The possession of land is intimately linked with distinctions of social status, kinship, and forms of social unity. Land can be held by an individual head of family, by the family itself, or by the community as a whole. Political forces inevitably have centered on land—its acquisition, expropriation, or redistribution. Consequently, land rights are carefully guarded.

Sorghum, barley, wheat, teff (a local grain), cotton, and citrus fruit are the primary crops. During the Italian colonial period, land was appropriated and put into plantation-style production. Coffee, a major export crop of Ethiopia, is central to traditional Ethiopian and Eritrean hospitality and community social networks.

Pastoral nomads (mobile herders) of Eritrea and Ethiopia, like those elsewhere, move their herds of cattle, goats, or camels in order to gain access to forage and water in an arid environment. In the fertile western lowlands, agropastoralism (a combination of farming and livestock raising) is especially common. Sedentary agriculturalists cultivate crops along the Gash and Setit Rivers and trade with neighboring nomadic groups. Water is always a source of tension in these dry lands. The cycle of war and drought has devastated the traditional subsistence patterns of many agropastoralists and, especially, the pastoral nomads. Many of these nomads have huddled in refugee camps in Sudan or around the Ogaden (eastern Ethiopia) town of Gode for years; the vast majority of these people are without camels or goats. Many of the former nomads, having lost their animals or access to traditional grazing lands, have taken up farming at the edges of the highland plateau. Cotton is also grown in the western lowlands, fed by waters of the Gash and Setit Rivers. However, Eritrea has historically imported food from its neighbors. Salt from the Denakil Depression bordering the Red Sea is a major export.

Social and Political Organization

Geography shapes subsistence strategies, and these strategies, in turn, shape social and political organization. Ethiopia and Eritrea are geographically divided into highlands and lowlands. Settled Christian farmers and nomadic Muslim pastoralists who are socially and politically diverse inhabit these regions. There are exceptions to these general patterns including Muslim farmers or animist nomads. Animists believe that all living things possess a soul. Agropastoralists serve as social and economic links between various sedentary and nomadic groups. In addition, at the end of Eritrea's war of liberation, highland people—former fighters—were given land in the western lowlands by the government. The peasant farmers, mostly Amhara and Tigray speakers, have a patrilineal kinship system, tracing descent and organizing descent through the male line. Social relations are overwhelmingly organized on the basis of hierarchical patterns and individualistic associations that are intensely patriarchal: That is, relationships are determined on gradations of honor, power, and authority, with authority given to men. Great value is given to independence and self-reliance. The pastoralists of various ethnic groups are also strongly patrilineal, tracing descent through the male line and passing goods from father to son.

The Kunama, now settled agriculturalists, occupy the southwestern Eritrean lowlands as well as the western edge of the plateau. In contrast to most of the people of the Horn, they are matrilineal, tracing descent and organizing descent through the female line. In addition, there are the former slaves from Sub-Saharan Africa who, although no longer slaves, are still a despised caste group within Ethiopia given their previous low status. They continue to be denied access to needed social resources and, clearly, do not have social respect.

Religion and World View

There is not a neat fit between regions, ethnic identity, language, and religion. Approximately half of Eritrea's population lives in the highlands and speaks Tigrinya and Tigre. The majority of these—usually the Tigrinya speakers—practice the Coptic Orthodox Christian religion. The Tigre speakers are usually Muslim and are divided into a number of tribes, some of which live in either the eastern or western lowlands, or between the highlands and the lowlands. The remainder of the population lives in the lowlands; the majority of these are Muslim. Many, but not all, speak Arabic. A number of people, in fact, live between the highlands and the lowlands, some in permanent villages and others—both Christian and Muslim—move there periodically with their livestock. The Bileyn are an example of how mixed such areas have become; they are often bilingual or trilingual and are equally divided between Christianity and Islam.

The Afar and Saho speakers are Muslim pastoral nomads of the eastern lowlands, although some have become settled agriculturalists in recent decades. The Rashaida are an Arabic-speaking Muslim tribe of pastoralists also living in the eastern lowlands. The adherence to Islam or to traditional African religion varies among these pastoralists. The Hadareb speakers or Beja in western Eritrea have traditionally farmed both in Sudan and Eritrea. The Kunama, a Nilotic people, are settled agriculturalists in the western region, many of whom have left their indigenous African religion and converted to Christianity. Those have become members of the Mekanayesus church that was initially founded by the Lutheran Church of Sweden. Another Nilotic group, the Nara, also living in villages in the western lowlands, were Islamized in the nineteenth century. Overall, Eritrea has two dominant linguistic/religious communities, Tigrinya-speaking Christians and Tigre-speaking Muslims. When all other other groups are included, the Eritrean population is approximately half Muslim and half Christian.

The religious affiliations in Ethiopia are similar to those of Eritrea. In 1999 the religions of Ethiopia included Muslim (45 to 50 percent), Ethiopian Orthodox (35 to 40 percent), animist (12 percent), and non-Orthodox Christians (5 percent).[6] In general, although with many variations, the highlands are home to the Ethiopian Orthodox peasants; the lowlands are home to the Muslims. Those who practice traditional African beliefs or are non-Orthodox Christians are found in scattered locations.

THREATS TO SURVIVAL

The geography of the Horn has had a profound effect on the history of these two countries, separating peoples and making conquest from the center difficult. For centuries, various emperors have tried, with varying success, to consolidate their power over the region that encompasses modern-day Eritrea and Ethiopia. The refugee-producing modern conflicts are not new but extensions of unresolved disputes from previous centuries.

Ethiopia traces its history back to the ancient Christian kingdom of Axum established in the north highlands in the first century A.D. This kingdom gradually declined between the seventh and twelfth centuries A.D., as Islamic influences grew. In the eleventh century a new power, the Amhara—a Semitic people of the highlands—established the Abyssinian empire, beginning the colonization of many non-Amhara people of the region, a political expansion coupled with a sociocultural expansion of the Amhara language, customs, moral values, and religion—Monophysite Christianity. For more than 700 years—1270 to 1974—all but one of the rulers of Ethiopia were Amhara. This Amhara expansion did not go unchallenged, and in fact, such challenges underlie much of the political and social tension within present-day Ethiopia. In 1525 a *jihad*, a holy war, was launched by a Muslim sultan, armed by the Turks and with support from many nomadic Somali clans.

This conflict and resulting religious turmoil set the stage for the expansion of the Oromo, who were a purely African, non-Semitic people, neither Christian nor Muslim. These nomadic pastoralists were among the area's most powerful lords by 1780 and today still constitute about 40 percent of the Ethiopian population.

During the nineteenth century, the powerful Amhara king of Shoa in the southern highlands, Menelik II, established a new capital, Addis Ababa, in recently conquered Oromo lands. The colonialization, the bloodshed, and the loss of their lands, all due to Amhara domination, fostered an animosity among the Oromo, Sidama, and Somali toward Amharas and a desire for independence that remain at the heart of many of the conflicts and refugee issues in the Horn today. During these expansions Menelik II put what is now Eritrea into Italian hands (1889), thus setting the stage for the Eritrean struggle for liberation (1961–1991) that began under Menelik II's successor, Emperor Haile Selassie, a struggle that produced thousands upon thousands of refugees.

Haile Selassie's fifty-eight years of rule of Ethiopia ended in 1974. Guerrilla activity in Eritrea had begun in 1961. Unrest among the Somalis, the Oromo, and the Afar was linked to the failure of Haile Selassie's government to deal with the widespread Wollo famine that killed 100,000 people and severely impacted over 800,000 others.[7]

The new military government, the Dergue, under Mengistu Haile-Mariam, was one of the world's most ruthless, repressive regimes. In a two-week period, 5,000 to 10,000 (some reports say up to 30,000) people were killed in Addis Ababa alone. As an Ethiopian refugee resettled in the United States recounted: "I was rounded up with my two brothers, my uncle and my father. . . . All of the men of my family were kept in jail over three months. I have never seen them since that time. . . . My older brother was shot in front of me and his body thrown on a pile of dead bodies.[8]

Literacy, prior to 1991 and the liberation of Eritrea from Ethiopia, was about 10 percent, and less than 1 percent of the elementary-aged children completed school. During the thirty-year civil war, education was even more severely disrupted. In 2000, 37 percent of elementary-age children and 11 percent of secondary school–age children were enrolled in school, and the overall literacy rate was 35 percent.[9] In 1999, the life expectancy was forty-five years in Eritrea and forty-two years in Ethiopia. Prior to the 1960s, Eritrea had flourishing small-scale industries and a well-developed system of roads and railroads built during the period of Italian occupation. These were destroyed during the thirty-year war.

Struggle for Self-Determination

The opposition of many national groups to the Ethiopian government's rule had its roots in centuries of imperial domination. National movements developed seeking either total independence or regional autonomy.

The Eritrean People's Liberation Front (EPLF) waged the longest-standing war in Africa, thirty years (1961–1991), to achieve the goal of Eritrean independence. The intense, brutal war forced over one-quarter of the Eritrean population to flee to Sudan, Saudi Arabia, and Italy. Much to the surprise of international observers, the EPLF, without outside military assistance, achieved their goal—the liberation of Eritrea from Ethiopia and the establishment of an independent nation.

The Tigray People's Liberation Front (TPLF) was formed in 1975 in order to achieve "national self-determination," partly in response to the Ethiopian government using famine as a weapon of war. The TPLF combined with other opposition groups to form the Ethiopian Peoples Democratic Forces (EPDRF). In May 1991, they drove Mengistu Haile-Mariam out of Ethiopia and became the government of Ethiopia. Subsequently, the Oromo Liberation Front (OLF) pulled out of the government, and they continue in active opposition to the EPDRF.

Current Events and Conditions

The long war between Ethiopia and Eritrea ended in 1991. Both countries had new governments that had liberated their people from oppression, dictatorship, and colonialism. In Eritrea the successful liberation struggle bound diverse peoples into a nation committed to self-determination and rebuilding. Differences of ethnicity and religion were overridden by a genuine sense of being Eritrean, a free people. The Eritreans put aside their weapons and tempered both ethnic and religious differences to become one people, bound by a shared national identity.

Fundamentalist Islam has not had a strong hold in the Muslim communities and groups within Eritrea or Ethiopia. Within the refugee camps in Sudan, however, Islamic fundamentalist groups have been proselytizing and politicizing, fomenting discontent and attempting to organize groups to oppose the current government of Eritrea especially.

In Ethiopia, a new ethnic group—the Tigray—was now in charge. The EPRDF invited other groups that had battled Mengistu's regime to join in forming a transitional government, perhaps the first time that a guerrilla army has seized power and offered to share it. This government ventured onto new paths of structuring a government that would provide significant political power to the major ethnic groups. Recent events, however, have threatened almost all of these efforts to establish peace and independence in the region. A two-year-long struggle between Ethiopia and Eritrea over territory along their common border ended recently, but tensions continue to be felt.

Food Security

Ethiopia and Eritrea are among the poorest countries in the world. As an example, a 1996 UN report notes that "Eritrea is one of the lowest per capita users of commercial energy. . . . Out of 7,000 kilometers of road, only seven to eight percent is paved or gravel covered . . . the present tele-communication system reaches only about 0.49 per cent of the population and is concentrated in the urban area."[10] Ancient feudal land policies that continued under the last Ethiopian emperor, Haile Selassie (1930–1974), required the farmers to till the land and pay taxes to absent landlords and to the Ethiopian Orthodox Church. Under Mengistu Haile-Mariam (1974–1991) the Ethiopian government maintained a centralized approach by tightly controlling the grain market. The oppression of farmers continued with the initiation of the "villagization" program. Thousands of farmers, mostly from the rebellious northern region of Tigray, were forcibly moved by government resettlement programs in the mid-1980s to southern areas just as these farmers were to plant their crops. Once again both the government and the people were reminded of the old saying, "God makes drought. Man makes famine." Despite its larger area and population, Ethiopia was drained of resources during the war with Eritrea and with the various opposition groups. Famine continues to occur frequently, often due to the diversion of resources to military purposes.

The populations of Eritrea have been even more severely impacted by war and famine. Many pastoralists and agropastoralists lost their animals and their land, fled to Sudan, or became settled agriculturalists; peasant farmers were uprooted, lost their plow animals, and were unable to farm. A severe consequence was the loss of food security; in 1995 nearly 80 percent of Eritrea's people were forced to rely on food aid.[11]

After 1991, when both nations' energies could turn to peace building, food production rose significantly. Tigrayans in northern Ethiopia terraced land that had been laid waste by Mengistu's army. Farmers resumed growing large amounts of wheat, barley, coffee, and teff in both countries. The harvests were good. Due to good harvests the Eritrean government cut its request for international food aid by 50 percent in 1993. The two-year "border war" (1998–2000) between Ethiopia and Eritrea has turned this all around. Food security took a dismal plunge after 1996, producing a grave humanitarian situation. Thousands of persons were killed; over a million people were displaced, and millions of dollars were diverted away from development. The percentage of Ethiopia's people depending on food

Men (not women) may collect food at distribution centers (Asmara, Eritrea). (Courtesy Joan Sullivan-Owomoyela)

aid increased markedly during 1998–2000, and the World Food Program (WFP) has sought to pressure the rest of the world to meet the need for international food aid for Ethiopia.

Both Eritrean and Ethiopian troops laid land mines, compromising the safety of returnees and the ability to plant crops. Ethiopian troops destroyed almost everything in the areas of Eritrea they controlled, including grain reserves, livestock, homes, equipment, and infrastructure. The displacement of over one-third of Eritrea's population made planting crops before the seasonal rains came difficult if not impossible. After the peace agreement, Ethiopian forces pushed thousands of farmers off of their land in the Gash-Setit area just prior to planting time. Famine has since struck the entire region.

Internal Displacement

The effects of displacement on human populations are devastating, resulting in untold misery. In Ethiopia over 350,000 people have been displaced, and in Eritrea over 1 million people have been displaced. Internal displacement means that people lack shelter, food, medicine, sanitation, and family networks. According to the United Nations High Commissioner for Refugees (UNHCR), 540,000 Eritrean people are living in twenty-four camps; 62 percent are under eighteen, and 57 percent are female. Another 500,000 are believed to be surviving in remote mountains in caves, outside under overhangs, and in makeshift shelters. With no roads through the high mountain passes, getting supplies into the area is a major project. When the rains come, the route is impassable. People must walk hours to get to distribution points, and even then, there are not enough supplies to go around.

During Eritrea's struggle for liberation, over 500,000 Eritreans fled to Sudan. After 1991, efforts to repatriate these refugees were stalled due to severe disagreements between the government of Eritrea, the UNHCR, and international donors. In 1994, formal repatriation was begun with the return of 28,000 Eritreans. Further repatriation was halted when diplomatic relations between the governments of Sudan and Eritrea were broken. Renewed repatriation efforts in 1999 involving Sudan and Eritrea were again halted due to the fighting between Ethiopia and Eritrea. The return of these refugees has caused some destabilization.

Political Instability

The new federal government of Ethiopia has strived to achieve self-determination and national autonomy for its people by dividing Ethiopia into ethnic regions. Ethnic tensions and hostility are still near the surface.

Some observers have suggested that Ethiopia engaged in the border war with Eritrea in order to divert attention from these ethnic tensions and weld the people together to fight a common enemy.

Fighting another war has seemed to strengthen the unity of the Eritrean people. However, the destruction of infrastructure, the bombing of a rebuilt power plant at Massawa, the lack of food security, and the forced removal of farmers from their land have set back basic development efforts in Eritrea severely. Peace and development are linked. Without peace there is no development; without development there is little hope for peace in the long run. In addition, many observers suggest that one of Ethiopia's aims in the border war was to undermine the influence of the current Eritrean government formed from the liberation fighters of the EPLF so that a government more amenable to control by Ethiopia could come into place. That has not happened. However, Eritrean opposition forces have been meeting, and the Eritrean refugees in camps in Sudan continue to be politicized on behalf of the opposition efforts.

RESPONSE: STRUGGLES TO SURVIVE CULTURALLY

Diaspora

Eritrean refugees in western countries such as the United States, Canada, Germany, Sweden, and Italy have, over the years, made significant financial contributions to their families and to political causes. These contributions have been made through the Eritrean People's Liberation Front and later through taxes to the Eritrean government. Some people have returned for short periods of time to volunteer with the government in the rebuilding of Eritrea. In response to the border war, refugees in the west have formed several organizations to collect funds for rebuilding Eritrea and to feed and shelter internally displaced people. Also, a new Eritrean nongovernmental agency, Haben, has been approved by the Eritrean government to use volunteers and funds in rebuilding.

The UNHCR is working closely with the Eritrean Relief and Refugee Commission (ERREC) to boost local capacity to deliver emergency relief aid to both displaced people and returning refugees. They have also registered and assisted Eritrean refugees in Kassala, Sudan, as well as Eritrean and Somali refugees in Yemen. The WFP is responsible for providing international food aid. Both Ethiopia and Eritrea have received shipments, albeit not in sufficient quantities to meet the extreme need under conditions of internal displacement and refugee flight.

The repatriation of some 500,000 Eritrean refugees from Sudan began in the mid-1990s, with a pilot project involving some 25,000 to 30,000 people. Initial indications were that the pilot resettlement efforts were relatively successful. The former refugees began to reestablish themselves, and they organized community-based institutions and established development projects and began participating in the political and social life of Eritrea. Following the end of the border war between Ethiopia and Eritrea in December 2000, repatriation efforts began again, and already sizable numbers of people have returned to Eritrea from the camps where they had lived. Ethiopians who lost their homes and fields have also begun to move back to their ancestral areas. Many people are hopeful that the conflicts and difficulties have been resolved so that they can get on with their lives.

FOOD FOR THOUGHT

Hundreds of thousands of people in Ethiopia and Eritrea have been displaced by military actions and government tactics. Many displaced people have been pushed into marginal areas within their own countries, and many have been forced to leave their countries as refugees. A majority of these displaced people face malnutrition and starvation. Internally displaced people, as well as refugees, have frequently been politicized and used to negotiate foreign aid and peace settlements.

Critical issues to consider in Africa, the Middle East, and other regions where there are large numbers of refugees are the questions of repatriation—the return of people to their own countries—and the alternative options of resettlement in the host country or in a third country such as the United States. In order to come up with the most viable options for the populations involved, several factors need to be considered, including the issue of safety and protection for the refugees, the availability of resources to support them, the willingness of the governments and agencies involved with the refugees to provide them with assistance, and critically, the attitudes and objectives of the people themselves.

Governments assess their national interests and construct their policies in order to protect or enhance such interests. In some cases, the interests of refugees and others who are affected by government policies and practices are not protected, and it is the people who pay the price. It is critical for international agencies, governments, nongovernment organizations, communities, and individuals to consider all of the factors that shape the ways in which people are treated. If they weigh these factors carefully, and they are equitable and socially just in their deliberations, it may well be possible to come up with policies that both protect and promote the interests of everyone. The challenge is now with donors and governments and individuals to support the new ray of hope in the Horn, a ray of hope that history teaches us is very fragile.

Questions

1. The crises in the Horn of Africa are given relatively little attention in the news headlines and on our television screens. Why is the Horn of Africa apparently

not important to people in the West? Why has the international community been so slow to respond?

2. Have we reached the point of compassion fatigue, the process whereby people become so tired of seeing humanitarian emergencies that they become disillusioned?

3. In recent years there has been much debate about the UN peacemakers being deployed to areas immediately after armed conflict. How can the United Nations protect human security when governments are abusing the rights of their own citizens as well as waging war on their neighbors?

4. It is essential that the international community plan in advance for increased repatriation aid to Eritrea. What can be done to ensure that Western governments and their citizens understand refugee crises?

5. How can governments and aid agencies work to build a stable peace to guarantee basic necessities of life? What elements are necessary to support peace with justice, to ensure that all groups of people have equal access to food, shelter, safety, dignity, and respect?

NOTES

1. The number of refugees and internally displaced persons is always contentious. Due to national concerns or government denial of access to the United Nations High Commissioner for Refugees (UNHCR) and other agencies, the number is assumed to be much higher than reported here. Unless otherwise noted, the statistics for refugees, asylum seekers, internally displaced, and those in flight but not recognized as refugees come from U.S. Committee on Refugees, *World Refugee Survey 2000: An Annual Assessment of Conditions Affecting Refugees, Asylum Seekers, and Internally Displaced Persons* (Washington, DC: Immigration and Refugee Services of America, 2000).

2. So called because the region resembles the horn of a rhinoceros.

3. Recent estimate (1993) of numbers of language speakers include Afar (300,000), Bedawi (120,000), Bilen (70,000), Kunama (140,000), Nora (63,000), Saho (144,000), Tigré (800,000), and Tigrigna (1,000,000); *www.ethnologue.com/show_country.asp?name=Eritrea.*

4. Also spelled *Bileyn* and *Bilen.* As with many of the place names, tribal names, and ethnic group names, the spelling in English varies.

5. Badege Bishaw, "Forest History of Ethiopia Past and Present," Ethiopian Tree Fund Foundation, 1990, *www.etff.org/history.html.*

6. CIA—The World Factbook 2001. *www.cia.gov/cia/publications/factbook/geos/et.html.*

7. Colin Legum, *Ethiopia: The Fall of Haile Selassie's Empire* (New York: Africana Publishing Company, 1975), 11.

8. Lucia A. McSpadden, *Ethiopian Refugee Resettlement in the Western United States: Social Context and Psychological Well-Being* (Ann Arbor, MI: UMI Dissertation Services, 1988), 39–40.

9. Government of Eritrea, *Ministry of Education, Statistical Abstracts, 2000* (Asmara, Eritrea: Government of Eritrea, Ministry of Education, 2000), 15–16.

10. CIA—The World Factbook 2001.

11. See M. Fahlen, *Interagency Cooperation and the Continuum from Relief to Development* (Asmara, Eritrea: United Nations High Commissioner for Refugees, 1995), 6–7; and United Nations Commissioner for Refugees, Country Operations Plan, State of Eritrea, May 29, 1995 (Asmara, Eritrea: UNHCR).

RESOURCE GUIDE

Published Literature

Allen, Tim, ed. *In Search of Cool Ground: War, Flight & Homecoming in Northeast Africa*. Geneva, Switzerland: United Nations Research Institute for Social Development, 1996.

Black, Richard, and Kalid Koser, eds. *The End of the Refugee Cycle? Refugee Repatriation and Reconstruction*. New York: Berghahn Books, 1999.

Kibreab, Gaim. *Ready, Willing . . . and Still Waiting: Eritrean Refugees in Sudan*. Uppsala, Sweden: Life & Peace Institute, 1996.

———. *Refugees and the Development in Africa: The Case of Eritrea*. Trenton, NJ: Red Sea Press, 1987.

McSpadden, Lucia Ann. *Conflict and Control in the Repatriation of Eritrean Refugees*. Uppsala, Sweden: Life and Peace Institute, 2000.

Moussa, Helene. *Storm & Sanctuary: The Journey of Ethiopian and Eritrean Women Refugees*. Dundas, Ontario: Artemis Enterprises, 1993.

Pool, David. *Eritrea: Towards Unity in Diversity*. London: Minority Rights Group International, 1997.

United Nations High Commissioner for Refugees. *Protecting Refugees: A Field Guide for NGOs*. Geneva: Author, 1999.

United Nations Research Institute for Social Development. *War-Torn Societies Project Research Update 2*. Geneva: War-Torn Societies Project, UNRISD, 1996.

U.S. Committee on Refugees. *Beyond the Headlines: Refugees in the Horn of Africa*. Washington, DC: Author, 1998.

———. *World Refugee Survey 2000: An Annual Assessment of Conditions Affecting Refugees, Asylum Seekers, and Internally Displaced Persons*. Washington, DC: Immigration and Refugee Services of America, 2000.

Videos and Films

Eritrea. 1990. Directed by Susan Kalish. Available from the Cinema Guild, 130 Madison Avenue, 2nd Floor, New York, NY 10016–7038. Telephone: (800) 723–5522. Email: TheCinemaG@aol.com. Web site: http://www. cinemaguild.com A film that examines the history of the thirty-year-long liberation struggle against Ethiopia and the challenges that face the Eritrean nation.

Eritrea: Hope in the Horn of Africa. 1993. Produced by Grassroots International. Available from First Run/Icarus Films, 153 Waverly Place, Sixth Floor, New York, NY 10014. Telephone: (800) 876–1710. Email: mail@frif.com. Web site: http://www.frif.com. A film that deals with how Eritrea is building a

93

nation after a long civil war and how they are attempting to construct a new model of democratic development.

Eritrean Artists in War and Peace. 1997. Directed by Brian Varaday. Available from the Cinema Guild. A film that focuses on the aesthetic development of a dozen artist-fighters in Eritrea and the role of art in the struggle of the Eritrean People's Liberation Front.

In Search of Cool Ground: The Mursi, the Kwegu, and the Migrants. 1985. Available from Audio-visual Services, Pennsylvania State University, 1127 Fox Hill Road, University Park, PA 16802–1824. Telephone: (800) 826–0132. Three films about people in southwestern Ethiopia and how they have adapted to their environment.

WWW Sites

Citizens for Peace in Eritrea
http://www.eanp.org/cpe.purpose.htm

The Humanitarian Times
http://www.giniel.sched.pitt.edu/htimes/index.htm

International Development Research Center
http://www.idrc.ca/

United Nations High Commissioner for Refugees (UNHCR)
http://www.unhcr.ch

United States Committee for Refugees
http://www.refugees.org

Organizations

Amnesty International
322 Eighth Avenue
New York, NY 10001
Telephone: (202) 807–8400

The Brookings Institute Project on Internal Displacement
1775 Massachusetts Avenue
Washington, DC 20036
Telephone: (202) 797–6483

Eritrean Development Foundation
1111 14th Street, NW, Suite 1000
Washington, DC 20005
Telephone: (202) 408–6995

Ethiopian Development Community Council, Inc.
1038 South Highland Street
Arlington, VA 22204
Telephone: (703) 685–0510

Horn of Africa Program
Life & Peace Institute
P.O. Box 1580
SE 751 45 Uppsala, Sweden
Telephone: (46) 169500
Web site: http://www.life-peace.org

United Nations High Commissioner for Refugees (UNHCR)
1775 K Street, NW, Suite 300
Washington, DC 20006
Telephone: (202) 296–5191

U.S. Committee for Refugees
1717 Massachusetts Avenue, NW, Suite 200
Washington, DC 20036–2003
Telephone: (800) 307–4712

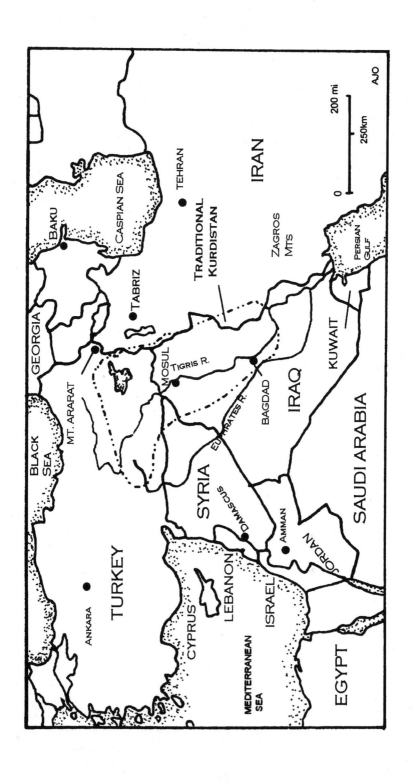

Chapter 5

The Kurds
Laurel Erickson

CULTURAL OVERVIEW

The Kurds, who today number some 20 million people, are the largest ethnic group in the world that occupies a geographically distinct area but who lack a nation–state of their own. The Kurds make up a "nation" in that they occupy a cultural territory made up of numerous communities of individuals who see themselves as "one people" and who share common ancestry, language, history, social institutions, and ideology.

The People

The Kurds are a non-Arab, mostly Muslim people with their own language and culture who have no state of their own but who live as a minority group in several different countries of the Middle East. Most of the Kurds live in the mountainous areas of northern Iraq, southeastern Turkey, and western Iran, but smaller numbers of Kurds live in Syria, Lebanon, Armenia, and Azerbaijan. Additional groups of Kurds have migrated to Europe (especially Germany, where their numbers are estimated at perhaps one-half million), the United States (where an estimated 35,000 have been resettled), and Canada. The population numbers are not completely clear and are controversial. The Kurds call the place they live "Kurdistan" ("home of the Kurds"), but that word cannot be found on most maps.

Historians disagree about how long the Kurds have lived in this part of the world. Arguments about timing range from 3,000 to 12,000 years. Archaeological finds include evidence that some of the earliest human steps toward animal domestication and the development of agriculture, as well

Kurdish father and son in traditional dress. (Courtesy Hanan Al-Nakshabandi)

as record keeping and technologies such as weaving, pottery making, and metal working, took place in the home of the Kurds as long as 8,000 to 12,000 years ago. Kurdish culture remains dominant in most areas where they live, and it has remained distinct in spite of repeated invasions by other peoples.

Although the origins of the Kurds are uncertain, they are thought to be related closely to Iranians. They are considered one of the most ancient people of the Middle East and may be descended from the ancient Medes. The Medes along with the Hittites, Mitannis, Haigs, Persians, Scythians and Alens were an Indo-European language–speaking tribe.[1] Newcomers to the area brought their own language and culture, which created a richer cultural mix. The Kurds were later conquered by Persians and then by the Arabic Muslims in A.D. 640, although the Kurds are said to have fought more vigorously than most against Arab domination.

The language of the Kurds is probably closest to Farsi, the predominant language of modern Iran. Kurdish, however, is divided into two primary groups, each with many dialects. The reason for this variation is the environmental setting in which the Kurds live: The high mountain ridges isolate the people in the valleys between, causing many tribes to interact very little with others. This isolation has contributed to the development of the various dialects, which of course cause difficulty in communication, something that makes it harder for the Kurds in different areas to work together. The Kurds have not yet agreed on a "standard" Kurdish language, but they have a large and rich (mostly oral) literature, consisting of poems and epic dramas.

Those who know the Kurds describe them as suspicious of strange things but quick to change their opinions if justified. They are considered self-sufficient and individualistic, proud of their attention to detail, joyous, free-spirited, romantic, hospitable, and generous (sometimes recklessly so, spending great amounts of money to entertain guests, for example). The arrival of visitors takes priority over any other plans a family may have, since providing hospitality brings honor to the family.

Kurds are very proud of their warrior tradition and think that, as ancestral nomads, they are freer, more proud, and alive than their agricultural neighbors. This tradition may be related to the emphasis that Kurds place on their honor, which they consider more important than life itself. Families and family honor and respect are very important, especially where women are concerned. Kurdish men and women from different families are never supposed to be alone together, to ensure that rumors of misbehavior will not be started.

Several writers describe what they call the Kurd's "traditionally high status of women," especially in comparison to other Muslim societies.[2] Kurdish women have commanded armies and distinguished themselves in battle, and some modern guerrilla groups include women in their ranks. Kurdish women have been active in politics from early on and have reportedly also played a primary role in religions, especially in the traditional "Cult of Angels" groups (see below). Others have described Kurdish women as having secure financial positions, even in a culture in which men make most of the decisions, family descent is through the father's line, and newly married couples live with the groom's parents. One author noted that in some isolated contemporary tribes the birth of a female child is more celebrated than that of a male.

Contradicting this rosy picture of the situation of women in Kurdish society are the words of Leyla Zana, a political activist and Kurdish leader in Turkey, who said, "Everywhere in the world women are ill-treated by men but amongst the Kurds it is especially bad. A woman is not even treated as a servant; she is a thing, almost an animal. For a Kurd, the birth of a girl is nothing."[3]

Modern Kurdish families often have six or more children, with the older children helping to care for the younger. Marriages are often arranged within a large extended family or clan, although the girl has some say in the matter. Family members help each other—if a husband dies, for example, other extended family members will help his widow and children.

Just as the mountains have resulted in a variety of language dialects, they have contributed to the great diversity in art and clothing styles that can be found among the Kurds. Their rugs are distinctive, with motifs particular to Kurdish artists. Most traditional Kurdish costumes, although they vary from region to region, are distinctively colorful. Women wear jewelry, often quite a lot and sometimes very elaborate.

The Setting

The history and culture of the Kurds are entwined with the mountains, their primary home. The mountains have provided some measure of freedom for the Kurds in several states, depending on how interested the various rulers were in dealing with them. However, the mountains, which have isolated and protected the Kurds, have also worked against them, keeping them uninformed about changes (political, economic, and social developments) in the rest of the world and retarding social and political change.

Because these mountains have prevented different Kurdish groups from communicating with one another, their history has been marked by continuous quarrels between persons or between communities, tribes, or factions, which are often suspicious of one another and sometimes hostile.

The area in the Middle East where the majority of Kurds live is a geologically active, earthquake-prone area, where the mountains are still growing several inches a year. "Kurdistan" is a land and climate of extremes, where altitude greatly affects the temperature and where the contrast in climate zones has been increased by the relatively recent destruction of forests and overgrazing at lower elevations. Precipitation in the area is relatively high (60 to 80 inches), and it comes mainly in the winter, largely in the form of snow. An important feature of the land of the Kurds is that it includes fertile river valleys where fruit trees, grapes, and other crops are grown. The headwaters of some of the Middle East's most important rivers are in the mountains where the Kurds live, including the Tigris and the Euphrates, which provide water to Turkey, Syria, and Iraq. These rivers were crucial to the origins of states and civilizations in what was known as the Fertile Crescent, and they continue to be of significance to the economic and environmental well-being of the modern Middle Eastern states of turkey, Syria, and Iraq.

Traditional Subsistence Strategies

For centuries, the Kurds lived as nomads in the mountains, moving regularly with their grazing animals from one good pasture to another. Those who lived at lower elevations did some farming to supplement their diet, but they were still usually seasonally seminomadic. Their nomadism decreased further in the early 1900s after World War I when some Kurds were forcibly resettled. At this time, France and Britain divided the Ottoman Empire. Since mechanization, agricultural work is mostly seasonal, and many Kurds are making a gradual transition from nomadic to sedentary life, especially in Iraq and Turkey.

The transition from a subsistence economy (supplying their own needs or bartering their goods for others) to a market economy (involving money) in the mid-nineteenth century meant that both mountain chiefs and landlords of plains and hills were incorporated into the modern state establishment. Most Kurds today can be described as predominantly peasants who depend on a combination of livestock production, crops, and cash-based employment. In recent years there has been some out-migration from the Kurdish regions to cities and towns in the Middle East, where Kurds work as bricklayers, builders, butchers, and traders. Some Kurds, mainly men, have gone to work in the oil fields of Iraq, Kuwait, Saudi Arabia, Iran, and the United Arab Emirates.

Social and Political Organization

There are strong loyalties among the Kurds to families and territories or tribal groupings, although the latter vary depending on the political and economical situation. Many tribes have been in existence, with the same names, for several thousand years. Traditionally, most political power was held by the tribal chiefs, called *aghas*, who, in the mountain tribes, were in charge of allocating grazing rights to tribal members. Kurdish loyalty first to tribal leaders and later to religious leaders, known as *sheikhs*, is considered one of the biggest obstacles to cooperation among different Kurdish groups, making it difficult to consolidate them in order to strive for political independence as a people.

Although some analysts believe that the traditional tribal structure is beginning to disintegrate, and may be fading considerably in Turkey, others believe that tribalism is stronger than ever among the Iraqi Kurds. Tribes may vary from several dozen households to large groups or confederacies of individual tribes.[4] Some scholars think that, in Turkey, the former tribal chiefs have remade themselves into politicians and administrators, some of whom are highly educated and quite worldly. A few Kurds—usually unaffiliated peasant families, rather than herdsmen—are not tribal, but they have never wielded much political power.

Religion and World View

Prior to the seventh century, most Kurds were Zoroastrians who became Sunni Muslims after conquest by the Arabs. Most Kurds are now Muslim; but some still practice one of several ancient faiths known collectively as the "Cult of Angels," three branches of which—including Yazidis, Yarsanis, and Alevis—survive today. There are also some Shi'ite Muslims, and both Judaism and Christianity have made inroads into Kurdistan.

Kurds have a reputation for being somehow less devoted to Islam than other groups, but they are probably about equally devout. Some Kurds, because of customs that derived from their traditional nomadic way of life, were perhaps less able to follow all of Islam's requirements, given their isolation and decreased access to Islamic scholars and teachers. Islamic fundamentalist teachings have influenced the Kurds, especially those in the towns and cities. A fairly sizable number of Kurds, estimated at 50,000 to 60,000, belong to the Yezidi sect, whose followers believe in reincarnation. These people have been subjected to persecution and discrimination in several parts of the Middle East where Kurds reside, including what used to be Soviet Armenia, Georgia, and northern Iraq.

An important national Kurdish festival is New Ruz, or new year, celebrated on March 21 with special foods, special flowers grown for the occasion, visiting, and gift-giving. Some celebrants light bonfires on the roof or in the streets to mark the passing of the dark winter season and the arrival of the light spring season. Firecrackers scare off evil spirits, and dead friends and family members are remembered.

THREATS TO SURVIVAL

Having no state, or country, to call their own, the Kurds are scattered throughout the Middle East, the former Soviet Union, and Europe. Others have fled as refugees to the United States or Canada. Those who have stayed in their original homelands have faced persecution and hardships. The conditions of Kurds in different countries vary widely, but most have suffered forms of repression ranging from cultural assimilation to physical annihilation. The Kurds have rarely enjoyed a period of peace and stability and have never been able to count on loyal allies.

A review of the threats to the survival of Kurdish culture and Kurdish people follows. Because they have had to deal with several different state governments, the Kurds in each country are discussed separately.

Kurds in Iran

Kurds in Iran, who represent about 8 percent of the population, live mostly in the Zagros Mountains along Iran's borders with Turkey and Iraq. Iranian Kurds acknowledge their close ethnic and ancestral ties with the Persians of Iran, the ethnic group to whom they are most closely related.

After World War II, an independent Kurdish state, the Mahabad Republic, was formed from a section of Iran, but it lasted only one year. The then-Soviet Union assisted this secessionist movement, hoping to pressure the Iranian government into granting them economic concessions, especially long-sought access to the Persian Gulf. The young republic collapsed when internal Kurdish disagreements kept them from resisting a newly powerful Iranian armed force.

After the 1979 overthrow of the shah and the establishment of the Islamic Republic in Iran, the Kurds, concerned about possible oppression, tried once more to establish a quasi-independent state. Again, it was short-lived, given a stronger Iranian army, the Iran-Iraq War that began in 1980, and internal Kurdish divisions and disagreements. The Kurds have not come close to even those modest efforts to establish independence after World War II. Today, Kurdish leaders in Iran generally insist that they are seeking autonomy within Iran, not independence.

Restrictions on Kurdish cultural expression were moderate in Iran during the time of the ruling Pahlavi dynasty (1925–1979), especially in comparison to restrictions on Kurds in Turkey (see below). Kurdish-language media were permitted, although political content was censored. Kurdish-language instruction was permitted in schools, although the main language of instruction was Farsi, the language of the Iranians. The Iranian government's attitude toward Kurdish autonomy has not changed much since the establishment of the Islamic theocratic government (a government based upon the beliefs of Islam) in 1979. The Kurds in Iran have developed a sense of a dual identity as Kurds apart from other Persians, and Iranian Kurds apart from other Kurds.

Economically, the Kurds in Iran remain quite poor and benefit very little from the oil extracted from the areas in which they live. As Iran became more isolated internationally, the country's economic decline made Kurdish poverty worse and dampened the possibilities for improvement in their economic well-being. There have been moderate economic gains made by some Iranian Kurds in the past few years as Iranian policies have been moderated by democratic forces.

Kurds in Iraq

In Iraq, where they represent about 15 to 20 percent of the population, the Kurds have suffered under a variety of non-Kurdish rulers. The area now known as Iraq has seen centuries of empires rising and falling. At the beginning of the twentieth century, it was part of the Ottoman Empire. After World War I, the Kurds were included, without any say-so, into the new kingdom of Iraq, which was made a British mandate after World War I. The new Iraqi government was under British advisers until 1932, when it became a constitutional monarchy headed by King Faisal I.

Although the 1920 Treaty of Sèvres, which established the kingdom of Iraq, called for Kurdish autonomy and independence, its provisions with regard to Kurdish autonomy were not implemented, and for a variety of reasons, the treaty was never ratified. This treaty, however, represented the first international recognition of the Kurdish movement and the Kurdish desire for self-determination.

In the new country of Iraq, many competing groups vied for power and economic benefits, and the Kurds resented both British and then Arab administration. Large Christian and Jewish communities, along with a variety of older religious groups, competed with the divided Muslim population (Sunni and Shi'ite). "These social and ethnic divisions, plus the economic and educational gaps between rural peasants and urban merchants and landowners, made the new state all but impossible to govern, let alone to develop politically."[5]

The Kurds of northern Iraq pressed the Iraqi government for self-rule several times during the period of the constitutional monarchy. Following World War II, they formed their own republic in Kurdish areas on the Iraq-Iran and Iraq-Turkey borders, but this lasted only a few months. In the 1960s, they rebelled against the Iraqi government when their demands for self-government, use of their language in school, and a greater share in oil revenues were refused. Fighting continued through the 1970s, during which time the Iranian government provided some arms to the Iraqi Kurdish rebels.

A revolution against the monarch in 1958 created the republic of Iraq, which has since seen many changes of leadership, with violence, intrigue, and political secrecy characterizing most periods of change. Saddam Hussain, now declared "President for Life," has control over the majority Ba'th Party, the army, and the secret services. During the Iran-Iraq War, from 1980 to 1988, hundreds of thousands of Kurds were drafted into both the Iranian and Iraqi armed forces to fight each other on the battlefield. Many deserted. During the war, however, Kurds established control over large areas while the Iraqi military was concentrating on the war. The Kurds allied with Iran, and they paid for this allegiance. When the Iran-Iraq War ended, the Iraqi government turned on the Kurds in what some analysts such as William Spencer have described as "a savage and deliberate campaign of genocide."[6] Reports indicate that the Iraqis started using chemical weapons against the Kurds, causing the deaths of thousands of civilians. In what was called the Anfal campaign (the word means "spoils of war"), the Iraqi government destroyed hundreds of villages, capped water wells, and poisoned the crops in the fields. At least 180,000 Kurds, and probably tens of thousands more, died or disappeared during this operation.

Kurdish fighters, known as *peshmerga*, were executed, and tens of thousands of Kurds were placed in concentration camps. When they were finally released, they were warned not to return to the Kurdistan area of Iraq. Iran opened its doors for Kurds fleeing Iraq, although it already had one of the largest refugee populations in the world. In 1991, a number of Kurdish uprisings in northern Iraq were again met with brutal violence and quashed by the Iraqi army. Hundreds of thousands of Kurds who left their homes returned when the United States and its allies provided troops and aircraft to protect the northern "no-fly" zone north of the 36th parallel in Iraq, the area where most of the Kurds were settled. During this period of protection, the Iraqi Kurds attempted a form of self-rule, but it failed as a result in part of internal divisiveness. One of the two major factions, the Kurdish Democratic Party (KDP), made an arrangement to cooperate with Saddam Hussain in order to get rid of their opposition, the Patriotic Union of Kurdistan (PUK) Party. Success was short-lived, as the PUK regrouped in the mountains and recovered most of their lost territory. Before Hussain withdrew, he rounded up opposition dissidents supported by the U.S. Central Intelligence Agency (CIA) who had sought to form the anti-Saddam Iraqi National Congress. In 1994, the northern Kurds began fighting among themselves, and many civilians as well as fighters were killed, perhaps as many as 5,000 or more.

The Kurds downplay the ferocity and extent of their civil war, because they rely on the West to help protect them from Baghdad. A cease-fire declared in 1995 slowed the fighting, but occasional skirmishes continue.

Kurds in Turkey

In Turkey, although they represent between 17 percent and 22 percent of the population, the Kurds are not officially recognized as a separate ethnic group. This is the case even though the Kurds were living in the southeastern part of modern Turkey before the first Turkic tribes arrived in the tenth century. Kurds enjoyed autonomy until the last years of the Ottoman Empire. When that empire was broken up after World War I, Turkey, afraid of being divided and reduced even further, determined to suppress all non-Turkish ethnic identities. Indeed, some believe that no country has ever been as preoccupied with eliminating minority Kurdish national identity as has Turkey in the twentieth century. As the Turkish minister of justice said in 1930, "I believe that the Turks must be the only lord, the only master of this country. Those who are not of pure Turkish stock can have only one right in this country, the right to be servants and slaves."[7]

For many years, the Kurds were almost completely excluded from national life in Turkey. Before 1991, it was against the law for them to speak their native language or display any symbols of the Kurdish culture. The ban was partially lifted in 1991, but Kurdish can still only be spoken in the home, not in public or in broadcast media. School classes are conducted only in Turkish. For many years, Kurdish place names were removed from maps, and parents were forbidden to give their children Kurdish names. Kurdish political parties were forbidden as well. Kurdish festivals, such as New Ruz, were forbidden or at least strongly discouraged.

As is true of the Kurds in Iran, the Kurds in Turkey are very poor, especially when they are compared to non-Kurdish Turks. This poverty shows up in high infant death rates and low literacy rates as well as in economic measures. In the 1970s, renewed feelings of Kurdish nationalism resulted in demands for a separate Kurdish state. The Worker's Party of Kurdistan (known as the PKK) was founded in 1978 by Abdullah Ocalan. This party was outlawed in 1980, when a military coup resulted in a change in government in Turkey. Ocalan took refuge in Syria, but the PKK, and the guerrilla warfare it espoused, grew quickly because the Turkish government shut down other Kurdish organizations and repressed all forms of Kurdish expression. In the warfare that followed, thousands of Kurds were killed, many of them civilians.

Since the 1980s, Turkish military and internal security forces have fought against PKK guerrillas in southeastern Turkey. For years, the PKK held the edge, staging hit-and-run attacks and escaping into their familiar mountains. In the 1990s, however, the Turkish army trained effective commando troops and outfitted them with new equipment, including helicopters, and the Turkish armed forces were able to get the upper hand. The continual fighting has resulted in many villages becoming ghost towns, and the countryside has been stripped of trees and crops.

The Kurdish sociologist and writer Ismail Besikci, imprisoned and tortured for publishing studies on Kurdish ethnic rights in Turkey, became a "prisoner of conscience" whose plight was publicized by the human rights organization Amnesty International. Other Kurds in Turkey have undergone large-scale forced migration from their southeastern villages to western Turkey, both for "military security" reasons and as punishment for involvement in behavior considered damaging to the state.[8]

On the other hand, the Turkish government has recruited Kurdish peasants into its army, promising regular wages to an economically depressed group and further setting Kurd against Kurd. Although the government claims that they have never forced anyone to enlist, independent human rights organizations dispute that claim. As mentioned previously, the two major Kurdish parties in northern Iraq, KDP and PUK, have been engaged in a civil war since 1994. The Turkish PKK has taken advantage of the resulting confusion and established bases in Iraq from which to conduct raids on Turkish territory. In 1995, Turkish government troops moved across the border into northern Iraq to harass the PKK. This was not a popular move with the rest of the world. The United States (Turkey's largest source of military aid) and its European and NATO (North Atlantic Treaty Organization) allies pressed for a withdrawal. The Turks had previously committed themselves to protecting Iraqi citizens from Saddam Hussein and had actively helped to end the Iraqi occupation of Kuwait, so this attack on Kurds in Iraq was a contradiction of policy.

In February 1999, PKK leader Abdullah Ocalan was arrested, tried, and sentenced to death by the Turkish government. Ocalan, who himself speaks little Kurdish, has been described by some as a power-hungry madman, but to many of the members of the PKK and their supporters, he is a hero, in spite of the fact that many international observers agree that he and his guerrillas wiped out rival Kurdish movements and potential personal rivals with ruthless determination. In May 2001, the PKK softened their position on establishing an independent Kurdish state. Many human rights groups have urged the Turkish government not to put Ocalan to death. The Turkish government is in a complex position on the question of capital punishment. On the one hand, if they do not carry out the sentence, it could be argued that the government is "soft on terrorism." If they do carry out the sentence, other countries and nongovernment organizations could question the degree to which Turkey is committed to human rights and pluralism, something that has implications for Turkey's potential candidacy for membership in the European Union. In late 2001, Abdullah Ocalan declared that the guerrilla war for independence was a mistake. He remains in Turkish prison.[9]

Kurds in Syria

Syrian Kurds, who number around 1 million, representing 8 percent of the population, are more assimilated into local Arab culture than Kurds in other Middle Eastern states, but they have suffered repression, imprisonment, and torture in Syria as well. This was the case especially between 1958 and 1976, a time considered the "heyday of Arab nationalism." Like Iraq, Syria was also a new state, mandated to France after World War I. Although postwar treaties encouraged the development of autonomy among minorities in the newly formed states, the Kurds had no international support, nor were they prepared to take a national approach. Some scholars have suggested that the Kurds' "tribal urge" was greater than their urge to become an autonomous nation and that *aghas* and *sheikhs* were worried more about maintaining their own authority than uniting for a common purpose.[10] After World War II, the Syrian mountain Kurds were ignored or left to fight among themselves. It was the detribalized Kurds in the cities who began to be active in political development of the Kurdish cause. In 1990, Kurds were first elected to the Syrian Parliament. They are, however, still considered inferior by some people in Syria, their language is suppressed, and many are unable to claim citizenship, identity cards, or passports. As in other Middle Eastern countries, there are efforts to promote the civil, political, and cultural rights of Kurds in Syria.

Kurds in Armenia, Azerbaijan, and Lebanon

Nearly all the Kurds in Armenia are followers of the Yazidi religion, and they and many of the Sunni Muslim Kurds and Kurds of other faiths were the victims of mass expulsion from Armenia. Some recognition of Kurdish culture has resulted in Kurdish-language broadcasting and a newspaper, but the majority of education is in the Armenian language, and there is inadequate representation of the Kurds at local and national levels of government.

In Azerbaijan, the Kurds may number as many as 200,000. In the earlier part of the twentieth century they enjoyed the status of an autonomous area within Azerbaijan, but recently they have been caught up in the Nagorno-Karabagh conflict and forced into the Azerbaijani army. This conflict erupted in the central province of Azerbaijan in 1988 killing tens of thousands of Azerbaijanis and Armenianis. A ceasefire was initiated in 1994.

Kurds in Lebanon, who number some 50,000, lack civil and political rights, but they have been less subject to overt oppression than Kurds in other parts of the Middle East.

Environmental Threats

The lands of the Kurds, once almost all forested, has been cleared in the twentieth century, and soil erosion and increased vulnerability to drought and economic downturns have resulted. In some areas, pasture lands are still in fairly good condition, but there are efforts to privatize the land, which is limiting the movement of stock and causing localized degradation. Ancient Kurdish forests, which began in a more humid past, cannot renew themselves once they have been clear-cut, because the microclimate and ecosystem that nurtured their growth literally evaporate. Although damage to the environment has been accumulating for centuries, that done in the last two centuries is the worst. The rich soil is being washed away, and the fertility of the area is threatened. Because of a nearly continuous state of siege or war, few resources are available to be spent to combat the ecological problems.

The rivers of the Kurdish region have been subjected to exploitation, and in the past several decades, large-scale dam projects have been initiated on the larger rivers. The Turkish government's Southeast Anatolia Project, which is one of the world's largest public works efforts, is estimated to have cost over $35 billion. Its centerpiece is the Ataturk Dam on the Euphrates River, the reservoir of which has inundated substantial amounts of fertile river bottom land and has led to the destruction of hundreds of villages, both ancient and modern. While Turkey will benefit greatly from the development of hydroelectric power and irrigated agricultural land as a result of this gigantic project, the Kurds will find themselves in an even more vulnerable position than they were before, with less productive land and higher population densities and greater poverty in marginal areas.

RESPONSE: STRUGGLES TO SURVIVE CULTURALLY

The Kurds have endured cultural repression and/or attempted genocide and ethnocide in all of the nation–states in which they live. Armies, rulers, and governments stripped them of their human rights. In virtually all of the states where they exist, the Kurds are considered second-class citizens. The response of the Kurds to the situations that they have faced varies both at a national and a local level. There has been political mobilization among Kurds for generations. They have formed political parties and organized formal resistance movements. The Kurds have a long reputation as fearsome warriors dating back thousands of years, a reputation of which they are very proud. Their divisiveness, however, gives regional powers a chance to play one group off against the other. In order to counteract these efforts, Kurdish resistance movements have sought to communicate with one another more frequently and have entered into intergroup dialogues and negotiations. Some Kurd support groups and political parties have also attempted to negotiate directly with governments.

One of the strategies that Kurds use is to draw attention to their situations by interacting closely with human rights organizations such as Middle East Watch, Amnesty International, and the Minority Rights Group. Like many minority groups, the Kurds have sought to use the media to their advantage, and in recent years they have been active on the World Wide Web. Kurds have engaged in peaceful (and sometimes not so peaceful) demonstrations in Europe and the United States as well as in the Middle East.

Kurds have run for office and in some cases have been elected to Parliament. At the grassroots level, Kurds have sought to teach their language and cultural traditions in spite of the repression that they faced. It is not unusual today to see publications in Kurdish in the Middle East and in Europe and the United States.

Some Kurds have had to flee their homelands and requested asylum in other Middle Eastern countries. Others have resettled in Europe (mostly in Germany, with half a million Kurds), Canada, and the United States. There are an estimated 35,000 to 40,000 Kurds in the United States, some of whom have resettled successfully in places ranging from New York to Lincoln, Nebraska. Resettling in a Western industrial nation is in itself a stressful choice.

What challenges do these refugees face? A female Kurdish refugee may resettle with her husband and children in the midwestern United States, where religion, language, expected behavior, dress, and attitudes about school and work are so utterly different from her own. She may believe that eye contact and shaking hands with a strange man is culturally inappropriate, but she is expected to impress an interviewer to obtain a job that may make the difference in adequate food for her family. She cannot read the signs in order to take the bus or speak the language to ask directions; she is afraid to venture out alone on the streets for fear of getting lost. She and her family do not understand the laws in their new home. Learning a new language may be an even bigger barrier if she came from a rural area and has had no or limited formal education in her own language. She is isolated, lonely, and depressed. Field workers have found that refugee resettlement has also shown that cultural adjustment of the women in a family is vital to the overall success of the family.[11] Although many are eventually quite successful, the most motivated refugees face significant adjustment stress in their new homes, even if they feel welcome by their neighbors.

FOOD FOR THOUGHT

The Kurds are the largest ethnic group in the world that occupies a geographically distinct area and does not have a country of its own. They have suffered cultural repression and attempts at genocide and cultural repression from the governments under which they have lived. Hopes for a successful pan-Kurdish nationalist movement are slim.

What Kurds need most depends on where they live. In Turkey, cultural autonomy is the most crucial issue. In Iraq, self-determination is a more pressing goal. In countries such as the United States, Germany, and France, the cultural and economic well-being of individual families and small communities is seen as crucial. The Kurds see themselves as engaged in a struggle against overwhelming odds. They are pitched against powerful nation-states in the Middle East, and they have relatively little support for their efforts to gain autonomy from the international community, which is dominated by states that are concerned about issues of sovereignty and autonomy within their own borders. While there is little indication that the Kurds will be able to establish their own state in the near future, there is no question that the Kurdish movement is still very much alive.

Questions

1. What if the Treaty of Sèvres, with its proposed development of a Kurdish state, had actually been ratified and implemented after it was signed in 1920? What differences would this treaty have made for the Kurds of today?

2. What do you think is the biggest obstacle to Kurds gaining autonomy in the modern world?

3. What do you think are the biggest barriers to Kurdish refugee resettlement success in their new countries of resettlement? How can these barriers best be addressed? How are they being addressed by refugee resettlement agencies?

4. What should U.S. foreign policy be regarding the Kurds, when the U.S. government interacts with Turkey, Iraq, or Iran?

5. Compare the plight of the Kurds, as discussed in this chapter, with the situation of other ethnic groups discussed in this book. What similarities do you find? Differences? Are there some survival strategies used by other groups that would be useful for the Kurds?

NOTES

1. "Iran-Kurds," 2001, *http://www.cyberiran.com/history/kurds.shtml.*
2. RSC Refugee Service Center, "Iraqi Kurds—Their History and Culture Refugee Fact Sheet," No. 13, 1999, *http://www.cal.org/RSC.*
3. Kurdistan Committee of Canada, *"The Status of Kurdish Women,"* 1995, *http://burn.ucsd.edu/archives/kurd-1/1995/0083.html.*
4. "Iran-Kurds."
5. William Spencer, *Global Studies: The Middle East* (Guilford, CT: Dushkin/ McGraw-Hill, 1998), 67.
6. Ibid.
7. *Milliet* (Turkish newspaper), September 30, 1930.
8. *Kurds and Kurdistan,* 2001, *http://w1.638.telia.com/~u638021/Xaneper/ Hemsida/Kurdistan/Kurdfakt.html.*
9. Michael Radu, "The Rise and Fall of the PKK," *Orbis* 45, no. 1 (2001), 47–64.
10. Barbara Robson, *Iraqi Kurds: Their History and Culture* (Refugee Fact Sheet Series No. 13, 1996), 3, *http://www.culturalorientation.net/kurds/*; Nader Entessar, *Kurdish Ethnonationalism* (Boulder, CO: Lynne Rienner Publishers, 1992), 78–80; Robert Olson, *The Emergence of Kurdish Nationalism and the Sheikh Said Rebellion, 1880–1925* (Austin: Univeristy of Texas Press, 1989), 145.
11. G. R. Rumbaut, "Portraits, Patterns, and Predictors of the Refugee Adaptation Process: Results and Reflections from the IHARP Panel Study," in *Refugee as Immigrants: Cambodians, Laotians, and Vietnamese in America,* ed. D. W. Haines (Totowa, NJ: Rowman & Littlefield, 1989), 138–182.

RESOURCE GUIDE

Published Literature

Bulloch, James, and Harvey Morris. *No Friends But the Mountains.* New York: Oxford University Press, 1992.

Ciment, James. *The Kurds: State and Minority in Turkey, Iraq and Iran.* (New York: Facts on File, Inc., 1991).

Entessar, Nader. *Kurdish Ethnonationalism.* (Boulder, Colorado: Lynne Rienner Publishers, 1992).

Izady, Mehrdad R. *The Kurds: A Concise Handbook.* (Washington, D.C.: Taylor & Francis, 1992).

Kashi, Ed. *When the Borders Bleed: The Struggle of the Kurds.* (New York: Pantheon, 1997).

Meiselas, Susan. *Kurdistan: In the Shadow of History.* New York: Random House, 1998.

Films and Videos

Dreaming a Nation: The Kurds. 1994. Part of the Nationalism: Blood and Belonging series.
Journey of Hope. 1991. Written and directed by Xavier Koller. Miramax Films.
Journey of the Sun. 1999. Film Directed by Yesim Ustaoglu. International Sales.

WWW Sites

American Kurdish Information Network
www.kurdistan.org/

Amnesty International's annual reports on human rights abuses in various countries.
http://www.amnesty.org/ailib/countries/indx514.htm

CNN interactive on the Turkish PKK and the arrest and trial of Abdullah Ocalan
http://cnn.com/interactive/specials/9904/ocalan.kurds/content/default.html

Human Rights Watch. Information on restriction of the use of the Kurdish language
http://www.hrw.org/reports/1999/turkey/turkey993–08.htm

Kurdish Worldwide Resources
http://www.kurdish.com

Kurdistan Democratic Party
http://www.kdp.pp.se/index.html

Meet the Kurds
http://cobblestonepub.com/pages/Kurds.htm

Özgürlük Press Agency. Press release about Kurdish filmwriter Yilmaz Guney
http://www.ozgurluk.org/press/msg00402.html

Patriotic Union of Kurdistan
www.puk.org/

Organizations

American Kurdish Information Network (AKIN)
2623 Connecticut Avenue NW # 1
Washington, DC 20008–1522
Telephone: (202) 483–6444
Email: wki@kurd.org
Web site: www.kurd.org

Amnesty International USA
322 Eighth Avenue
New York, NY 10001

Cultural Survival
215 Prospect Street
Cambridge, MA 02139

Human Rights Watch
350 Fifth Avenue, 34th Floor
New York, NY 10118–3299

Institute Kurde
106 Rue La Fayette
75010, Paris, France

Kurdish Cultural Center
14 Stannary Street
London, SE11 4AA, United Kingdom

Kurdish Human Rights Project
Linen Hall, Suite 236
162–8 Regent Street
London W1R, United Kingdom

Turkish League for Human Rights
Yildrim Palas No. 17/10
Aksaray-IST, Turkey

Washington Kurdish Institute, 605 G Street, SW
Washington, DC 20024
Telephone: (202) 484–0140
Email: akin@kurdish.org
Web site: www.kurdistan.org

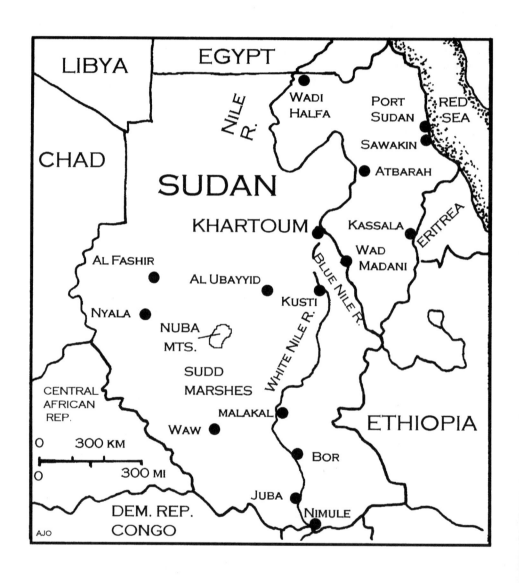

Chapter 6

The Nuba of Sudan

Mona A. Mohamed and Margaret Fisher

CULTURAL OVERVIEW

The People

Sudan, the largest country in Africa (967,499 square miles), is characterized by high levels of ethnic and linguistic diversity and, in some cases, by intergroup tensions. The Sudanese population is made up of over 200 different ethnic groups who speak 134 languages. Some of the Sudanese peoples are considered by themselves and by the state to be indigenous, that is, peoples who are culturally distinct, who are the descendants of the earliest residents of the areas in which they reside, and who seek to maintain their land, resources, and identities. One such population in Sudan is the Nuba, non-Arab peoples who reside in a hilly and mountainous region in the central part of the country.

From an ethnographic perspective, Sudan can be divided into two major regions, the north and the south. The groups in the north are predominantly Muslim urban dwellers and rural agricultural and cattle and camel herding groups who claim Arab heritage. Those in the south of Sudan are farmers and agropastoralists (people who combine livestock herding with crop production) who are mainly Christians or followers of indigenous religions and who are considered to be of African heritage.

The Nuba peoples of Sudan are the indigenous inhabitants of the Nuba Mountains in the central part of South Kordofan Province. Numbering approximately 1.6 million, the Nuba consist of a variety of ethnic groups, some fifty in number, who collectively are labeled Nuba. The Nuba speak an array of language dialects and practice a farming adaptation that distinguish them from surrounding Arab herders and Nilotic peoples (e.g., the Nuer and Dinka) who live along the White Nile River in southern Sudan.

The Nuba are located in an area that is essentially a geographic and cultural frontier zone between the north and the south of Sudan. After the collapse of the ancient Christian kingdoms of Nuba, Alwa, and Dotawo, and the Islamic invasion of the north of Sudan around the fifteenth century, some of the survivors retreated to the Nuba Mountains, an area that has long represented a place of refuge. About 70 percent of the population of the Nuba Mountains today is made up of Nuba; the balance of the population of the region includes Arabic-speaking Baggara herders, Jellaba, and a sizable number of Fellata, West Africans who migrated into the Nuba Mountains in the early part of the twentieth century to work in the cotton fields.

Since 1983, there has been an ongoing civil war in Sudan that has seen the people of the southern part of the country struggling against the people of the north, where the government is located. The Nuba have had to cope with attempts by the government of Sudan to Islamicize them (that is, to require them to become Muslim and to learn Arabic). The Sudanese government imposed Sharia, or Islamic law, throughout the country, including the Nuba Mountains, in the 1980s. The Nuba, who had a long history of religious and cultural tolerance, were put in a position where they had to accept the religion, language, and cultural rules of external societies. Slave raids, which were an issue for the Nuba in the past, became increasingly commonplace, as did the alienation of land by non-Nuba peoples such as the Jellaba.

Over the past two decades, and especially since 1989–1990, the Nuba have been subjected to attacks by Sudanese government forces that have resulted in the destruction of villages and homesteads and the deaths of large numbers of people.[1] Sizable numbers of Nuba have been displaced, and some of them have had to seek refuge in other countries. Many Nuba have been imprisoned, often for long periods of time. In addition, the Nuba, like a number of other central and southern Sudanese peoples, have to face efforts by the government and by liberation groups to prevent the distribution of food, medicines, and other goods provided by international and local organizations that were supposed to be used to aid people who were suffering. In spite of these problems, the Nuba have maintained their identity and resilience, and they have sought actively to resist the imposition of external policies and practices through community organizing and the use of the media, including the World Wide Web, to make the public aware of their situations.

The Setting

The Nuba Mountains region covers an area of more than 19,305 square miles, a region about the size of Scotland. The highest peak in the Nuba Mountains is more than 4,921 feet above sea level. The environment of the region is semitropical, and droughts are fairly common. The rainy season lasts from approximately mid-May to mid-October, and rainfall during this period averages 16 to 31 inches. Periodic shortfalls of rain during the growing season affects crop yields, and people buffer themselves against scarcity by collecting wild plants and doing a limited amount of hunting.

The Nuba Mountains contain hills, ridges, and high plateaus that are dissected by streams and rivers. The gradual degradation of the mountain rocks has resulted in very fertile alluvial or water-deposited soils that can support a wide variety of crops. The introduction of mechanized farming in the 1950s has had impacts on the environment, with some parts of the Nuba region becoming increasingly degraded, with losses of top soils and the expansion of sand dunes.

Traditional Subsistence Strategies

Some Nuba families, such as the Miri, have two kinds of agricultural land: a small plot close to the family homesteads, in which vegetables and fruits are grown, and a larger field away from the homestead, in which they grow crops such as sorghum, millet, sesame, pumpkins, and various kinds of beans. Farmland is held in the name of the family. Generally, it is women who cultivate the gardens close to the homesteads, whereas men cultivate the fields located further away. Some of the watering of the crops is done by hand; in other cases, small irrigation furrows are dug that channel the water to the fields. Some crops may be grown in terraced fields on hillsides. Mechanized farming was introduced in the Nuba Mountains region during the colonial period. Cotton was grown and marketed to places in Sudan and elsewhere. Cotton still represents a source of income for a portion of Nuba households, and some Nuba work on cotton schemes or forms.

Sorghum is used in making local porridge and brewing local beers. The porridge is eaten with very thick okra and meat stews. The Nuba peoples have diversified socioeconomic systems in which some of their subsistence and income is derived from a combination of their crops and, in some cases, poultry and animal herds, and cash is earned through sales of goods or raised through migratory labor. When life becomes difficult in their region many Nuba migrate to the capital and various cities in Sudan to help boost their incomes through working for other people.

The process of labor migration has affected the viability of the livestock industry in the Nuba Mountains. Now that young men are going to the cities as laborers, they are no longer able to care for the cattle and small stock (sheep and goats) in the mountains. Livestock losses are a major problem for many Nuba, and the sizes of livestock herds have declined over time. Besides the losses of livestock due to accidents and theft, various kinds of livestock diseases have reduced the herds, including rinderpest, lungsickness, and foot-and-mouth disease. Such herd losses have dire economic consequences. A major issue facing the Nuba has been the gradual loss of their agricultural land, some of which was taken over by immigrant populations who borrowed or purchased it, and some of which was taken over by the colonial and postcolonial state governments and turned into agricultural schemes aimed at the production of cash crops such as cotton.

Social and Political Organization

Nuba social and political organization is diverse, with some groups organized around males (i.e., they are patrilineal in their orientation, with descent traced through the male line) and others organized around families (i.e., they are matrilineal in their orientation, with descent traced through the female line). Most Nuba are organized into what are known as clans—groups of related people who trace their descent either through the male or the female line. These clans are corporate groups that are exogamous, meaning that marriage within the clan is forbidden. The clans each have names and symbols to which the members owe allegiance, and each clan has specific rules by which the members are supposed to operate. Together, a number of clans are combined into the largest social unit in Nuba society, the tribe. Members of the tribe see themselves as belonging to a single group that speaks the same language, follows the same customs and traditions, and in many cases, have shared rights to ancestral territories or lands.

Nearly all Nuba villages have their own chief or traditional authority, a person who is responsible for resolving conflicts and overseeing legal cases at the local level, who has the authority to maintain order, and who serves as an arbiter in disputes such as those over land. In 1971, the Sudanese government passed the People's Local Government Act, which was geared toward integrating grassroots political representation, administration, and decision making from the level of the province downward. As a result of this act, People's Councils were formed that contain representatives from each village in specific localities. In some cases, these People's Councils organize and distribute supplies of sugar and salt, and they often function as linkages between the provincial authorities and the people at the village level.

Religion and World View

The Nuba practice a number of different religions, including Christianity, Islam, and indigenous religions. Most Nuba actually practice a mixture of religions, combining a belief in a single god with indigenous sets of beliefs and practices. Many Nuba believe that there are spiritual beings who speak through priests; in other words, they believe in spirit possession, a not uncommon belief in much of Africa. There are also rain priests in many, if not most, Nuba villages. These individuals perform rituals aimed at bringing the rains. Certain Nuba clans are known for being excellent rain-makers, and their rain priests are sometimes employed by other clans to perform rain magic. Failure to produce rains can cause rain priests to lose their reputations, and extended drought periods in the Nuba Mountains have witnessed local communities taking out their frustrations on the unfortunate rain priests.

Magic and religion are tightly woven systems in the world view of the Nuba. Some Nuba are known for their abilities to heal the sick. In some cases, they call on the spirits to restore the health of an ill person; in other cases, they administer medicinal herbs. Some traditional healers among the Nuba have become powerful political figures and have played important roles in Nuba history, for example, leading resistance against external threats.[2]

One of the issues that has raised concern among women's human rights groups around the world and in Sudan specifically is the practice of female circumcision, which a number of Nuba groups, as well as other Sudanese groups, practice. Female circumcision—or as some human rights activists describe it, female genital mutilation (FGM)—in the Nuba Mountains involves what is known as clitoridectomy, the practice of removing, often with the use of a knife, razor blade, or scalpel, a portion of a young woman's genitalia, specifically the clitoris, as part of a coming-of-age ceremony. This practice, which has been justified on religious and cultural grounds, has been opposed by some groups and individuals because it is seen as having harmful physical and psychological effects on young women. An important social movement in Sudan and elsewhere in Africa has as its major goal the eradication of female circumcision.

In April 1990 a cabinet reshuffle in the Sudanese government resulted in a strengthening of fundamentalist Islamic influence at the national level. In early 1992, the governor of South Kordofan, Lt. General Sid Ahmed al-Hussein, formally declared a *jihad*, a holy war, in the Nuba Mountains. Over 25,000 Nubian villagers were sent to what in Sudan are known as "peace camps" (or, as some describe them, concentrated camps) where reeducation was to take place. Sudan's Islamic militia and army targeted Christian churches in the Nuba Mountains, desecrating them and looting doors, windows, vestments, Bibles, and catechism books. These actions have been condemned widely by human rights groups and governments from around the world as an assault on religious freedom. In 2001, the Nuba continued to be the targets of aggression, violence, and oppression by the dictatorial government in Khartoum. The world's longest civil war continues to destabilize the region.

THREATS TO SURVIVAL

Demographic Trends

The population of the Nuba Mountains is growing relatively rapidly in spite of some of the difficulties that people face. The average population growth rate is about 2.7 percent per annum. Life expectancy ranges from forty-seven to fifty-three years. The infant mortality rate is 77 per 1,000 births. Population and family planning measures have had some effects on population growth rates, although the availability of reproductive health information and birth control devices is not widespread in the region. Diseases such as malaria and tuberculosis have long been a problem for the Nuba, who have sought international assistance in combating these problems.

A factor that affects the Nuba and other populations in central and southern Sudan is famine, the lack of food and other resources that is a product of either human factors (prevention of the movement of goods into an area) or natural factors such as prolonged drought. Tens of thousands of Nuba and other people in central Sudan reportedly have starved to death or have experienced severe privation as a result of the inability to obtain sufficient food to meet their needs. As of May 2001, an estimated 42,000 Nuba once again faced starvation.[3] In some cases, the famine-related deaths are a direct result of the policies of the government or of liberation organizations that have purposely prevented the distribution of food and medicine. Famine in the conflict zones of Sudan was also a product of deliberate efforts by government and opposition forces to prevent people from planting crops. In some areas, relief food became a major source of support for the local populations, a substantial proportion of whom had been displaced from their homes.

It is apparent that food is being used as a weapon in the civil war in Sudan. Food stores have been looted by armies and militias. A permanent government blockade, in place since the beginning of the war, barred all UN relief operations and even traders from the rebel areas of the Nuba Mountains.[4] Local people have resorted to creative means to survive; these means range from selling off livestock and household assets to engaging in labor migration and joining—often briefly—the various armies or nongovernment organizations operating in the region in order to get access to food and cash. Together with the war and other crises, some 4 million people in Sudan have been internally displaced, and many of them are at risk.

Investigations by the United Nations Special Rapporteur and foreign government dignitaries and human rights organizations have indicated that slave raids continue to occur in the Nuba Mountains and in other parts of central and southern Sudan. The abduction of persons, mainly women and children from various racial, ethnic, and religious groups, has become—as it was in the eighteenth and nineteenth centuries—a major human rights issue, with various agencies, including Anti-Slavery International, Survival International, and Amnesty International, condemning the practice of forced servitude in Sudan.[5] In some cases, nongovernment organizations, some of which are Christian relief agencies, have initiated the practice of buying back enslaved Nuba people from their owners and freeing them. This strategy apparently created another problem, since some local people consider this as a good source of income and hence they continued the practice for their own benefit. In this way, it might be said that the nongovernment organization efforts could have contributed to the enhancement of the practice of slavery instead of demolishing it, though this conclusion is still the subject of widespread debate.

Environmental Crises

A major problem facing the people of the Nuba Mountains is environmental degradation. In some areas, the tree and shrub cover has been removed by people seeking fuel wood and building materials. There are parts of the Nuba Mountains that have been affected heavily by the grazing of domestic livestock. In these areas, the loss of grasses, and the encroachment of bush due to grazing pressure, has become a major problem, leading to a process known as desertification—the spread of desertlike conditions. In some parts of the Nuba Mountains, surface water sources such as wells have seen their water levels decline, and droughts—both seasonal and longer term—have become a major constraint on agricultural production.

One of the major projects in the Nuba area that caused environmental damage was the Habila Mechanized Agricultural project that was initiated in the 1970s. The project objective was to grow sorghum for export to the Arab Gulf states, mainly Saudi Arabia. The project's initial phases resulted in widespread deforestation as people cleared forests for cultivation purposes. The project also limited the grazing areas and minimized the possibilities of traditional farming expansion in the future.

Another source of environmental crisis is the continuing war between the Sudan People's Liberation Army (SPLA) and the government. Both sides have been accused of burning villages and farms and stealing animal wealth from their opponents in the region. The burning and bombing of villages and the destruction of wells have had major effects on the wildlife and vegetation of the Nuba region. The restructuring of the population—caused in part by deliberate policies of forced relocation—has led to heavy concentrations of people in some parts of the Nuba Mountains and surrounding areas, which has exacerbated the impacts of environmental change.

The exploration of the Nuba Mountains for minerals and petroleum began in earnest in the past decade. The discovery of diamonds, gold, oil, or other high-cost natural resources could well lead to an expansion of the activities of multinational corporations in the Nuba region. Some Nuba community-based organizations have attempted to bring attention to the threat of the operations of multinational corporations. In June 2001, the U.S. House of Representatives voted overwhelmingly (422–2) to support legislation that would ban investments and trade by U.S. multinationals in Sudan. While this legislation will probably not go before the U.S. Senate and be signed into law until early 2002, the U.S. government has indicated its support for human rights standards to be observed by multinational corporations. The U.S. government continues to re-evaluate its policy toward Sudan. Key factors in the George W. Bush administration's policy include publicizing Khartoum's harsh treatment of its civilians, modifying the ways that humanitarian food relief is supplied, and implementing strict sanctions against assistance to Sudan's dictatorial regime.[6]

RESPONSE: STRUGGLES TO SURVIVE CULTURALLY

Although the Nuba are undoubtedly in a precarious position, they are seeking actively to promote their human rights and to enhance their cultures and standards of living. Some Nuba have sought audiences with government officials and have pressed for peace agreements to be negotiated. Nuba nongovernment organizations have been formed that are aimed at drawing attention to the situations of the Nuba and other Sudanese populations. Some of these nongovernment organizations are made up primarily of women who cooperate in their efforts to resolve conflicts and implement sustainable development projects at the community level.

Some Nuba organizations have engaged in literacy programs and the collection of oral history information that they plan to use in the development of school curricula. While the Islamicization of the Nuba area has affected the ways in which education is practiced, the Nuba have been able to argue relatively effectively for a multicultural approach to education and development.

There has been a resurgence in the practice of traditional Nuba customs, beliefs, and rites. One of their well-known dances is the Kambla, which consists of pure African rhythm with beautiful movements. The male dancers put bulls horns and ostrich feathers on their heads to symbolize animals, and they wear beads and other materials such as laces made from metal bottle tops on their arms and legs. These cause a musical sound when the dancers strike the ground with their feet. The Kambla used to be considered one of the most praiseworthy forms of Sudanese traditional dancing. Today, it is being practiced in some Nuba communities, in part in order to generate the interest of tourists and to honor the cultural traditions of the various Nuba groups. The Nuba have been a favorite subject of filmmakers since the 1920s and 1930s (e.g., *Nuba Gathering* by J. G. Mayrogordsto, 1935), in part because of their physical appearance, body ornamentation, and community-oriented work, play, and rich ceremonial life.

Although most Nuba now are Muslims and Christians, Nuba customs and traditions have not been erased. While there are fewer bracelet and stick fights, less nudity, and little in the way of elaborate body paintings, the Nuba continue to be proud of their rich cultural heritage. Group celebrations such as the *sanda* combine sporting events, harvest feasting, music, and dances. Nuba crafts have become highly prized items in international markets. The Nuba have begun to negotiate with film companies for fair compensation in exchange for being filmed. Discussions have been held in a number of Nuba communities about establishing rules for the activities of tourists, researchers, and filmmakers.

From the perspective of the Nuba, the most pressing issues they are facing are survival, resistance to genocidal policies, sovereignty, the right to make their own political decisions, and the rights to practice their own cultural traditions and speak their own languages. Strategies employed in order to reach these goals have varied. Some Nuba have joined the liberation organizations such as the Sudan People's Liberation Army. Others have withdrawn further into the mountains in an attempt to avoid being affected by conflict and cultural transformation efforts. Some Nuba groups have forced local networks of human rights monitors to report on the treatment of people in their areas.

Various political groups and parties in the Nuba region, northern Sudanese political opposition parties, and the academics in different universities inside and outside Sudan are struggling against the government not only for freedom and democracy but also for keeping the rich culture of Nuba alive. Collaboration with human rights organizations such as African Rights has helped lift the veil of secrecy surrounding Sudanese government policy toward the Nuba. Reporting on human rights violations against the Nuba and documentation of witness testimony by African Rights, Human Rights Watch, and other human rights organizations has proven to be remarkably effective in generating international support for the causes of the Nuba people.[7]

FOOD FOR THOUGHT

The experiences of the Nuba raise questions about the ways in which people respond to external threats and local problems. The Nuba have not sat idly by while outside forces have sought to exploit their human and natural resources. They have organized themselves to resist policies of domination, and they have sought actively to promote their human rights and maintain various cultural traditions, customs, and values. In some cases, this was done through military means; in other cases, it was achieved by the act of withdrawal. In still other cases, it was brought about by collaborating—on a limited basis—with the agencies and organizations that were attempting to dominate and control them.

The Nuba have formed community-based institutions that build on traditional systems of cooperation, reciprocity, and collaboration. While the benefits of development—the process whereby the standards of living of people are raised through various means—are valued by the Nuba, they are not unaware of the fact that development has its costs. They do not want to lose their identities in the face of rapid modernization. They also do not want to give in completely to the forces that would promote massive social and economic change.

The issue that arises is, What kinds of development policies are most appropriate for multiethnic communities like those of the Nuba? Is it not possible for the Nuba and other peoples to come up with culturally appropriate and sustainable development programs that will enable them to enhance their living standards while at the same time allowing them to maintain their cultural traditions and identities?

The challenges facing the Nuba are many. Without the support of the international community and the strength and resilience of the people of the Nuba Mountains and the organizations and individuals with whom they work, it might have been difficult to reverse the negative political, economic, environmental, and social trends affecting the Nuba. The willingness of the Nuba to collaborate with others and to employ diverse means to achieve their goals will undoubtedly enable the Nuba to survive over the long term. What remains to be done now is for the government of Sudan and the opposition groups to go into a real peace and reconciliation process. After that, it will be necessary to rehabilitate the countryside and promote sustainable, balanced, and equitable development in the Nuba Mountains.

Questions

1. Do you think that the practice by some nongovernment organizations in Sudan of buying back slaves from their owners and releasing them is a legitimate and effective strategy to stop slavery?

2. What kinds of help do you think that international organization can provide for peoples such as the Nuba who are caught in conflict situations?

3. It has been pointed out that the Nuba have been under severe threat for over two decades, caught between rebellious factions and the government of the Sudan. The United States and the North Atlantic Treaty Organization (NATO) intervened in a similar situation in Kosovo in 1999. Why do you think that a similar intervention has not occurred in Sudan?

4. Do you believe that access to food and medicine is a human right? If so, how would you ensure that people such as the Nuba could exercise this human right? If not, how would you ensure the survival of those Nuba who were starving or sick?

5. Suppose that you are sent on a mission by an international organization such as the United Nations to help in conserving the Nuba culture. What would your plans involve?

NOTES

1. "Nuba Survival," *http://www.nubasurvival.com/news&events/New*; The Nuba Mountains Homepage, *http://go.to/NubaMountains*.

2. "Ingessana Hills," *http://www.sudanupdate.org/REPORTS/Peoples/Ing.htm*.

3. Cathy Matenyi, "Food Situation Precarious in Embattled Nuba Mountains," *AfricaOnline*, May 2001, *www.africaonline.com/site/Articles/1,3,2644jsp*.

4. Amnesty International, "Africa: Regional Country Index—Sudan," 1998, *http://www.amnesty.org/ailib/aireport/ar98/afr54.htm*.

5. Ibid.

6. James Phillips, "To Stop Sudan's Brutal Jijad, Support Sudan's Opposition," *The Heritage Foundation Backgrounder*, No. 1449, June 13, 2001, *www. heritage.org/library/backgrounder/bg1449.html*.

7. Mohamed Suliman, Part 3: "Land Use—The Nuba Mountains of Sudan: Resource Access, Violent Conflict, and Identity," *http://www.idre.ca/books/899/ 310sulim.htm*; Amnesty International, "Africa: Regional Country Index—Sudan"; "Nuba Survival"; The Nuba Mountains Homepage.

RESOURCE GUIDE

Published Materials

African Rights. *Facing Genocide: The Nuba of Sudan*. London: African Rights, 1995.

Human Rights Watch/Africa. *Behind the Red Line: Political Repression in Sudan*. New York: Human Rights Watch/Africa, 1996.

Musa Rahhal, Suleiman Musa. *The Right to Be Nuba: The Story of a Sudanese People's Struggle for Survival*. Lawrenceville, NJ: Red Sea Press, 2001.

Nadel, Siegfried F. *The Nuba: An Anthropological Study of the Hill Tribes in Kordofan*. New York: Oxford University Press, 1947.

Riefenstahl, Leni. *The Last of the Nuba*. New York: Harper and Row, 1973.

Verney, Peter. *Sudan: Conflict and Minorities*. London: Minority Rights Group International, 1995.

Voll, John Obert, and Sarah Potts Voll. *The Sudan: Unity and Diversity in a Multicultural State*. Boulder, CO: Westview Press, 1995.

Films and Videos

Female Circumcision: Human Rites. 1998. Available from Films for the Humanities & Sciences, P.O. Box 2053, Princeton, NJ 08543–2053. Telephone: (609)

275–1400. Fax: (609) 275–3767. Email: custserv@films.com. Web site: www.films.com.

Kafi's Story. 1989. Depicts Nuba life prior to the beginning of Sudan's civil war during the 1990s. Produced/Directed by Arthur Howes and Amy Hardie; 53 minutes. United Kingdom. California Newsreel, 149 Ninth Street, San Francisco, CA 94103. 1–800–621–6196. Telephone: Fax: 415 621 6522. Email: *contact@newsreel.org.*

Nuba Conversations. 2001. A follow-up to *Kafi's Story*, filmed ten years previously by Arthur Howes. Produced/Directed by Arthur Howes, 5 minutes. United Kingdom. California Newsreel, 149 Ninth Street, San Francisco, CA 94103 Telephone: 1–800–621–6196. Fax: 415 621 6522. Email: *contact@ newsreel.org.*

The Right to Be Nuba. 199. Peekaboo Pictures Production, directed by Hugo D'Aybaury. Available from the Filmakers Library, 124 East 40th Street, New York, NY 10016. Telephone: (212) 808–4980. Fax: (212) 808–4983. Email: info@filmakers.com. Web site: www.filmakers.com/.

Sudan: Black Kingdoms on the Nile. 1999. Available from Films for the Humanities & Sciences, P.O. Box 2053, Princeton, NJ 08543–2053. Telephone: (609) 275–1400. Fax: (609) 275–3767. Email: custserv@films.com. Web site: www.films.com/.

WWW Sites

Africa Christian Faith in Action. "Sudan: A Country of Contrasts." 1999
http://www.liaafrica.org/aboutsudan.htm

Africanews. "Sudan: A Cry in the Silence." 1996
http://www.peacelink.it/afrinews/3-issue/p4.html

American Anti/Slavery Group
http://www.anti-slavery.com/oil

"The Crises in Nuba Mountains." Press release, 1993
http://www.halcyon.com/pub/FWDP/Africa/nubal.txt

Dietrich, S. "The Nuba Mountains of Sudan: Hell on Earth." 1999
http://www.africanews.org/east/sudan/stories/1999038-feat4.html

International Women's Committee. Nuba Mountains Letter in support of Nuba women and children. Drafted by Sondra Hale, Asma Abdel Halim, and Laura Nyantung Beny. 1997
http://www.africapolicy.org/docs97/sud9710.nub.htm

Nuba Mountains. A Lost Paradise
http://i-cias.com/m.s/sudan/nuba.htm

Nuba Mountains Solidarity Abroad
http://www.halcyon.com/pub/Africa/nuba2.txt

PetersVoice. "Personal Appeal of Bishop Macram Gassis." 1999
http://www.petersvoice.org/appeal.html

Suliman, Mohamed. "Resource Access: A Major Cause of Armed Conflict in the Sudan: The Case of the Nuba Mountains." 2000
http://www.idrc.ca/minga/case-su.html

Organizations

African Commission of Human and Peoples' Rights
c/o Organization of African Unity (OAU)
P.O. Box 3243
Addis Ababa, Ethiopia

African Rights
11 Marshallsea Road
London SE1 1EP, United Kingdom
Telephone: (44) 171–717–1224
Fax: (44) 171–717–1240

Africa Policy Information Center (APIC),
110 Maryland Avenue NE, No. 509
Washington, DC 20002
Email: apic@igc.org
Web site: http://www.africapolicy.org

Africa Watch
c/o Human Rights Watch
350 Fifth Avenue
New York, NY 1118–3299
Telephone: (212) 290–4700
Web site://www.hrw.org

American Anti/Slavery Group
198 Tremont Street, No. 421
Boston, MA 02116
Telephone: (800) 884–0719
Web site: www.anti-slavery.com

Anti-Slavery International
Thomas Clarkson House
The Stableyard
Broomgrove Road
London SW9 9TL, United Kingdom
Telephone: (44) (0) 20–7501–8920
Fax: (44) (0) 20–7738–4110
Email: antislavery@antislavery.org
Web site: http://www.antislavery.org

International Nuba Coordination Center (INCC)
Windmill Place, Suite 38
2–4 Windmill Lane

Hamwell, Middlesex UB2 4NJ
United Kingdom
Telephone/Fax: (44) 20-8993–5809
Email:Suleimanrahhalincc@compuserve.com

Minority Rights Group (MRG)
379 Brixton Road
London SW9 7DE, United Kingdom
Telephone: (44) 171–978–9945
Email: minority.rights@mrgmail.org
Web site: http://www.minorityrights.org

Sudan Human Rights Organization (SHRO)
USA Branch
c/o Nurredin Mannan
8511 60th Place
Derwin Heights, MD 20240

Chapter 7

The Ogoni of Nigeria

A. Olu Oyinlade and Jeffery M. Vincent

CULTURAL OVERVIEW

The People

The Ogoni are a minority ethnic people who live in the Western Niger Delta Region of southern Nigeria. During the 1970s, Ogoniland, or the Ogoni Nation, became part of the Rivers State of Nigeria. There are approximately 500,000 Ogoni who represent less than 0.05 percent of Nigeria's 100 to 120 million people. The population density of this region equals 1,233 people per square mile, making it one of the most densely populated areas of Nigeria.

Reliable information about the origin of the Ogoni is limited. Archaeological and oral historical evidence suggests that the Ogoni have inhabited the area for over 500 years. Presently, two theories exist about the origin of this people. First, the Ogoni may have migrated into their present territory from across the Imo River sometime around the eighteenth or the nineteenth century. Vestiges of this migration are two Ogoni villages, Warife and Utetuk, that still exist at the other side of the river. Warife still speak Khana, whereas Utetuk have adopted the customs and language of Annang, a neighboring tribe in the Akwa Ibom State. When they arrived in the region, the Ogoni did not find this area to be occupied. As a consequence, they were able to keep their identity from their neighbors—the Ibibios in the southeast, the Igbos to the north, the Ikwerres to the west, and the Andoni and Ijaws to the south. According to this theory, the first Ogoni settlement was in the Khana kingdom, followed by Tai, Gokana,

129

MALI

NIGER

LAKE CHAD

CHAD

NIGER RIVER

SOKOTO

KANO

MAIDUGURI

BENIN

ZARIA

NIGERIA

KADUNA

NIGER RIVER

JOS

YOLA

ABUJA

ILORIN

OGBOMOSO

IBADAN

OSOGBO

MAKURDI

CAMEROON

BENIN CITY

LAGOS

Ogoniland

GULF OF BENIN

WARRI

PORT HARCOURT

0   100 200 KM

GULF OF GUINEA

AJO

EQUATORIAL GUINEA

0   100   200 MI

Ogoni family. (Courtesy Fred Idamkue)

and Eleme, respectively. The Ogoni Nation grew from these first settlements.

The second theory claims that the Ogoni people came on the trading ships, which often visited Bonny, a small city-state island in the delta. They began to settle in Bonny until their population began to outgrow the little town. This necessitated their migration further inland. Once they arrived at Bonny, the resident Ibani people referred to the new arrivals as the "Igoni" or "strangers." As time passed, the Ibani then became known as the "Ogoni." Today, in Bonny, people say that the Ogoni and the Ibani are "brothers." It is quite possible that Ogoni residence on this island in the delta prevented them from being captured during the slave raids that ravaged the mainland.

Following the signing of the Berlin Treaty in 1885, the European colonial powers divided Africa among themselves. Many tribal leaders in Nigeria were coerced into signing treaties with the British. The Ogoni were possibly the last tribe to come into contact with the Europeans due to the precolonization ban on European penetration for trade imposed by the powerful king Jaja of Opobo in the southern point of the delta region. When it eventually came time to enter into treaties with the English colonial ruler of Nigeria, the Ogoni chiefs refused. British colonial records indicated that the Ogoni fiercely resisted colonization until the early 1900s.

Their resistance to colonization may have contributed to the woes that eventually befell the Ogoni Nation and continued to affect it until the present time. The English did not meet with much resistance to colonization from other Nigerian tribal populations in the region. During the late 1880s, tribal leaders representing the Hausa and Fulani tribes in northern Nigeria, the Yorubas in the southwest, and the Igbos in the southeast established treaty relations with the English. As a result, the English facilitated the economic development in these tribal territories. Schools were built, and trading relationships were put into place. At this time, for example, the Nigerian Military Academy (now a military university) was built in the Hausa city of Kaduna, and Nigeria's first university and medical college was established in the Yoruba city of Ibadan. On the other hand, the English provided little assistance to the Ogoni people since they had resisted colonization.

During the colonization period, the English generally recognized only three major tribal populations—the Hausa-Fulani, the Yoruba, and the Igbo. More than 250 other tribes in Nigeria were largely ignored. As the English began to withdraw from Nigeria, they divided it into three major arbitrary regions (North, West, and East). Each region was dominated by one of the three major tribes. The other 250 tribes within Nigeria were then governed by one of these three dominant groups and were further marginalized and given minority status.

The Ogoni people are organized into traditional political systems referred to as kingdoms. There are six kingdoms that are divided into three separate yet united divisions. First, the Khana division is situated in the eastern as well as the northern-most portions of Ogoniland. It consists of four separate kingdoms—Babbe, Ken Khana, Nyo Khana, and Tai. Each kingdom speaks a dialect of the language Khana and maintains separate territories. Second, the Gokana division and kingdom lies in the south-central part of Ogoniland where the people speak Gokana, a language similar to, but not identical to, Khana. Third, the Eleme division and kingdom is found in western Ogoniland. Although the Eleme language is closely related to both Khana and Gokana, it is distinctly different.

Today, there are over 124 villages and towns in the Ogoni Nation, each headed by a chief. The town of Bori serves as the capital of Oganiland. Other important towns include Bodo, Dere, and Bomu in Gokana; Nonwa in Tai; Nchia in Eleme; Bane, Baen, Kono, and Kpean in Southern Khana; and Tabangh, Okwali, and Beeri in Northern Khana.

The Setting

Ogoniland is bounded on the north and east by the Imo River, on the south by the coastal sand plains (occupied by the Andoni people), and on the west by the Aba-Port Harcourt highway. The delta region contains a range of environmental zones including coastal sand plains, deltaic and floodplains, mangrove forests, and barrier island habitats. Ogoniland currently includes about 404 square miles. The climate for the southern coastal region of Nigeria is hot and humid. Average temperatures in the Port Harcourt area range between 77.0°F in August to 81.0°F in March and April. This area receives 93 inches of rainfall during the year; heaviest rains arrive during the months of July and August.

Traditional Subsistence Strategies

Ogoniland had abundant, fertile soil and the delta plateau within Rivers State was known as the "bread basket" of the region prior to the oil drilling in the late 1950s and early 1960s. The extraordinary fertility has historically enabled the Ogoni to make a good living as subsistence agriculturalists. Fertile plateau soil has supported agricultural endeavors, while the rivers that empty into the Gulf of Guinea provide ample fish and other seafood. The agricultural economy has mainly consisted of yam and cassava (manioc) production.

At the height of its agricultural production, people came from all over the region to buy Ogoni-produced and -processed food. With their cooperative efforts, Ogoni fishermen typically work together in small groups to enhance their catch and improve their share of the fish market. The main source of income for an Ogoni family, however, is the sale of agricultural products. They make substantial money from Gari (which is processed from cassava) and palm oil (which is processed from palm fruits). They also make money by trading in coconuts, pottery, and palm wine (processed from the sap of certain palm trees). Ogoni palm wine tappers are known to migrate hundreds of miles, sometimes as far as Lagos and Ijebu-Ode in Yoruba land, in search of good-quality palm trees for tapping.

Social and Political Organization

The social organization of the Ogoni is centered around the family. The typical Ogoni family consists of a father, a mother, and eight children. Unlike most other tribes in Nigeria, polygyny (the marital custom whereby a male has two or more wives) is uncommon among the Ogoni, making the line of descent and inheritance less complex than in the polygynous tribes. Unlike the more dominant tribes like the Yorubas and the Igbos, however, Ogoni mothers have larger families. On average, Ogoni women have three to four more children than women in the dominant tribes. Like most of Nigeria, the role of the Ogoni family is very crucial in socializing a child to become a good tribesperson and a good citizen of Nigeria. Anecdotal sources suggest that from childhood the Ogoni are raised to respect their parents, older siblings, older relatives, and elders of their community. Ogoni families are arranged internally into a hierarchy that includes father, mother, and then children according to birth order. The privileges range from choice pieces of meat during meals to more complex issues revolving around marriage. Younger siblings, for example, may delay marriage based on the marriage plans of older siblings. By tradition, younger siblings are obligated to perform as instructed by older siblings. In fact, in many cases, it is the younger ones who go to their older siblings to offer their services as a sign of respect. Although Ogoni accept such priority rules based on the family hierarchy, it does not prevent some degree of conflict or unhappiness. On occasion, birth order privileges may be modified so that a younger child, usually a female, can marry and begin to have children while she is young.

The traditional political structure of the Ogoni Nation, like most other cultures in Nigeria, can be described as benign dictatorship by the monarchy. This political system is hierarchically arranged and extends downward and outward from the *Gbenemene*, or "king." Under the *Gbenemene* in each kingdom is the *Mene Bua*, a high chief who oversees a group of villages and towns. Each village and town, then, is directly governed by its own chief called the *Mene Buen*. In turn, each village or town is subdivided into many compounds, each headed by a compound chief (or lower chief) called the *Mene Zeu* who reports directly to his *Mene Buen*.

The *Gbenemene* has the highest authority over all matters in his kingdom, and all the chiefs pay homage to him and allow him to subordinate them as a sign of respect for his position. For example, they would defer authority to him in matters dealing with the development of his kingdom and the relationship between state government and the kingdom. It is the chiefs that oversee each village or town in matters that are most germane to each locality. Since there are many chiefs within each village and town, the Ogoni have the largest number of chiefs in the council of chiefs in the Rivers State of Nigeria.

The traditional political system is classified as benign dictatorship because the king is appointed by a council of king makers rather than being democratically elected by the people. Typically, there is a ruling family from which the king and his successors are appointed, with the crown prince being the oldest male alive. In order to ensure traditional succession pattern, it is imperative for the king to have a son. Aside from the symbol of power and prestige that polygyny accords the king, the desire to have a crown prince often contributes to his having many wives at the same time.

Since both the king and his chiefs are appointed, the Ogoni traditional political system qualifies as a dictatorship of monarchy. They are, however, very generous in serving the people by giving very freely of themselves to work for progress of the people. Like the king, the work of the chief is endless. They are frequently called upon to help resolve a range of problems including family disputes, marital discord, or land claims. For all their services, the king and his high chiefs are nominally paid by the city council, with the king being better paid than the high chief. The positions and services of the compound chiefs are purely voluntary. They must combine their responsibilities for the people with making a living from other sources. It is because of their benevolence that the term *benign* is appropriate in describing the chiefs and the entire monarchy system. In return for their selflessness, the people usually give the king and the chiefs gifts including farm produce, fish, ornaments, jewelry, cloths, goats, cattle, and substantial cash. In many cases, coupled with their own personal income, the chiefs receive enough gifts to enable them to live above the average living standards of other Ogoni. The monarchy is highly respected; Ogoni people hardly ever challenge its authority and prefer to take instructions from the monarchy rather than from the officials of the state government. This is especially true of the *Gbenemene*, whose rulings on disputes and issues concerning his kingdom are deemed the final word.

Religion and World View

The fertile land and rivers of the region not only provide sustenance for the Ogoni but are regarded as a spiritual inheritance. The land is a god, and it is worshiped as such. Despite Christianization, many aspects of indigenous culture persist. Colorful masks and decorative arts, for example, are used to demonstrate the strength of Ogoni during ceremonies. If someone is ill, the Ogoni still consult the shamans and voodoo priests for cure. Although various denominations of the Christian Church abound throughout Ogoniland, most people are traditionalists who worship a common deity, Bari (Obari-Eleme), the creator of Heaven and Earth. Also, various groups in the different villages and towns worship other more immediate gods and ancestral spirits.

The planting season is regarded as more than a time of preparation; it is a spiritual, religious, and social occasion. The waters that flow throughout the region not only provide life and food, but the Ogoni view the rivers and streams as an integral life force intricately bound with the life of the whole community. Common myths of origin are found within the subgroups, but not within the Ogoni as a whole. Ogoni tend to feel stronger ties within subgroups.

THREATS TO SURVIVAL

Impacts of Oil Production

I hereby appeal to the international community to come to the assistance of the Ogoni people who are threatened in a very real way by the activities of Shell, on the one hand, and the insensitivity of successive military dictators in Nigeria on the other hand. There are signs that the government of President Bahangida is at last waking up to the dire plight of the Ogoni people but there is still need for men and women of goodwill throughout the world to come to the aid of the Ogoni people before they are driven to extinction. More so as Ogoni leaders have been harassed and arrested by Nigerian Security agents.[1]

The Dutch Shell Oil Company first discovered oil in Ogoniland in 1958, and since then, the lives of the Ogoni people have been changed. Since drilling began in the late 1950s, Shell and its partners—the Nigerian National Petroleum Company (NNPC), Elf Aquataine, Chevron, Willbros of Tulsa-Oklahoma, and the British Oil Corporation's Agip—have been responsible for 50 percent of all extracted oil from Nigeria, and Ogoniland specifically. Records of the Shell Petroleum Development Company of Nigeria Limited (SDPC) show that Shell owns five major oil fields—Bomu, Korokoro, Yorla, Bodo West, and Ebubu—and about 100 wells in Ogoniland. According to SDPC, about 900 million barrels of crude oil have been extracted from Ogoniland, yielding by 1996 over U.S. $30 billion for Shell.[2]

For decades, the Rivers State region has been the "goose that lays the golden egg." As the costs of oil exploitation escalated and violence ensued, however, the Ogoni area has become a thorn in Nigeria's side. In the early 1990s, the Ogoni began to speak of the "ecological war" that the Nigerian government and Shell Oil were waging against them. They then accused both the government and Shell of "mounting a campaign of intimidation and terrorism against the Ogoni people."[3]

The presence of Shell and its partners in Ogoniland have led to both industrial development and environmental degradation of the area. For development, one can cite the establishment of two oil refineries, one petrochemical plant, a fertilizer plant, and a power plant in Ogoniland. The positive contributions of Shell to the development of Oganiland can be disputed. While Ogoni people complain of not having pipe-borne water, electricity, hospitals, and schools, Shell believes it has exhibited considerable goodwill toward Ogoniland. Shell continued to argue that they had devoted considerable time, energy, and capital to community assistance programs, education scholarships, health and water treatment programs, agricultural development, and road construction.[4]

The response to this claim by Shell was cynicism by the Ogoni. One thirty-four-year-old man from Bianu in the Nyo-Khana kingdom responded by saying "[W]e would be better off today if Shell had never come and taken one drop of oil." Despite the good intentions that Shell might have had in improving the livelihood of the Ogoni people, very little of their efforts have resulted in tangible gains for the Ogoni. Even in the refineries and other plants run by Shell in Ogoniland, few Ogoni were employed in these establishments.

Environmental and Sociocultural Crises

The heavy production of oil in Ogoniland as well as the Niger Delta has resulted in intensive ecological damage of the areas. The environmental effects of having eight oil fields, over 100 oil wells, numerous oil pipelines, and four flow stations in Ogoni have been severe. Between 1976 and 1991, nearly 3,000 separate oil spills, averaging 700 barrels each, have occurred in the Niger Delta.[5] Shell's response to spills has been reported to be slow and insufficient. Oil spills can be traced miles from the source. Reports claim that more than 6.4 billion liters (1.6 million gallons) were spilled in Nigeria between 1982 and 1992. Much of the land has been stained black, destroying the once fertile soil and continually limiting agricultural productivity. Waters in the area flow black-brown and are void of fish. According to Shell, of the total number of spills recorded by the company worldwide in 1995, 40 percent were in Nigeria alone.[6] Shell's response to criticism has been to largely deny that there is a problem, although they do admit to the 3,000 sites affected by drilling operations and the occurrence of acid rain one month a year in the Delta.

Many of Shell's practices and equipment would be prohibited under the environmental laws of most countries. But under Nigerian law, companies are not required to clean up or compensate for the effects of spills caused by sabotage. This makes it easy for the oil companies to operate with less regard for the environment and its people since spills can easily be attributed to local sabotage. The entire delta region is plagued by the careless flaring of gas, poorly placed aboveground pipelines, and unlined toxic waste pits. A major blowout at Kegbara Dere in 1970 spewed oil for several weeks, destroying a large part of Ogoniland in a densely populated area. According to the 1992 United Nations Conference on Environment and Development, the Niger Delta is the most endangered river delta in the world.[7] The Ogoni maintain that, within Ogoniland, both Shell and the Nigerian government have instituted a policy of ecocide (the purposeful destruction of the environment). The Ogoni have continually pushed for self-determination and autonomy through statehood, in order to benefit from the region's oil reserves and drilling operations.

As a direct result of considerable environmental degradation, Ogoni health and livelihood have been greatly threatened. Oil spills and the intense venting of toxic gases have continuously destroyed the traditional means of subsistence farming.[8] The World Wide Fund for Nature has calculated that the gas flares in Nigeria are a major contributor to global warming. More than 75 percent of the natural gas that is vented from the oil wells is burned off, as opposed to 20 percent for the wells in Libya, Iran, and Saudi Arabia. In the United States, most of the natural gas is captured and used for domestic and commercial purposes.

The burning of methane and other hydrocarbons has produced a sharp increase in respiratory diseases, and the noise from burning has led to hearing problems for many Ogoni. Many flares are located near villages and give inhabitants around-the-clock light. The flares also give off so much heat that it is sometimes impossible to go near them, thereby preventing local farmers from having access to many parts of their land. Even though the environmental impact assessment has not been fully documented, the impact of gas flares and oil spills on local ecology and climate, as well as on people's health, is quite significant. Some studies, for example, have indicated that blood-lead levels of many inhabitants are at near toxic levels. Also, respiratory problems, coughing, skin rashes, tumors, gastrointestinal problems, and various forms of cancer have been linked to pollution in the land.[9] Many children exhibit the symptoms of kwashiorkor (a protein deficiency ailment) with their distended stomachs and light hair. Worse still, the death rate in Ogoni escalated as many people began to die from the consequences of environmental pollution and "barrow pits," which companies dig to extract gravel for road construction. These pits are left uncovered, so during the heavy tropical rains of the raining season, they are filled with mud and water, causing the drowning of unsuspecting children. By the middle of the 1990s, the death rate in Ogoniland deteriorated to a state of natural decline (more people dying than were being born each year).[10]

In similar manner, animal life throughout the region has also been destroyed along with their habitat(s). The mangrove forests of the Nigerian Delta is home to a number of endangered species including the Delta elephant, the white-crested monkey, the river hippopotamus, and crocodiles.

Nigerian Political Structure

Nigeria gained its independence from the United Kingdom in 1960. Since then its people have lived under the control of a military government. Such dictatorships struggled to secure and to maintain power, and little attention was given to the people of Nigeria. The armed forces have retained power through continuous military coups and have utilized the large oil reserves in the south to finance their regimes.

The recent regimes of General Ibrahim Babangida (1986–1993) and General Sani Abacha (1993–1998) were held as violent, rights repressive dictatorships that allowed few freedoms for their citizens and quickly stifled internal critiques. The untimely death of Abacha brought Nigeria under the current leadership of General Abdulsalami Abubakar in June 1998. For the most part, General Abubakar continued the repressive tactics used by the Babangida and Abacha regimes; however, his reign was short-lived. He announced a timetable for democratic elections and soon after relinquished power to a democratically elected civilian government in 1999.

Under the 1989 Nigerian Constitution, the federal government holds all mineral rights within the country. Oil companies buy shares of the land from the government in order to extract oil. The successful extraction of mineral wealth requires assistance from both parties. Every day Shell alone sends nearly 300,000 barrels of crude oil through 3,800 miles of pipeline out of the region. Oil revenues represent over 90 percent of Nigeria's total exports and supply over 80 percent of the nation's revenue.

During the economic boom of the 1970s, Nigeria enjoyed great wealth from its share of oil revenues. This enabled the nation's economy to boom and strengthened the Nigerian currency, the Naira, significantly. Throughout the 1970s and 1980s, Nigeria's military and civilian governments were extremely corrupt. Stealing from the national treasury in the billions of dollars, wasteful spending, misappropriation of funds, and gross mismanagement of the economy became the norm in Nigeria.[11] It is a well-known fact that oil made General Abacha, the former military head of state, a billionaire and kept him in power for many years. The value of the Naira plummeted from U.S. $2 in the 1970s to a mere $.0095 in the late 1990s. Consequently, the Nigerian economy collapsed.

With the election of 1999, Nigeria returned to civilian rule under a democratically elected president, congress, and many public officials. The new president, a retired military general and former Nigerian military head of state in the 1970s, Olusegun Obasanjo, has been very active in rebuilding the country and heading it toward economic recovery. So far, the economic recovery has been very slow and not yet felt by the Nigerian masses. Economic and political pundits are optimistic about Nigeria's future, assuming that future presidents will continue with the recovery efforts of the present administration.

Human Rights Abuses

In addition to widespread environmental impacts, the Ogoni have been the victims of intense human rights abuses by the federal government. These abuses began as a consequence of the government's failure to resolve the initial tension between the Shell and Ogoni farmers on whose land oil was discovered. As competition for land escalated between the two sides, the Nigerian government intervened by forcefully taking land away from the farmers, especially the illiterate ones, and appropriating it for the oil companies. In some cases, limited monetary compensation was given to the landowner.

There is a strong belief by many members of the international community that the Nigerian government has engaged in systematic oppression in Ogoniland since May 1994 to silence protests of oil-related environmental hazards and mishaps.[12] Since the beginning of oil exploitation in their area, the Ogoni have repeatedly demonstrated for improved extraction methods, some local input in the drilling, and compensation for both the land and resources taken or destroyed. Most of these public protests have been met with state-sponsored violence.

The crackdown on Nigerian protestors initially began in 1990 when Shell called for military assistance under fears that the company's operations were going to come under attack by protestors from a village just outside the Ogoni territory. Although the protest was peaceful, military forces opened fire, killing at least eighty villagers. Shortly afterward, military forces swept through the village, destroying or badly damaging nearly 500 homes. This was a clear warning to the people that hindrance of oil production would be swiftly countered with harsh punishment.[13]

As further protests ensued, they were repeatedly met with government-sanctioned violence. Villages throughout Ogoniland and the entire delta have been subject to repeated military raids. These raids were characterized by flagrant human rights abuses, including extra judicial executions, indiscriminant shooting, arbitrary arrests and detention of outspoken individuals, floggings, rapes, looting, and extortion. Strong evidence exists that links government forces with Shell in an attempt to crush this community movement for environmental justice (equity and fairness in the treatment of the environment and the people in those environments by companies, governments, and individuals).[14]

For nearly a decade, Ogoniland has been under military occupation by the Rivers State Internal Security Task Force in order to protect oil facilities and quell any uprisings. Since the start of the attacks on the Ogoni by the security forces, access to the region has been closed off to outsiders. The refusal to allow reporters, human rights monitors, or environmental researchers into the area to document the claims of human rights abuse, military sweeps, and environmental destruction is an important aspect to this situation.

RESPONSE: STRUGGLES TO SURVIVE CULTURALLY

Organizing to Survive

Since the beginning of oil exploitation in their homeland, the Ogoni have repeatedly asked for improved extraction methods, some local input into the drilling, and just compensation for both the land and resources taken. As already mentioned, however, under Nigerian law, the government holds subsurface mineral rights. The Ogoni people who take no part in the oil operations, feel their lands are being ravaged while they receive no benefit in return.

The Ogoni people had experienced the effects of a corrupt partnership between the Nigerian government and Shell Oil that destroyed portions of the Niger Delta environment, its wildlife, and many people.[15] As a result, the Ogoni formed the Movement for the Survival of Ogoni People (MOSOP) with the launching of the Ogoni Bill of Rights (OBR) in 1990.[16] The OBR was signed by all of the Ogoni leaders, and it outlined the people's demands for environmental, social, and economic justice. It especially emphasized the need for Ogoni political autonomy (mainly in the form of statehood) in all political matters that affect them within Nigeria as well as the right "to the control and use of a fair portion of Ogoni economic resources for Ogoni development." Other demands laid out in the document include "adequate and direct representation as of right in all Nigerian national institutions, the use and development of Ogoni languages in Ogoni territory, the full development of Ogoni culture, the right to religious freedom, and the right to protect the Ogoni environment and ecology from further degradation." In August 1991, MOSOP amended the OBR to internationalize their campaign as well as affirm their commitment to nonviolence by stating that "the Ogoni people abjure violence in their struggle for their rights within the Republic of Nigeria."

In October 1990, MOSOP presented the OBR to the then military president of Nigeria, General Ibrahim Babangida, and members of the Armed Forces Ruling Council. This was MOSOP's first attempt at getting governmental response to the problems of the Ogoni Nation, but unfortunately, the government was silent on the matter by not giving any reply to MOSOP. The next step taken by MOSOP was to present some of its demands (mainly economic) directly to the oil companies operating in Ogoniland.

The movement specifically demanded the NNPC, Shell, and Chevron to pay back royalties totaling U.S. $10 billion within thirty days or quit operating in Ogoniland. The oil corporations did not acknowledge this demand.

The silence of the government and the oil corporations to MOSOP's demands did little to deter the movement from continuing its struggle. On January 4, 1993, the inaugural day of the United Nation's Year of the Indigenous People, MOSOP organized its first annual Ogoni day. The activities of the Ogoni day, which included speeches by Ogoni leaders and a march with 300,000 participants, signaled the determination of the Ogoni people to have their demands heard by the Nigerian government and the oil companies. Despite so many people participating in the event, the event was completely free of violence. Since the demonstration by MOSOP remained violence free, it was recognized as the official voice of the Ogoni people during the Unrepresented Nations and Peoples Organization (UNPO) general assembly meeting at The Hague in January 1993. This gave MOSOP and the Ogoni their first major international press coverage by Cable News Network (CNN) and *Time* magazine.

MOSOP played a central role in creating a number of grassroots organizations. These organizations were designed to give each Ogoni individual a role to play within the political movement. The first president of MOSOP was Dr. Gary B. Leton, a highly respected and well-decorated scientist, as well as a conservative traditional leader. Serving with Leton at the behest of MOSOP at this time was Chief N. Kobani, the first vice president and a leading conservative traditional chief in Gokana Kingdom. Like Leton, Chief Kobani had also served in many important government roles.

During the Leton-Kobani leadership, MOSOP's steering committee faced several issues that eventually led to a factionalization of the committee and the movement in general. Most notable among their concerns was the erosion of the power of the traditional rulers, which they alleged was happening. The conservative leaders believed that the community-based grassroots organizations compromised the power of the chiefs by making community decisions that normally were under the authority of the chiefs. In a society where the chiefs are paramount as well as significant in leadership, this was a serious matter. To make matters worse, during the national presidential election of 1993 (which was eventually annulled by the seating military president), the conservative leaders wanted the Ogoni people to participate in the elections, but other committee members, led by Ken Saro-Wiwa, successfully convinced the rest of the movement not to vote. This was Saro-Wiwa's way of protesting against the government for not addressing Ogoni concerns earlier presented to it.

Other problems such as the personality clash between Ken Saro-Wiwa and the conservative chiefs, as well as disagreement over the continuing acceptance of government contracts by individual MOSOP leaders, pushed the two sides further apart. In the past, many Ogoni leaders, conservatives and "radicals" alike (including Ken Saro-Wiwa), had benefited from big government and private contracts from the oil companies. Often, these contracts served as a way to silence opposition to drilling activities in the area since most of the time, the contracts were never fulfilled and neither the government nor the oil corporations would complain. This is a common patronage system across Nigeria.

With the determination of MOSOP to represent adequately and honestly the Ogoni Nation, Ken Saro-Wiwa stopped accepting any further contracts and called on his fellow committee leaders to do the same. Reportedly, they feared that open attacks on the government would threaten their contracts; hence, they preferred to split from MOSOP in an effort to protect their economic interests. In June 1993, Dr. Leton, Chief Kobani, Chief Orage, Mr. Badey and many conservative chiefs left MOSOP, even though they remained committed to the objectives of the OBR.

Ken Saro-Wiwa became leader of MOSOP in the early 1990s. Many people had believed that Saro-Wiwa was a traitor for supporting the federal government against Biafra during the Nigerian Civil War. On the other hand, Saro-Wiwa was a highly charismatic leader who regained the trust and love of the Ogoni masses. Saro-Wiwa spoke a number of regional languages, so he could address the people in different kingdoms in their local mother tongues, which enhanced his charisma and respect among the Ogoni masses.

Under the leadership of Ken Saro-Wiwa, MOSOP took a strong stand against the environmental degradation and repression in Ogoniland. The movement contended that Shell and the Nigerian government had actively participated in a cooperative effort to ravage the land while providing little, if any, benefit in return. Saro-Wiwa demanded that power be returned to local communities. For example, although Nigeria ranks among the largest oil producers in Africa, it is one of the poorest nations on the basis of its per capita income—U.S. $260 per year.[17] Year after year, MOSOP resubmitted its demands as outlined in the OBR to the federal government with no response. "MOSOP's protests provoked a violent and repressive response from the federal government, for which any threat to oil production is a threat to the entire existing political system."[18]

In May 1994, Ken Saro-Wiwa and eight other MOSOP activists were arrested and detained by the military. The government contended that the group had ordered Ogoni youth to murder four conservative, government-sympathetic Ogoni elders. MOSOP and the nine defendants strongly denied any connection to the murders. Within a day, security forces swept through Ogoniland, killing over 1,000 Ogoni and displacing thousands more over the next few days in the name of "restoration of law and order."[19] Leaders of the Movement for the Survival of Ogoni People contend that government agents carried out the killings in order to incriminate Saro-Wiwa and to polarize the MOSOP.

The nine defendants were held without trial for eight months before a specially constituted quasi-military tribunal was formed. It was no surprise that the defendants were found guilty of murder in November 1995 and sentenced to death by hanging. Calls for leniency came to the Nigerian government from across the world, but General Abacha ordered that the verdict be carried out as quickly as possible. Ken Saro-Wiwa and eight other defendants were hanged on November 10, 1995.

Many governments threatened economic sanctions against Nigeria, and international calls for a worldwide boycott of Shell Oil were made. The global community, including world leaders and environmental and human rights groups, united in pronouncing the hangings as unacceptable and un-justified. Immediately after the hangings, as thousands of Ogonis wandered the streets in mourning, 4,000 military troops were deployed throughout Ogoniland to beat anyone found mourning in public. During the following week, many countries withdrew their ambassadors from Nigeria.

In the years following the executions, Ogoniland has continued to op-erate under military control, and the security forces maintain a strong hold on any opposition. Shell has yet to officially resume its operations in the area, claiming it will produce oil only if there is a genuine and broad-based agreement with communities and groups in Ogoni. MOSOP has claimed, however, that in 1998 some oil facilities had been reactivated without ad-dressing claims of alleged ecological damage.

Since the death of Ken Saro-Wiwa and some MOSOP leaders, coupled with the imprisonment and exile of other leaders, anecdotal evidence show that the movement lost its cohesion. Many movement leaders and partici-pants still remain in refugee camps, some returned from exile and refugee camps to Nigeria, while many others were relocated by international or-ganizations in Western countries (about 1,500 in the United States). It is suggested that MOSOP still continues to operate but in various factions and under different leaders, with the more popular factions being head-quartered in Nigeria, Great Britain, and the United States.

International Advocacy on Behalf of the Ogoni

As a passive resistance movement, the Ogoni uprising followed a vigor-ous campaign at the local and international levels to popularize the Ogoni plight and solicit support. Given the powers of global electronic commu-nication, the Ogoni were able to communicate with other groups facing similar situations and people and organizations that could lend assistance. The Ogoni Bill of Rights was presented to the United Nations Subcom-mittee on Human Rights on the Prevention of Discrimination against and

Protection of Minorities, to the African Human Rights Commission, and to several human rights and environmental organizations in Europe. In response, the Rain Forest Action Groups and Greenpeace wrote to Shell regarding environmental destruction in Ogoni.

Human Rights Watch/Africa, Amnesty International, and the Sierra Club all launched campaigns to spread information on the Ogoni situation and put international pressure on Shell and the Nigerian government. The Ogoni also presented their case at the tenth session of the Working Group on Indigenous Populations in Geneva in 1992 and the General Assembly of the Unrepresented Nations and Peoples Organization at The Hague in 1993. The massive propaganda effort brought intense media attention to Shell and the Ogoni. The international profile gave the struggle its much-needed legitimacy as it faced off against two very powerful and wealthy opponents.

Some of the tensions within Ogoniland were calmed on September 1998 when General Abubakar ordered the release of twenty Ogoni activists. The "Ogoni 20" had been detained for four years on charges of murder. These charges were the same as those made against Saro-Wiwa and eight others. Since then, reports of periodic government-supported military raids on Ogoni and other area villages have continued to surface throughout 1999.

In May 1999, the family of Saro-Wiwa filed a lawsuit in the United States seeking damages as a result of the hanging, which, they say, is partly Shell's fault. Shell denies all wrongdoing and is appealing on jurisdictional technicality to stop the lawsuit from being heard. These raids and earlier arrests of MOSOP activists led many Ogoni to flee Nigeria and seek refuge in neighboring African countries like the Republic of Benin.

FOOD FOR THOUGHT

The environmental change that occurred among the Ogoni can be described as environmental ethnic discrimination. Environmental ethnic discrimination is the unequal treatment of the environment by a majority ethnic society such that the environment of the ethnic minority is treated with less regard. This may include engaging in environmentally destructive practices in areas dominated by minority populations. It may also include ethnic discrimination in environmental policy making, differential enforcement of regulations and laws to the detriment of ethnic minorities, the deliberate targeting of minority communities for toxic wastes disposal, and the exclusion of minorities from leadership of the environmental policy making.

The cultural context of environmental ethnic discrimination finds powerless peoples and their rights to land, resources, health, environmental protection, and their future "expendable" in the name of national security and national debt. A striking commonality in many cases is the Nigerian government's resort to claims of protecting national security as a means of covering up environmental degradation and silencing environmental activists. This, in turn, has led to the devaluation of economic, social, and political rights.

Vast reserves of crude oil were discovered in Nigeria during the 1950s. It is currently believed that Nigeria possesses estimated crude oil reserves equal to 16 to 22 billion barrels. Most of these reserves lie beneath the Niger Delta including Ogoniland. Western Africa has become more important in the global energy picture during the past two decades. It is now, for example, the fifth largest supplier of crude oil to the United States. Crude oil represents a very significant component of Nigeria's economy and, by extension, its political system. Oil exploration and extraction have been carried out by well-financed, powerful multinational oil companies including Shell (Dutch-British), Chevron, Mobil, Elf (French), and Agip (Italian).[20] Crude oil is the basis for a disproportionate amount of Nigeria's total federal revenues, export earnings, and the gross national product (GNP). Consequently, these multinational oil companies have had a considerable influence upon the economic and political systems within Nigeria. The people of Nigeria, however, have not only been denied the benefits of the country's oil wealth, but they have also suffered under repressive governments. A 1999 Human Rights Watch report stated, in this regard, that "Successive governments have misspent the oil wealth which the oil companies have helped unlock, salting it away in foreign bank accounts rather than investing in education, health, and other social investment, and mismanaging the national economy to the point of collapse."[21] Furthermore, the inhabitants of the Niger Delta such as the Ogoni have also had to endure the devastating impacts of oil spills, natural gas flarings (burning of vented gas), ill-planned construction, and toxic waste upon the soil, water, air, vegetation, animal life, and people. Multinational companies must be held accountable for the adverse impacts that their worldwide activities have upon the people and the lands from which they extract resources.[22]

The Ogoni have taken their struggle to the international level with the formation of MOSOP. Their plight is unique in its success in recruiting international assistance and could mark a new era of indigenous and minority mobilization for the protection of rights and put the realities of self-determination within reach. A new imperative combines profit with sustainable development, economic growth, and social equity.

Questions

1. How should the United Nations Universal Declaration on Human Rights be enforced in situations like those of the Ogoni?

2. Discuss the concept of self-determination. Should the Ogoni as a minority population have the right to self-determination?

3. In such a case of natural resource extraction, who should own the rights to those resources? Those who live on the land, the government, private companies, or someone else? Should people receive compensation for the resources that are extracted from their lands?

4. What Are the roles and responsibilities of multinational corporations operating in Third World countries that may not have the environmental laws of the industrialized nations?

5. Discuss how environmental degradation is directly linked to human rights. For example: right to a secure livelihood, right to adequate food and water, the right to a healthy ecosystem.

NOTES

1. Statement made by Ken Saro-Wiwa, leader of the Movement for the Survival of the Ogoni People (MOSOP), at a press conference in The Hague, May 24, 1993.

2. "The Destruction of a People: Dictatorship, Shell Oil, and Princeton," *http://www.princeton.edu/~progrev/96–97/nov96bdlm.html/*.

3. "Ogoni and Oil," Trade, Environment, Development (TED) Case Studies, *http://gurukul.ucc.american.edu/TED/OGONI.HTM*.

4. Ibid.

5. "Shell in Nigeria: What Are the Issues?" *www.essentialaction.org/Shell/issues.html*.

6. "Ogoni and Oil."

7. "Harnessing Abundant Gas Reserves," *http://www.un.org/ecosocdev/geninfo/afrec/vol13no1/gas.htm*.

8. "The Price of Oil," Human Rights Watch Report, 1999, *http://nigerianscholars.africanqueen.com/opinion/oilhrw/hrw.htm*.

9. Ibid.

10. Ibid.

11. Ibid.

12. Ibid.

13. Ibid.

14. Ibid.

15. Ibid.

16. "Ogoni Bill of Rights," Urhobo. Historical Society, *http://www.waado.org/NogerDelta/RightsDeclaration/Ogoni.html*.

17. "The Price of Oil."

18. "The Price of Oil: Summary," Human Rights Watch Report (1999), 7, *http://nigerianscholars.africanqueen.com/opinion/oilhrw/hrw.1summary.htm*.

19. "Shell in Nigeria: What Are the Issues?"; "Communication from The Secretary, African Commission on Human and Peoples Rights," *http://www.cest.org/text%20files/nigeria.PDF*.

20. "The Price of Oil"; "Ogoni and Oil."

21. "The Price of Oil: Summary," 2.

22. "Shell-Shocked: The Environmental and Social Costs of Living with Shell in Nigeria," 1994, *www.greenpeace.org%Ecomms/ken/hell.htm#cont*; "The Price of Oil."

RESOURCE GUIDE

Published Literature

Human Rights Watch/Africa. *Nigeria. The Ogoni Crisis: A Case Study of Military Repression in Southeastern Nigeria.* New York and Washington, DC: Human Rights Watch/Africa, 1997.

Kretzmann, Steve. "Nigeria's Drilling Fields: Shelling Oil's Role in Repression." *Multinational Monitor* (January–February 1995), www.essential.org/monitor/hyper/issues/1995/01/mm0195_01.html.

Sachs, Aaron. *Eco-Justice: Linking Human Rights and the Environment.* WorldWatch Paper 127. Washington, DC: WorldWatch Institute, 1995.

Saro-Wiwa, Ken. *A Month and a Day: A Detention Diary.* New York: Penguin Books, 1995.

United Nations. *Declaration of Principles on Human Rights and the Environment.* Declaration drafted by an international group of experts on human rights and environmental protection at a meeting convened on May 16, 1994, by the United Nations in Geneva, Switzerland.

Unrepresented Nations and Peoples Organization. *Ogoni.* Report of the UNPO Mission to investigate the situation of the Ogoni of Nigeria, February 17–25, 1995. The Hague: Office of the General Secretary, 1995.

World Press Review. (February 1996), 28.

Films and Videos

Delta Force. 1995. A Catma Films production. Available from Essential Action, P.O. Box 19405, Washington, DC 20036. Documentary that provides evidence for the environmental destruction of the Western Niger Delta region of Nigeria.

The Drilling Fields. 1994. A Catma Films Production. A documentary on environmental destruction in Ogoniland. Jane Balfour Films, Ltd. *www.oneworld. cz/oneworld/1999/english/delta.htm.*

WWW Sites

Environmental Rights Action
www.essentialaction.org/era/Field50.html

MOSOP Canada
www.mosopcanada.org/index1.html

"The Ogoni 20 Are Free."
www.oneworld.org/mosop/

Report from Essential Action and Global Exchange. Provides links to sites describing Shell's controversial past and present in Nigeria.
www.essentialaction.org/shell/report

Shell Nigeria
www.shellnigeria.com

Unrepresented Nations and Peoples Organization
www.unpo.org/

Organizations

African Commission of Human and Peoples' Rights
% Organization of African Unity
(OAU)
P.O. Box 3243
Addis Ababa, Ethiopia

Movement for the Survival of the Ogoni People (MOSOP)
24 Odu Street
Ogbunali, Port Harcourt, Rivers State, Nigeria
Telephone: (234) 84–232609

ANGOLA ZAMBIA LAKE KARIBA

CAPRIVI STRIP

Kasane

Okavango
Delta

ZIMBABWE

NAMIBIA

Maun

Francistown

Ghanzi

Bobonong

BOTSWANA Serowe

Mamuno

Mahalapye

Kalahari
Desert

Gaborone

0   100 MI

0   100 KM

Tshabong

SOUTH AFRICA

AJO

Chapter 8

The Okavango Delta Peoples of Botswana

John Bock and Sara E. Johnson

CULTURAL OVERVIEW

The People

The Okavango Delta Peoples of Botswana consist of five separate ethnic groups, each with its own language and ethnic identity. The ethnic groups are Bugakwe (Kxoe, Bugakhoe, Kwengo, Barakwena, Mbarakwena, Mbarakwengo, G/anda, /anda); Dxeriku (Dceriku, Diriku, Gceriku, Gciriku, Vagciriku, Giriku, Mbogedo, Niriku, Vamanyo); Hambukushu (Mbukushu, Bukushu, Bukusu, Mbukuschu, Mamakush, Mampakush, Ghuva, Haghuva, Gova, Cusso, Kusso, Hakokohu, Havamasiko); Wayeyi (Bayei, Bayeyi, Bakoba, Bajei, Jo, Hajo, Tjaube, Yei); and Xanekwe (Gxanekwe, //tanekwe, tannekhoe, River Bushmen, Swamp Bushmen, G//ani, //ani, Banoka). For each of these groups, there are many different spellings (and pronunciations). Some of these are names from another language; others are corruptions or misinterpretations. Since many outsiders have contributed to the written history of these groups and people have moved across national boundaries, it is important to recognize this disparate nomenclature to preserve the breadth of each group's cultural history. In this chapter, the spellings that members of these ethnic groups in Botswana use in referring to themselves are used.

Understanding the historical distribution of people and their patterns of migration and association are key elements to interpreting the present. Members of all of these ethnic groups live outside of Botswana as well. Bugakwe, Dxeriku, and Hambukushu live in northern Namibia and southern Angola. There are also Hambukushu people in southwestern Zambia.

Okavango people of Botswana. (Courtesy John Bock)

Some Xanekwe and Wayeyi people also live in northern Namibia. Due to the Namibian war for independence and the Angolan civil war, communication and travel between Botswana, Namibia, and Angola has been difficult since the 1970s. As a result, the ethnic communities in these countries have grown apart. Although now travel along the Okavango River is easier between Botswana and Namibia, the ongoing civil war in Angola has left Angolan members of these ethnic groups relatively isolated.

Aside from the distinct ethnic identities of these groups, there is a further important distinction. Bugakwe and Xanekwe are Bushmen peoples (also called San or Basarwa). Bushmen are the aboriginal inhabitants of southern Africa and have lived in small groups as nomadic hunter-gatherers. Dxeriku, Hambukushu, and Wayeyi are Bantu peoples who speak distantly related Central Bantu languages. This suggests that the Dxeriku, Hambukushu, and Wayeyi are more recent inhabitants of the area, having separately migrated from central Africa several hundred years ago.

Today, people from all five ethnic groups live throughout the Okavango Delta. Historically the Bugakwe, Dxeriku, and Hambukushu lived in the Panhandle and eastern edge of the delta. The Xanekwe lived in the Panhandle and along the Jao and Boro Rivers in the central and western Delta, and the Wayeyi lived along the Jao River in the northern Delta, on the northwestern side of the Delta, and on the southern edge of the Delta.

The Setting

The Okavango Delta is a lush tropical wetland surrounded by Kalahari desert savanna. At around 7,700 square miles, it is recognized as one of the world's largest inland deltas, with over 98 percent of the water evaporating. The water starts its journey in the highlands of southern Angola. There, the Okavango River (called the Cubango in Angola) rises and flows south. It cuts through Namibia's Caprivi Strip and then enters northwestern Botswana. This area is extremely flat, and with such a small gradient, the water fans out. The northern part of the Delta is called the Panhandle. Here there is still enough of an elevation change that the river fans out for only 9 miles or so. This swampy area has immense stands of densely packed papyrus and reeds. Hippopotami, crocodiles, sitatunga (an aquatic antelope), and otters are plentiful. Elephants and buffalo are seasonal visitors. Fish are plentiful, and there are several hundred species of birds present, including African fish eagle and malachite kingfisher. On either side of the Panhandle, Kalahari desert savanna extends for hundreds of miles. These areas are forested with acacia and mopane trees, but standing water is very scarce. African mammals are plentiful in these areas, including many types of antelope, elephants, zebra, giraffe, and predators such as lions, leopards, cheetah, hyena, and African wild dogs.

South of the town of Seronga, the narrow Panhandle gives way to the wide Delta, which spreads out for more than sixty miles to the south, east, and west. This area is a patchwork of swampy areas and islands. The swamp is similar to that of the Panhandle. The islands are heavily forested with acacia, palm, and figs. Animal life here consists of mostly the same species as both the Panhandle and the desert savanna, with hippo, crocodile, sitatunga, and lechwe (another aquatic antelope) in the swamps and other types of antelope, elephants, zebra, baboons, and giraffe and predators such as lions, leopards, cheetah, hyena, and African wild dogs on the islands.

Central to this ecosystem is the annual flood, which brings water and nourishment to the Delta. The summer rains in Angola bring a flood in the winter months (June through September, since this is the Southern Hemisphere). The flood makes travel for both people and wildlife difficult, and the islands become surrounded by water. Once the flood recedes, the area can become quite dry, the formerly riverine floodplain becoming grassy plains. In many ways, this flood determines the life cycle, not only for the animals and plants but also for the people of the Delta.

Traditional Subsistence Strategies

The five different ethnic groups all pursue different traditional subsistence strategies. Bugakwe and Xanekwe are both hunter-gatherers, but the Bugakwe forage in both the desert savanna and the swamps, while the Xanekwe historically had a riverine orientation in their foraging. Dxeriku, Hambukushu, and Wayeyi peoples all engage in mixed subsistence strategies of farming, fishing, hunting, collecting wild plant foods, and cattle and goat herding.

Bugakwe men hunt in the desert savanna using poison darts shot from a bow. Using these darts requires immense skill to track the animals, get close enough to shoot, and accurately deliver the dart. Men may be away from their communities for days hunting. Tracking animals in the Delta environment is a challenging task. Footprints may leave clear demarcations in the sand of a floodplain, and then the trail seems to end with the start of an open grassland or a wooded island. A successful hunter needs to know enough about the behavior of his prey to anticipate their movement and be so familiar with the environment as to detect the slightest alteration in the soil or vegetation that indicates the distance and direction the prey has traveled. In this environment the stalker also has to guard against becoming the prey of several large carnivores, crocodiles, or an accidental encounter with a territorial hippo or black mamba (a highly poisonous snake). This knowledge acquisition begins with small children tracking each other and builds through a lifetime

Xanekwe men also hunt using poison darts in the desert savanna and hunt using spears in the river. Here they lie in wait for aquatic antelope and even crocodiles and hippo. Balanced in a dugout canoe, a man harpoons an animal, holding it while his hunting companions attack the animal with their spears and arrows. Dxeriku, Hambukushu, and Wayeyi men also use this hunting technique. Beginning in the late 1800s men began using firearms in hunting, but the traditional methods persist to this day. Men from all of these groups also are expert fishermen, using bow and arrow, spear, hook and line, or nets to catch bream and catfish.

Dxeriku, Hambukushu, and Wayeyi men have historically built fences from acacia thorn trees to protect their agricultural fields from elephants, buffalo, hippo, cattle, and rhinoceros. Men from these ethnic groups also plow the fields and tend cattle. Men from all five ethnic groups are expert craftsmen, making axes, weapons, and canoes.

Xanekwe women are adept at collecting foods from the swamps, such as bird eggs, roots, and small animals caught with snares. Women specialize in fishing using conical baskets, called weirs, in shallow water. Fish are herded into the baskets; the mouth of the basket is then lifted out of the water, trapping the fish. Women also use poison to catch fish. Bugakwe women collect some foods from the swamps but also collect foods from the savanna. These include eggs, roots, fruits, birds, and small game in addition to mongongo and marula nuts. While Dxeriku, Hambukushu, and Wayeyi women are also adept at these collecting activities, especially fishing, historically women from these groups also tended the fields and processed grain and other produce. This entailed planting, weeding, harvesting, separating the grain from the chaff, and finally, processing grain into flour. This processing is done using a mortar and pestle, sometimes referred to as a stamping block, to pound the grain. Once the outer husk has been removed, sifting begins using specialized baskets. After several cycles of pounding and sifting, flour is produced and the chaff discarded.

Boys and girls are able to contribute to the household economy to varying degrees, depending on the subsistence ecology. For instance, Bugakwe and Xanekwe children historically could contribute relatively little. This is because in a hunting and gathering subsistence ecology high levels of skill are required to be a competent producer. These skills take a long time to acquire, and for many types of hunting and gathering activities adults do not become capable until their twenties and expert until their thirties. While young people can catch some fish, collect some plant foods, and do some hunting, they are consuming far more than they can produce. Children and teenagers are still learning, and adults, in a sense, are paying for their learning by providing food that children and teenagers are not yet skillful enough to acquire. In the mixed subsistence ecologies of the Dxeriku, Hambukushu, and Wayeyi, children can contribute more to their households since some of the tasks take less time to learn. Boys and young men do the bulk of the labor in herding and taking care of the cattle and goats. Girls and young women can perform many of the agricultural-related tasks at the same level as adult women. For instance, fourteen-year-old girls are as good at grain processing as thirty-five-year-old women. Contrast this to foraging-related tasks, such as processing mongongo nuts, where fourteen-year-old girls are only one-tenth as competent as adult women. Among all the ethnic groups, young people do a great deal of the domestic chores, such as collecting water and firewood.

In addition to traditional forms of food collection and production, people from all groups have been involved in the market economy to some extent for nearly 100 years. Xanekwe people used their great hunting skill to acquire pelts of leopards, zebras, and other animals to trade for consumer goods such as pots, axes, knives, and clothing. Members of all these groups were heavily involved in elephant hunting for the ivory trade from the late 1800s. Men from all these groups participated in migratory labor to work in the South African mines beginning in the 1930s. Hambukushu and Wayeyi women are famous all over the world for their skill at basketry, and selling baskets to tourists and collectors has been an important source of income for some women since the 1960s. Since the 1960s, men from all of these ethnic groups have worked in safari lodges as guides and at other jobs, while women have worked in the lodges as maids, cooks, and other occupations.

Today, the distinctions in subsistence ecology between these groups are less clear. Partly due to living in multiethnic communities and partly as a result of education, government programs, and modernization, members of all these groups are converging on a common mixed subsistence strategy of fishing, farming, collecting wild foods, herding, and hunting. Government regulation of hunting has greatly diminished the hunting component of all these groups' subsistence regime. Still, Bugakwe and Xanekwe peoples are substantially more oriented toward foraging, with far fewer cattle and smaller fields than members of the other ethnic groups.

Social and Political Organization

Bugakwe and Xanekwe people historically lived in small groups centered on extended family relationships. These family groups moved periodically in response to local depletion of game animals, and groups would sometimes camp together for several months or even years before going their separate ways. There was no central authority figure. Dxeriku, Hambukushu, and Wayeyi people all lived in semipermanent, patrilocal extended family settlements. Within a region of several miles most families were related, and a hereditary headman was the political focal point. Beginning in the late 1700s, the chief of the Batawana, a Tswana-speaking group, began to exert political control over the peoples of the Okavango Delta. This external control resulted in changes to the traditional political structure of these peoples that is ongoing, and many matrilineal-oriented customs regarding property and the family were replaced by patrilineal Tswana traditions. In the early 1900s British civil servants also began to exert political control over the Okavango Delta, integrating traditional political institutions into government-based ones. It was not until after Botswana became independent in 1966, however, that government political institutions became formalized in much of the Okavango Delta. Today headmen are government employees and are assisted in their duties by police, court personnel, and citizen committees. The Tswana *kgotla* (community council) style of government has been universally adopted.

Political and social relationships with members of these ethnic groups in other countries have been limited. In Namibia and Angola, Dxeriku and Hambukushu people have had paramount chiefs, that is, a leader who exercises authority over all others for that people. Since before Botswana's independence, members of these groups in Botswana have not recognized this authority and have had no such central authority within or outside Botswana. In recent years, Bugakwe people in Namibia have had a chief. This is an artifact of the period before Namibian independence when South Africa administered the Namibian government. Bugakwe in Botswana do not recognize this authority.

Religion and World View

Bugakwe and Xanekwe peoples have historically had religious practices similar to those of many other Bushmen groups. These practices incorporate a strong belief in the supernatural with a deep reverence for the natural world. Dxeriku and Wayeyi peoples historically practiced religions that placed a great deal of importance on the spiritual connection with ancestors. Hambukushu people also saw these relationships as central to their religion. Dxeriku and Hambukushu traditionally had matrilineal totem clans related to certain animals such as elephant, crocodile, and lion. Members of a totem clan did not hunt or eat the totem animal. Moreover, people could not marry within their clan but only married people from specific clans. In this century many Bugakwe, Xanekwe, and Wayeyi peoples have also adopted this tradition. The Hambukushu also believed that certain individuals had the power to make rain, a precious commodity in this arid environment. These "rainmakers" exercised great religious and political authority, not only among Hambukushu but also among the other groups and even Batawana and Ovaherero (a nearby group of pastoralists).

To members of all these groups, physical and emotional health are but facets of spirituality. To varying degrees, shamans and herbalists (traditional healers who use medicinal plants) occupy important positions for their connection to the supernatural world and their healing abilities. Hambukushu and Wayeyi shamans are also expert herbalists and are sought out by people from within all five ethnic groups and also by others.

Today, most members of these groups practice their traditional religions. Many people also practice forms of Christianity, ranging from Western denominations or missionary organizations to indigenous forms of Christianity. The largest example of the latter is the South African-based Zion Christian Church (ZCC). By the late 1990s, the ZCC had become the largest and dominant denomination in many of the communities around the Okavango Delta, and members in their khaki (men) or white (women) uniforms could be seen marching to and from services. This affiliation has in some cases created a voting block, and in many communities, ZCC members exercise substantial political clout.

THREATS TO SURVIVAL

Loss of Traditional Life Ways, Language, and Cultural Traditions

The Okavango Delta Peoples face a number of challenges to preserving their traditional life ways, languages, and cultural traditions. These challenges have their roots in the Okavango Delta Peoples' integration into national political, social, and economic institutions. People have been experiencing this to some extent since Botswana's independence and far more intensively since the mid-1980s. Two of the major influences are interrelated: market incorporation and universally available primary and secondary education. As stated above, even today the main economic activities are traditional subsistence strategies. While some people have had access to cash for many years, this has been more of a supplemental source of income. Surveys of cash market participation were conducted in 1992 in a traditional community, and it was found that the greatest amount spent by a family during any one month was 3 Pula, then worth a little over one U.S. dollar.[1] Currently, however, many people see full participation in the national monetary-based economy as the most desirable route in the future.

People all over the world have changed their economic orientation from traditional forms of subsistence to participation in cash market economies. A driving force may be that people find the stability of resources attractive. Compared to traditional economic systems, which are subject to great variation due to weather, disease, and other environmental factors, cash market economies provide a more stable flow of resources. This is not to say that economic downturns cannot affect that flow; however, rather than the total loss a drought might bring in a traditional economy, cash market resource flow might only be reduced or disrupted for relatively short periods.

This shift to a cash market economy means that there is also a shift in the types of skills and knowledge that are important for children to acquire. Instead of becoming skilled at hunting, fishing, farming, or herding, children and young people attend school to acquire skills and knowledge such as proficiency in language, math, social sciences, and sciences. Rather than obtaining detailed knowledge about animal behavior and the natural world that is intrinsic to a traditional lifestyle, children and young people acquire knowledge about politics, geography, and cultures outside the Okavango Delta, Botswana, and Africa. The survey research has shown that these changes occur very quickly when people believe that an education will lead to employment in the cash market economy. Comparing girls who grew up in a traditional community and those who grew up in a community where their parents worked in wage labor, it was found that only girls in the traditional community knew how to process grain. Whereas only a few girls in the traditional community had attended school, all the girls in the wage labor community had attended school since they were six or seven. It was also found that there were great differences in children's and young people's knowledge of animals, plants, and the environment. Children in the traditional community had detailed knowledge about animal behavior, how to track and hunt animals, the food and medicinal qualities of plants, and where to find those plants. In the wage labor community, children knew no more of African animals and plants than children in the United States or Europe.

A key to this shift is the availability of education. The government of Botswana has made education accessible to all children. Even in the most remote parts of the Okavango Delta, there are primary schools. Most children board at secondary schools in the larger towns. Setswana, the national language of Botswana, is the language of instruction in primary school. Children also start to learn English during the last three years of primary school. English is the language of instruction for secondary school and is the language of government, business, and commerce in Botswana. The investment of time in learning Setswana and English has caused young people to invest less in learning the language of their ethnic group. Because children in remote areas now attend primary school, Setswana is more and more the language of play and camaraderie and in some cases is becoming the language of home.

A further consequence of formal education is the loss of cultural traditions. Customs marking life events, music and dance, and other customs that define a group's ethnic identity have come under pressure as more and more young people receive formal education. There are several reasons for this change. In addition to the Setswana language being taught in schools, Tswana customs, songs, and dances are also taught. Young people find that a mastery of not only the Setswana language but also Tswana culture may open doors both economically and socially in this predominantly Tswana country. In addition, as stated above, the customary law of Botswana that is applied to civil and minor criminal cases, especially in rural areas such as the Okavango Delta, is based in Tswana customs. These factors together mean that more and more young people are adopting Tswana language and cultural traditions in their daily lives. The Batswana are justifiably proud of their great literary and musical heritage, and being able to participate in this proud tradition may also attract young people from other ethnic groups to Tswana language and culture.

Land Reform and Development Schemes

In addition to these changes in children's pattern of learning and socialization, there have been external factors that have affected people's relationships with the land and traditional subsistence economies. Foremost among these have been changing government policies with regard to land utilization. Prior to Botswana's independence, land use in the Okavango Delta was governed by traditional practices and by the chief of the Batawana, whose greatest interest was in regulating hunting. After independence, much of the authority over land and many of the regulatory functions passed from the Batawana chief to the government. The Okavango Delta was seen as an underdeveloped region containing natural resources important to the development of Botswana's economy such as water, large herds of cattle, and large numbers of wildlife. Compared to many countries around the world, both developed and developing, Botswana is widely recognized as having pursued farsighted policies regarding wildlife and habitat conservation. Balanced against these policies have been the need to utilize natural resources and provide for the population. In the Okavango Delta, this has meant that environmental policies have been implemented along with policies to encourage cattle raising and exploitation of the Okavango River's water resources and to promote nature-based tourism.

An important consequence has been the increasing formalization of land use classification into wildlife management, commercial hunting, and nature-based tourism; agricultural; protected parkland; and settlement areas. To separate wildlife and cattle, ostensibly to prevent the spread of disease from wild buffalo to cattle, a series of "veterinary cordon fences," popularly known as "buffalo fences," have been erected around the Okavango Delta since the 1940s. The northern series of fences, erected in the 1990s, effectively demarcate the interior Delta as a cattle-free area. Botswana's National Development Plans 7 and 8 along with other legislation and regulations allocated the land in the Okavango Delta to these purposes with little consultation with local people and without what the Okavango see as sufficient consideration of traditional use patterns. Large parcels of land were leased to concessionaires for hunting and photographic safari businesses. As a result, people were no longer able to live in or participate in traditional activities such as hunting and collecting wild reeds and grasses for building materials in these areas.

Some land was set aside for community-based natural resource management (CBNRM), with mixed results. There are several communities in the Okavango region, such as Mababe and Sankuyo, that have had sizable sums of money and some jobs come from safari hunting and ecotourism (environmentally-oriented tourism). At the same time, there have been disputes over what to do with the money. Some of the other problems with the CBNRM approach were the aggregation of separate villages into artificial communities, disputes with enterprise partners, slowness in the distribution of benefits generated, and allegations that the land set aside for CBNRM was inferior.

The Okavango Pipeline and Dredging

Southern Africa is extremely arid, and thirsty countries in the region periodically eye the Okavango River as a wasted source of much-needed water. As stated above, 98 percent of the Okavango Delta's water evaporates. Faced with water shortages in the town of Maun and farther south at the Orapa diamond mine, the government of Botswana planned to dredge the Boro River in the southern Okavango Delta in the 1980s. This plan was shelved as a result of impact assessment and lobbying by the World Conservation Union (IUCN). The social impact assessment focused attention on the negative impact dredging would have on the traditional lifeways of the Okavango. In 1996 Namibia was faced with a dire water emergency due to continuing drought. The Namibian government announced plans to build a pipeline from where the Okavango flows through the Caprivi Strip to Namibia's capital Windhoek. This plan was shelved when well-timed rains ameliorated the water shortage and after considerable objections by nongovernmental organizations (NGOs) and the government of Botswana. Again, the negative social impact of decreasing the water level of the Okavango River and Delta in Botswana was a major objection.

Two of the results of the debate over the use of the Okavango River waters were the decision to establish a regional research center in the Okavango and the effort to plan a transboundary environmental impact assessment involving all three countries that use the waters of the Okavango River (Angola, Botswana, and Namibia). These three countries have an agreement that is overseen by a Permanent Okavango River Basin Water Commission (OKACOM) to manage the waters of the Okavango, established in 1994. It remains to be seen whether or not OKACOM can help alleviate some of the tensions among the three countries over the waters of the Okavango River.

The HIV/AIDS Pandemic

Perhaps the greatest threat facing the Okavango Delta Peoples is HIV/AIDS. In 1998, the HIV/AIDS prevalence rate in the Okavango Delta was estimated at between 25 percent and 40 percent of adults, one of the highest in the world.[2] Over 90 percent of hospital deaths were HIV/AIDS related. Several factors common to the African HIV/AIDS epidemic contribute to this high rate: a long-standing high rate of STD (sexually transmitted disease) infections; high levels of multipartnered sexuality; and no male circumcision. Infrastructural improvements in transportation that have occurred throughout the 1990s also contribute to the high rate of transmission. In 1990, there were only a few miles of paved roads in northern Botswana. Today there are well over 600 miles, and many more of improved gravel roads. This means formerly remote and difficult-to-reach villages have become easy to visit. Tourists, merchants, and truckers all ply these roads, and some of them bring HIV with them. In addition, the improved transportation means that people travel from remote villages to large towns, the capital Gaborone, and even Johannesburg to work, to go to school, or to purchase consumer goods. Again, this can provide a means of rapid increase in HIV/AIDS prevalence.

The rise of nature-based tourism in the Okavango Delta since the mid-1980s means that even the most remote areas are affected. Previously inaccessible areas have thousands of tourists visiting each year. Small planes constantly travel between bush camps and the town of Maun, providing another vector for HIV. Although the government of Botswana has a good AIDS education and health plan in place, it has not kept pace with the dramatic increase in movement afforded by improved transportation to remote areas of the Okavango Delta.

One of the most tragic features of the HIV/AIDS epidemic in Botswana is the pattern of mortality. Younger, educated, highly motivated people in the prime of their lives are the main casualties. This serves to deplete families, communities, and the workforce, leaving the very old and the very young. It is estimated that by 2006 Botswana will have over 50,000 AIDS orphans.[3] The Okavango Delta is one of the most remote and least developed parts of Botswana and is perhaps least prepared to handle this disaster. Among the Okavango Delta Peoples, traditional lifeways and extended families are already under great pressure, and the HIV/AIDS epidemic adds a further burden.

Economic Development and Modernization: A Two-Edged Sword

In the Okavango Delta, as in many places around the world, people are in a process of integration into national-level political, social, and economic institutions, partly within and partly outside of their control. When these issues have been discussed with people in the Okavango Delta, they say that economic development has benefits and it has costs and that the benefits outweigh the costs. People see development and modernization as unstoppable and irreversible and say they wish there was a way to maintain

162

their individual cultures while participating in Botswana's national institutions. One Xanekwe man said that he would like to return to the bush and be a full-time hunter-gatherer. When we asked why he did not do this, he said, "But what would my children do? They don't know how to hunt, they don't know the bush. All they know is school. There is nothing for them in the bush."[4]

Economic modernization has brought with it competition for land and resources, and it has contributed to growing social and economic stratification in the Okavango region. There are certainly people who have done very well, having established lucrative businesses and expanding their holdings of land, livestock, and capital. There are others who have become poorer and who have lost access to land and natural resources. The issue facing the people of the Okavango and the district council that oversees the region, the North West District Council, is how to ensure that economic development and modernization can provide for a better life for all people, not just the wealthy few.

Ironically, the development of the mining industry has been a key reason that the Republic of Botswana has done so well economically, but it is also the reason that there are threats to the well-being of the peoples of the Okavango. The sale of diamonds has contributed to the stability of Botswana. At the same time, the sale of diamonds excavated in Angola has helped fuel the civil war that has wracked that country for over twenty-five years. Now, the fighting in Angola is starting to spill into the Okavango region, with attacks by armed groups on civilians occurring in the West Caprivi region of Namibia. Diamonds have been used to purchase the weapons that at least some of these groups are using. Several hundred people, including members of the Xanekhwe and Bugakwe communities, have had to flee the fighting in West Caprivi and are now living in a Botswana refugee camp at Dukwe. As one refugee put it, "In Africa, diamonds have become war's best friend."[5]

RESPONSE: STRUGGLES TO SURVIVE CULTURALLY

Preserving Language and Cultural Traditions

Although preserving language and culture in the face of integration into national-level political, social, and economic institutions is a daunting task, there are many among the Okavango Delta Peoples who are working toward this goal. Bugakwe and Xanekwe representatives are active participants in organizations, workshops, and conferences regarding Bushmen peoples throughout southern Africa. There are several NGOs dedicated to this issue, among them Kuru Development Trust, Kgeikani Kweni (The First People of the Kalahari), Kalahari Peoples Fund, Working Group of Indigenous Minorities in Southern Africa (WIMSA), the International

Work Group for Indigenous Affairs (IWGIA), and Survival International. While there are common elements to the struggle to maintain cultural identity, the situation of the Bugakwe and Xanekwe is somewhat unique. More than most other groups, they are at the heart of issues concerning economic development, especially in regard to nature-based tourism. Many Bugakwe and Xanekwe people live in communities that are involved in community-based natural resource management. Moreover, many people work in safari camps. For many years Bugakwe and Xanekwe were the last to reap the benefits of economic development and modernization. Today, they have come farther faster than almost any other group in Botswana. Thirty years ago, many were nomadic hunter-gatherers who had little contact with other groups. These days, many Bugakwe and Xanekwe have secondary educations, and some have attended technical schools or university.

The challenge will be to preserve their languages and to begin teaching them to younger people. A group of linguists at the University of Cologne in Germany is compiling orthographies and studying the languages of the Bugakwe and Xanekwe. This documentation, in conjunction with the participation of local people, will be of primary importance in preserving these languages. The skills and knowledge of the hunter-gatherer life ways must also be taught to younger people. Both of these will take concerted effort to encourage young people to see the benefits of acquiring these traditional skills and knowledge in addition to a formal education. These same challenges are evident for Dxeriku, Hambukushu, and Wayeyi peoples.

While Dxeriku and Hambukushu in Botswana are struggling with these issues, members of these groups in Namibia are in somewhat different circumstances. There, Rudxeriku (the Dxeriku language) and Thimbukushu (the Hambukushu language) are official languages. There are dictionaries, school books, literature, and radio broadcasts in these languages. These are also languages of primary education. As contact between members of these groups in Botswana and Namibia increases, there may be more opportunities for people on the Botswana side to utilize these materials. While the language of primary instruction in Botswana has been Setswana, recently the law has been changed to allow the use of other languages. Although only Ikalanga has been used, languages of the Okavango Delta Peoples may be used in schools in the future.

The Hambukushu people have an excellent forum for the preservation of their cultural traditions such as craftwork and dance in the Botswana Christian Council's (BCC) Etsha Project in the town of Etsha 6. At the BCC's center there, people can learn and refine traditional skills such as basketry, pottery making, and leather work, as well as participate in traditional cultural activities. Artists from North America and Europe stay in residence for one to two years as resource persons and teachers. Hambukushu artists have visited North America and Europe demonstrating their outstanding basketry, and some baskets sell for substantial sums of money in these markets.

A group of Wayeyi educators and students formed the Kamanakao Association to preserve Wayeyi language and culture. In their language, Shiyeyi, *kamanakao* means "remnants," symbolizing the remnants of Wayeyi culture. Of all the languages of the Okavango Delta Peoples, Wayeyi has suffered the most. In the early 1990s, it was spoken mostly by the elderly and was in danger of disappearing. Through the efforts of the Kamanakao Association, an orthography of Shiyeyi has been compiled, and in many communities lessons in Shiyeyi are conducted for both children and adults. The Kamanakao Association is planning a Wayeyi cultural center in Maun, and efforts are being made to collect data on the Wayeyi, including oral history information.

Conservation, Traditional Lifeways, and Economic Development

A principle of CBNRM is that community control and preservation of natural resources when preserving wildlife and habitat is profitable to people. Because much of the nature-based tourism industry and concession land is controlled by people from outside the Okavango Delta, there are risks that the interests of the inhabitants will not be given the highest priority in the decision-making process. And without active benefits from the preservation of wildlife and habitat, local people will lose incentive to participate in conservation and natural resource management.

Traditional subsistence pursuits, especially hunting, have come under a great deal of pressure from land reform and conservation policies. Hunting is heavily regulated, and in some years, licenses are not issued in certain areas. This is based partially in the belief that subsistence hunting and "poaching" have equally detrimental effects on animal populations. One camp believes that subsistence hunting has little, if any, negative effect on animal populations due to the low population density of people in the Okavango Delta and the low-tech weaponry people are using. It may have a positive effect in weeding out old and sick animals. Poaching of elephants and rhinos usually entails organized bands using high-tech, often military, weaponry and killing large numbers of animals. According to the Botswana Defense Force, most of these bands have come from outside of Botswana.[6]

In response to these concerns, the Okavango Peoples Wildlife Trust (OPWT) was founded under the leadership of Kgosi Tawana II, chief of the Batawana and paramount chief of Ngamiland (Ngamiland is the district, similar to a province, that contains the Okavango Delta). The OPWT has been active in bringing together the headmen from all of the communities in the Okavango Delta to present a united front regarding policies on CBNRM, subsistence hunting, the "buffalo" fences, and utilization of the Okavango water resources. It is the only grassroots-based conservation organization operating in the Okavango and as such gives high priority to the interests of area peoples.

Preparing for the Future

The Okavango Delta Peoples stand at a crossroads. While working to preserve their languages, traditional skills and knowledge, and cultural traditions, people do not want to be left out of Botswana's dramatic economic achievements and political stability. The organizations working toward these ends are small and underfunded. Yet everywhere in the Okavango Delta people point with pride to their ethnic identity and to being a Motswana—a citizen of Botswana. Paradoxically, as more and more members of these ethnic groups become educated, these organizations will become stronger. And as more people receive educations, the learning materials available will become more widely accessible.

The threat of HIV/AIDS, however, is not ameliorated by ethnic pride or school education. Efforts are being made to cope with the AIDS crisis through government of Botswana–, UN-, and NGO-sponsored programs. These programs range from HIV/AIDS education to the provision of specialized health services for AIDS victims and condom distribution efforts. Work is also being done on providing high-protein foods to people and antiretroviral drugs to individuals who are HIV-positive.

In the face of this epidemic, it is crucial to preserve the languages of the Okavango Delta Peoples, their traditional skills and knowledge, and their cultural traditions for the rebuilding period that is bound to follow and for the thousands of AIDS orphans who are facing life without parents to teach them.

FOOD FOR THOUGHT

The five ethnic groups who make up the Okavango Delta Peoples face a number of challenges in the preservation of their traditional lifeways, languages, and cultural traditions. Some of these challenges are common to indigenous peoples all over the world. Others are specific to the case of the Okavango Delta. Still others are specific to only one ethnic group. The linchpin of this variation is economic development. The effects of economic development and modernization are felt in the loss of traditional lifeways and language, changes in the utilization of land, the threat of dredging and water offtake, and the devastation of the HIV/AIDS epidemic.

Many people and organizations are responding to these threats. They face an uphill battle but are making inroads in documenting and teaching the five languages, preserving and teaching cultural knowledge, demanding a greater voice in decision making, and working to preserve this unique ecosystem. Education can work for or against this process; it is up to governments to make educational systems responsive to local needs.

The Okavango Delta Peoples provide an example to the world of how a multicultural society can function successfully. Even under grave threat to their cultures, people live and work together and know and respect one another's traditions, lifeways, and languages.

Questions

1. Does the historical experience of the five ethnic groups who comprise the Okavango Delta Peoples parallel that of other indigenous peoples?

2. What are some of the major main threats to the preservation of the languages, traditional lifeways, and cultural traditions of indigenous peoples?

3. Does education improve or diminish a group's ability to preserve its language, traditional lifeways, and cultural traditions?

4. How have economic development and modernization impacted the HIV/AIDS epidemic among the Okavango Delta and other rural peoples?

5. Could more be done to help the Okavango Delta Peoples in their efforts to preserve their languages, traditional lifeways, and cultural traditions? By whom?

NOTES

1. These surveys were conducted as part of a dissertation research project by John Bock titled "The Determinants of Children's Activities in a Southern African Community," Department of Anthropology, University of New Mexico, Albuquerque, which was completed in 1995.

2. United Nations (UNAIDS), *Report on AIDS* (New York: Author, 1998).

3. Ibid.

4. Interview of Xanekwe man, personal conversation, Okavango Delta region, 1992.

5. Sources for diamond information: Douglas Farah, "Diamonds Are a Rebel's Best Friend," *The Washington Post*, April 16, 2000; Kate Dunn, "Tainted Gems Lose Sparkle as Prices Fall," Christian Science Monitor, October 27, 2000, pp. 1, 8; Blaire Harden, "Africa's Gems: Warfare's Best Friend," *New York Times*, April 4, 2000, pp. 1, 10.

6. Interview with Ian Khama, Brigadier of the Botswana Defence Force, 1992.

RESOURCE GUIDE

Published Literature

Bock, John. "Economic Development and Cultural Change among the Okavango Delta Peoples of Botswana." *Botswana Notes and Records* 30 (1998): 35–47.

Brenzinger, M. *Moving to Survive: Kxoe Communities in Arid Lands.* Cologne, Germany: University of Cologne Institute for African Studies, 1997.

Cowley, Clive. *Fabled Tribe: A Voyage to Discover the River Bushmen of the Okavango Swamps.* New York: Atheneum, 1968.

Larson, Thomas H. *Bayeyi and Hambukushu Tales from the Okavango.* Gaborone: Botswana Society, 1995.

Ross, Karen. *Okavango: Jewel of the Kalahari.* London: BBC Books, 1987.

Films and Videos

AIDS in Africa. 1990. Roger Pyke Productions. Filmmakers Library, 124 East 40th Street, New York, NY 10016. Telephone: (212) 808–4980. Fax: (212) 808–4983. email: info@filmakers.com. Web site: www.filmakers.com/.

Okavango: Jewel of the Kalahari. 1988. British Broadcasting Corporation and Public Broadcasting Service.

Wildlife Warriors: Defending Africa's Wildlife. 1996. National Geographic Society.

WWW Sites

Kalahari Peoples Fund (KPF)
http://www.kalaharipeoples.org

The Kamanakao Association
http://www.mindspring.com/~johnbock/kamanakao.html

The Okavango Delta Peoples of Botswana
http://www.mindspring.com/~johnbock

Okavango Peoples Wildlife Trust
http://www.stud.ntnu.no/~skjetnep/opwt/

The Republic of Botswana—The Government of Botswana Web Site
http://www.gov.bw

University of Cologne project: Hunter-Gatherers in Transition: The Conceptualization of Space and Environment
http://www.uni-koeln.de/phil-fak/afrikanistik/sfb389/c5-section.html

Working Group of Indigenous Minorities in Southern Africa
http://www.san.org.za

Organizations

First People of the Kalahari (FPK)
P.O. Box 173
Ghanzi, Botswana
Telephone: (267) 596 101
Email: fpk@info.bw

Kalahari Peoples Fund (KPF)
P.O. Box 7855
University Station, Austin, TX 78755
Telephone: (512) 453–8935
Fax:(512) 459–1159
Email: kalahari@mail.utexas.edu
Web site:http://www.kalaharipeoples.org

Kuru Development Trust
P.O. Box 219
Ghanzi, Botswana
Telephone: (267) 596 308
Fax (267) 596 285

Kuru Development Trust-Shakawe
P.O. Box 472
Shakawe, Botswana
Telephone: (267) 675 085
Email: shakkuru@info.bw.

Ngwao Boswa Basket-Weavers' Cooperative
P.O. Box 43
Gumare, Botswana
Telephone: + 267–674 074

Working Group of Indigenous Minorities in Southern Africa (WIMSA)
P.O. Box 80733
Windhoek, Namibia
Telephone: (264) 61–244 909
Fax: (264) 61–272 806
Email: wimsareg@iafrica.com.na
Web site:http://www.san.org.za

Chapter 9

The Palestinians
Lema Bashir

CULTURAL OVERVIEW

The People

The Palestinians are the Arab people indigenous to historic Palestine, the region of the Middle East that currently includes Israel, the West Bank, and the Gaza Strip. The Palestinian population currently is estimated at 8.4 million. Many of these are refugees. There are nineteen refugee camps in the West Bank and eight in the Gaza Strip, with a combined (registered) population of 570,896, according to 1998 figures. Approximately 3.6 million Palestinians are refugees in thirty-two camps in the surrounding Arab states (e.g., in Lebanon, Syria, the Gulf region, and Jordan).

The term Palestinians refers to those people—Muslims, Christians, and Druze—who occupy the Middle Eastern region from Lebanon south to the Sinai Peninsula and including areas that are now in Jordan, Israel, the West Bank, and the Gaza Strip. The Palestinians are a people descended from the Canaanites, who settled along the eastern coast of the Mediterranean Sea in Greater Syria (present-day Palestine, Syrian Arab Republic, Jordan, and Lebanon) around 3000 B.C. At various times throughout their history, the Palestinians and their ancestors have been under occupation of Assyrians. Babylonians, Persians, Greeks, Romans, Islamic Caliphs, the Crusaders, the Ottoman Turks, the British, and most recently, the Israelis.

Zionism is a movement for Jewish national self-determination aimed at restoring the rights of Jews to live in the lands of their ancestors. The Zionist movement began in the late nineteenth century in Europe, in part as a response to anti-Semitism. In 1882, in response to dangerous living

Palestinian family. (CIDA Photo: Peter Bennett)

conditions for Jews in Russia, a group calling itself "The Lovers of Zion" began the first organized migrations of Jews to their biblical homeland of Palestine. They settled in the northern part of the country and established approximately eleven settlements, the first of which was named "Ptah Tikva"—the gate of hope. However, due to worries about the dangers of moving to Palestine with no economic or military protection, the Lovers of Zion slowed their migrations.

On November 2, 1917, the British issued what came to be known as the "Balfour Declaration"—a communiqué from Lord Arthur James Balfour, the British foreign secretary, to Lord Rothschild, a Frenchman who had funded Ptah Tikva, declaring Britain's support for the Zionist Federation in creating a Jewish homeland in Palestine, while maintaining the "civil and religious rights of existing non-Jewish communities in Palestine." By May 1920, most of the Middle East had been divided up into two spheres of influence belonging to France and Britain, called mandates. The British Mandate area included Palestine, Trans-Jordan, and Iraq, and the supposed reason for the establishment of these mandates was to ease the Arab governments into independence after Turkish rule. All of the Arab governments in Greater Syria (Syria, Lebanon, Palestine, and Jordan) were opposed to the mandates and protested them vehemently. Under the British Mandate, the British began to aid the Zionist Foundation in moving European and Russian Jews to Palestine to establish their national home.

In just seventeen years, from 1922 until 1939, more than 300,000 Jewish immigrants entered Palestine and began to establish settlements, calling themselves *halutzim*, or pioneers. Fighting began between militant Arab groups, who protested this immigration to and settling of the land by foreigners, and three new Jewish strike forces; the Haganah, Irgun, and Stern Gang.

In 1936, all of the Arab nationalist groups in Palestine met to create the Arab High Committee, a permanent executive organ, under the leadership of Hajj Amin al-Husayni. The British had named Hajj Amin the permanent president of the Supreme Muslim Council in Jerusalem, but after he led the organization of a huge general strike by Palestinians of British goods, the British removed him from the presidency of the council and declared the council illegal. In 1939, after the huge pressure of the boycott, the British Mandate government decided not to establish Palestine as a Jewish state but to instead permit immigration to continue for five years and then would rely on Arab consent for further immigration allowances.

In the 1930s the British established the Palestine Royal Commission, also known as the Peel Commission, to investigate the Palestinian situation. The report recommended the partition of Palestine into two separate states in order to accommodate both the Jews and the Palestinians. The plan, which was announced in 1937, was eventually abandoned by the British after fierce opposition from all sides.

Unable to settle the dispute between Zionists and the Arab governments after World War II, Britain decided to withdraw from Palestine, which it did in 1947. In the same year the United Nations, under Resolution 181, came up with a partition plan that outlined the division of the region into a Jewish state and an Arab state. This plan was approved by the United Nations General Assembly on November 29, 1947. The partition plan was opposed heavily by the Palestinians and some Jews. The UN vote on participation sparked widespread violence, which eventually escalated into full-scale war. In 1948, heavy fighting began between the Arabs and the Zionists in Palestine, and after the massacre by the Irgun of 250 men, women, and children in the village of Deir Yassin in northern Palestine, around 700,000 Arabs fled the country. These events set the stage for the establishment of Israel in 1948.

The State of Israel was unilaterally declared on May 14, 1948, a date remembered by the Palestinians as "Al-Nakbeh," meaning "the catastrophe." It was not recognized by any of the neighboring Arab states nor by most other countries around the world at the time. The Arab states declared war on Israel, and when the fighting ended, Israel had added sections of the Galilee as well as the towns of Lydda and Ramle to the borders proposed by the United Nations in 1947. Another war took place in June of 1967, when Israel launched an attack on Egypt, Syria, and Jordan, resulting in Israeli reclamation of Jerusalem and territory on the West Bank. Nearly half a million Palestinian refugees fled into the surrounding Arab states.

The Setting

For the sake of convenience, the Palestine that is being referred to here is the pre–1948 Palestine, presently known as Israel and the Occupied Territories of the West Bank and the Gaza Strip. It is located just west of the Jordan River and south of Lebanon. It has a total land area of 10,166 square miles. Palestine in general can be characterized as a dry area that contains rolling, desert plains, rocky hills, and mountains.

Palestine has two seasons, a long dry summer and a short, rainy winter. The southern part of Palestine is arid desert. Water resources are extremely limited. The main sources of consumable water in the Occupied. Territories are the Jordan River and various aquifers in the West Bank and Gaza, providing 56,500 to 63,600 million cubic feet of water per year. Israel itself can be considered a "water-scarce" state, and it gets around 50 percent of its water resources from outside of its borders, mostly from the West Bank aquifer.

Traditional Subsistence Strategies

The Palestinian people are traditionally subsistence farmers, raising cash crops of olives, figs, and pomegranates, as well as goats and chickens, on small farms. Recently, however, increasing numbers of Palestinian men have begun to work in Israeli factories, fields, and other places of employment, since it has become more and more difficult for them to obtain land to farm. The Palestinian economy has become very dependent on these Israeli factories, and so when borders between the West Bank, Gaza Strip, and Israel are closed, Palestinian workers cannot get to their jobs and are sometimes unemployed for months.

Also, "cottage industry" became popular during the Intifada (the Palestinian uprising and general strike of Israeli goods in the late 1980s and early 1990s), as families began to produce simple products, mostly foodstuffs, in their homes and sell them in local markets. The large flow of Palestinians out of the country during the Intifada led to a great deal of earning and working abroad, creating an influx of foreign-earned money. This economy has been affected by the Arab-Israeli tensions toward the end of the 1990s and into the new millennium, with a reduction in exports from Palestine and restrictions on imports, resulting in economic difficulties for a sizable proportion of the Palestinian population. Many Palestinians today employ a mixed economic strategy, combining wage work with crop production and dependence on income obtained from relatives who are working either inside or outside of Palestine.

The Palestinian use traditional nonirrigation agricultural techniques, cultivating olive groves and dryland crops of various kinds. Land access has remained relatively static since the 1967 War, in part because of constraints on the availability of water and the difficulty of bringing new land under production. A fairly sizable number of Palestinians grow gardens near their homes, which they water with wastewater from their residences. Some Palestinian houses have cisterns to collect water during the rainy season. Palestinians have artesian wells that average between 200 and 400 feet deep from which they water their livestock and crops.

Social and Political Organization

In 1964, the Arab states decided to form the Palestine Liberation Organization (PLO) in order to bring together the Palestinians politically. The best-known PLO leader was Yasser Arafat, a Palestinian engineer. After 1967, the PLO became the umbrella organization for the Palestinians. The Palestinian National Authority (PNA) was established after the passage of the Oslo Accords, a set of principles and an agenda for negotiations between Jews and Palestinians announced in 1993. The PNA had its first elections in January, 1996.

Palestinian society is very much patrilineal (descent traced through the male line), with the eldest male relative acting as a guardian over his family. Interestingly, though, a movement away from patriarchy has begun, as men travel abroad to find work and their wives stay behind to run their households. However, the new somewhat dominating role of the woman in Palestinian society is still an informal one, and in the public sector, women still tend to take more passive attitudes.

Socioeconomic status also plays an important role in Palestinian society. City dwellers are often wealthier and more educated than village dwellers and as a result often claim a higher class status. Also, city dwellers generally have better access to education and thus more stable and lucrative jobs. Villagers and farmers are often less educated than city dwellers and have lower incomes and are more at the mercy of a variable market. The difference between these two groups can be delineated by many factors, but most noticeably by their dress (a more traditional style for the villagers, a more Western-style for the city dwellers) and their dialects. However, people enjoy great mobility in their class status, and education and travel have lessened the contrast between these two groups, so that a person's current occupation is no longer the sole definitive factor of their status.

In discussing the situation of the Palestinian people, it is important to note that more than half of them do *not* live in Palestine, but rather are spread throughout the world. According to the United Nations Relief and Works Agency (UNRWA), the operational definition of a Palestinian refugee is: "Palestine refugees are persons whose normal place of residence was Palestine between June 1946 and May 1948, who lost their homes and means of livelihood as a result of the 1948 Arab-Israeli conflict, and who took refuge in Jordan, Lebanon, the Syrian Arab Republic, the Jordanian-ruled West Bank or the Egyptian-administered Gaza Strip."[1] UNRWA is a special agency established by the United Nations and funded by state government and European Union contributions that provides assistance to Palestinian refugees. However, in December 1999, only 5.5 percent of Palestinian refugees qualified for relief assistance. Even that relief assistance only adds up to approximately $136 per person annually. According to the UNRWA definition, the thousands of Palestinians living outside of refugee camps or whose lands and homes were taken after the June War of 1967 do not qualify as refugees and thus are not allowed the benefits of refugee status, including housing, medical treatment, and education.

Refugees living inside and outside of camps in all the Arab states surrounding Palestine, except Jordan, do not have citizen status. In Lebanon and the Syrian Arab Republic, refugees are not granted citizenship even if they were born there. They are granted "travel documents" that are not recognized by many countries' governments. In Lebanon, Palestinian refugees are not allowed to work in the public sector at all, due to the government's desire to ensure sufficient jobs for its own citizens. Even in Jordan, citizens of Palestinian origin have a different citizenship classification.

Palestinian-Israeli peace negotiations began in Madrid, Spain, in 1991, in theory aiming at establishing some sort of long-term sustainable status for the area. However, Palestinians felt that the negotiations were biased in favor of Israel, and complained that the agreements signed gave the Palestinians far less land than necessary to accommodate their population and fewer rights than Israelis. The talks are ongoing, although they often break down after outbreaks of hostilities. The violence in the Middle East has intensified in the new millennium, with attacks and counterattacks by Palestinians and Israelis. The violence has included suicide bombings and other acts of terrorism and air and ground attacks on Palestinian facilities including the headquarters of the Palestine National Authority and Palestinian police stations by the Israeli military.

Portions of the West Bank are presently in a transitionary state, as Israel redeploys its forces and turns over powers to the newly established Palestinian National Authority (PNA). The PNA intends to establish a Palestinian state in these areas. The areas from which the Israeli army has so far withdrawn, known as "A areas," are technically under total control of the Palestinian Authority. They consist of six towns far from each other. Israeli military checkpoints control the flow of Palestinians to and from them. The "B areas" are under the shared jurisdiction of the Palestinians and the Israelis, while the "C areas," which make up over 70 percent of the West Bank, are fully under Israeli control.

Religion and World View

Palestinians are predominantly Sunni Muslims, with a minority of Christians and Jews. In the West Bank, approximately 75 percent of the population is Muslim, 17 percent is Jewish (the vast majority of which being settlers living in segregated areas), and around 8 percent is Christian. In the Gaza Strip the population is almost entirely Muslim. In the northern part of Israel proper, there are also a small number of Jewish Palestinians, whose ancestors had been living in Palestine prior to the immigrations beginning in 1882.

Islam is not only a religion to these Muslim Arabs; it is a way of life. During and after the Intifada, after being politically frustrated for so long, there was a mass return to religious conservativism among Palestinians. Women began to wear the *hijab* (Islamic headcovering) to declare their loyalty to their country and culture, to distinguish themselves from Israelis, and to increase their sense of nationalism.

THREATS TO SURVIVAL

After the wars in 1948 and 1967, the demographics of Palestine changed dramatically, as economic and political conditions pressured Palestinians to move out of the country, and Jewish settlers moved in. The biggest problems in the Palestinian diaspora are unemployment and lack of educational facilities. During the Intifada and during the new Al-Aqsa Intifada beginning in September of 2000, the Israeli government attempted to halt terrorist activities by restricting Palestinian entry to Israel. Schools and universities were closed for months at a time, and Palestinians were not permitted to leave their "A areas" to attend schools elsewhere, visit relatives, get medical treatment, or pray at mosques or churches in Jerusalem and Bethlehem, or in some cases, even to harvest crops in their own fields.

Palestinian communities suffered, and continue to suffer from, "brain drain," as those who had the means to travel abroad for education did so. The Israeli government restricts the right of return of Palestinians, as, it might be noted, does the Palestinian National Authority. Those with Jerusalem identification cards are not allowed to leave Jerusalem for more than two years before their ID cards are revoked, and any Palestinian who obtains a dual citizenship will lose his or her Palestinian ID card and thus their right to live in Palestine. The large majority of educated Palestinians do not live in Palestine at all, because of better job opportunities and security elsewhere, so a great part of the Palestinian population in the Middle East is involved in manual labor. It is a vicious circle, where the job market offers few opportunities for the educated, who then leave. This results in a dearth of educated Palestinians to support a service- or professional-oriented economic structure.

In September 1993, the Oslo Accords were signed by the Palestinians and the Israelis, establishing autonomy for Palestinians in the city of Jericho and in the Gaza Strip. However, the power granted to the PNA is limited. Since the signing of the Oslo Accords, over 500 Palestinian homes in the West Bank and Gaza Strip have been demolished by the Israeli government for being built without permits. It is almost impossible for Palestinians to obtain building permits to build homes on land that they own legitimately, so most are forced to build homes without permits. After the demolitions, they have the option of either spending thousands of dollars rebuilding their homes, which may be redemolished at any time, or leaving the area to live elsewhere. The Israeli Coalition Against Home Demolitions (ICAHD) has been working with Palestinians against the Israeli authorities, developing a program of civil disobedience to stop the demolitions and rebuild these homes. However, programs like ICAHD's can do very little to prevent the demolition of homes, which continues all over Palestine.

On September 28, 2000, Ariel Sharon, the chairman of the Israeli Likud Party and former minister of defense and now the prime minister of Israel, guarded by heavily armed soldiers, visited the "Noble Sanctuary" of the Al-Aqsa Mosque in Jerusalem, Islam's third holiest site. His visit to the mosque triggered a new wave of Arab terrorist violence in Palestine, termed the Al-Aqsa Intifada, leading to the deaths of hundreds of Palestinians and dozens of Israelis. Attempts at "peace" negotiations were halted, and Israeli

Prime Minister Ehud Barak resigned from office and called an emergency election. Ariel Sharon was elected prime minister of Israel.

Water rights issues are becoming an increasingly important issue in Palestine. In recent years, drought conditions have made water a valuable commodity in and around Palestine. Although 10 percent of households in refugee camps have access to water via networks, the networks are often dry, or when water is available it is often unsafe for consumption. In 1999, Palestinians encountered serious problems with access to safe drinking water, as Israeli settlements siphoned off Arab municipal supplies to their settlements. Since the aquifers under the West Bank extend into Israeli territory, Israel pumps around 90 percent of the annual recharge of the West Bank aquifers. Also, Israel's use of the aquifers amounts to overpumping and is slowly destroying the aquifers. Palestinian use of water has been capped by the Israeli government at 4,400 million cubic feet per year for the entire West Bank, that being only 14 to 18 percent of availability, regardless of population growth.[2]

Refugee camps in Arab countries, though assisting Palestinians in many ways with some medical care and almost adequate food rations, have their own set of problems. The average number of household members in a tiny refugee camp home is eight, and 18 percent of these homes do not have indoor bathrooms. Streets are unpaved and sewage systems are open, so diseases are very easily spread among camp populations. Crowded conditions continue to increase, as refugee camps are usually surrounded by urban areas and have no room to expand. Even the aid provided by UNRWA is barely sufficient, and most of the Palestinian refugees do not even qualify to receive aid.

Palestinian farmers have been encountering problems recently associated with the drought conditions. Because the rainy season is rather short, and only very poor irrigation systems are available to the Arabs in the West Bank and Gaza, even subsistence farming is becoming more and more difficult. Moving from the agricultural sector to other occupations is often not an option because the farmers tend to have minimal education, and few training programs are available to them.

Palestinians have experienced psychological damage as refugees. Over 100,000 Palestinians were jailed during the Intifada. According to Palestinian and Israeli human rights groups and international human rights organizations, 90 percent of the Palestinians arrested and jailed underwent, and still undergo, torture in interrogation.[3] "Mild" torture is still permitted in Israeli law. The effects of this treatment are beginning to appear in the dealings of the Palestinian National Authority police with the Palestinian people: They practice the same torture techniques on their fellow Palestinians that they suffered from in Israeli jails. Psychology is not a science that is widely accepted nor popular in Arab culture, and so these thousands of cases of posttraumatic stress generally go untreated.

Palestinians in the diaspora face a totally different set of challenges to their society. Their culture and traditions become more and more difficult to maintain as they assimilate into their surrounding cultures. Generations of Palestinian youth growing up in the United States or in Europe often do not learn to speak Arabic or to be proud of their ethnicity. Palestinians living in other Arab countries also lose a great deal of their Palestinian traditions and replace them with the traditions and customs of the people around them. Thus is created a hybrid culture—Palestinians in Lebanon have a distinctive culture and dialect, as do Palestinians in the Gulf countries, and so on.

Palestinians are irked that Israelis often refuse to use the word "Palestinian" and instead use the generic term "Arab." This negation of identity decreases Palestinian self-esteem and makes them more susceptible to denying their own culture and adopting elements of non-Palestinian cultures.

RESPONSE: STRUGGLES TO SURVIVE CULTURALLY

As the Palestinian people attempt to hold on to their culture and way of life, many organizations have been formed or have moved into the Middle East to aid them. Nongovernmental organizations like the International Council of the Red Cross, UNRWA, and UNICEF (United Nations Children's Fund) continue to work to try to better the human rights conditions of Palestinians in all parts of Palestine. Many other groups like the Badil Center for Refugee and Residency Rights, Shaml, The Holy Land Foundation, and B'Tselem (an Israeli human rights organization) have been organized in Palestine to secure Palestinian human and legal rights.

Group responses to problems faced by the Palestinians are becoming more common. It should be stressed that the vast majority of these responses are peaceful and they are aimed at resolving conflicts and promoting the well-being of Palestinian communities. Community-based organizations have been formed in most, if not all, Palestinian areas, and these organizations undertake a variety of activities, ranging from managing water to dealing with health, education, and welfare issues. Palestinian community representatives come together periodically to discuss their problems and prospects with one another. They also interact with Israeli government officials, oftentimes positively. These meetings and discussions have facilitated the flow of information between Arabs and Israelis and between local communities and the state, thus helping to alleviate some of the stressful conditions that people have sometimes had to operate under.

Organizations such as the Israeli Campaign against Home Demolitions, the Palestinian Land Defense Committee, and the Christian Peacemakers have begun active nonviolent campaigns against the Israeli authorities' demolitions of Palestinian homes. With extensive media involvement, they have staged protests. The nonviolent protests and media attention are bringing them more and more support from Palestinians, Israelis, and foreigners and drawing attention to Israel's persisting policy of Palestinian house demolitions.

The Tamer Institute for Community Education is a relatively new organization in the West Bank and Gaza Strip dedicated to promoting literacy among Palestinian youth. Its work in the past decade has triggered a movement among youth to concentrate on education and to popularize it.

Thousands of Palestinians suffer from posttraumatic stress. The Gaza Community Mental Health Program (GCMHP) began work in 1990 to lessen both the severity of it and the number of Palestinians who suffer from it Most prominently, the GCMHP has been holding group therapy sessions and training courses for PNA prison guards and police officers. Three years ago, Mandela Institute in Ramallah began a series of training sessions for PNA security forces, covering the topics of international and local law and law enforcement, search and seizure, interrogation, and human rights. These sessions were attended by approximately 1,000 Palestinian security enforcers.[4] The effect of these training and therapy sessions is beginning to show in the conduct of the PNA security forces, particularly with interrogators, as they begin to better understand the concept of human rights.

The movement of Palestinian youth and popular culture toward Westernization has been addressed by a trend attempting to repopularize traditional Palestinian dance, art, folklore, clothing, and architecture. The Popular Arts Centre in Ramallah holds activities and yearly festivals, and their dance troupe tours widely, both in the Middle East and abroad. Many organizations and private groups, like a new organization called Riwaq, have become involved in the restoration of historic buildings to be used as museums, music centers, restaurants, and even office buildings, to preserve the old architectural styles.

In the United States, negative media stereotypes of Palestinians and Arabs are being opposed by groups like the Arab Anti-Discrimination Council (ADC) and the Institute for Palestine Studies (IPS). The stance taken by many Arabs in the United States in the past tended to be a passive one, under the assumption that their stay here is not permanent and so they need not actively correct these negative stereotypes. This situation, however, has begun to change as Arab Americans have sought to rediscover their roots and to promote their cultural identities.

FOOD FOR THOUGHT

The history of the Palestinian people has been a difficult one, dominated by occupying forces and ongoing difficulties with coping with a high-risk arid environment. Their old lifestyle, as it was before 1948, is becoming more and more obsolete, as they struggle to create stable and viable economic and political systems. The mass exodus of Palestinians from Palestine as a result of the wars in 1948 and 1967 created a serious impediment to the attempts to maintain and develop their culture. Deliberate attempts by the Western media to portray negative images of the Palestinians cause a lowering of esteem for Palestinian culture not only outside of their culture but among their youth as well.[5] The current situation of the Palestinian government in trying to create a successful system leaves precious little time and energy to devote to environmental and sociocultural problems, and so they remain unresolved. Palestinians living in refugee camps have barely adequate access to food, medical facilities, and education—often because Arab host countries refuse to aid them—while their status as refugees prevents them from becoming citizens of any state. Palestinians living outside of refugee camps in the West Bank and Gaza Strip suffered from school and university closures during the Intifada, unemployment then and now, and the slow but deliberate erasure of their identity as a culture. Nongovernmental organizations, while beginning work on much-needed tasks, have only begun to scratch the surface of the multitude of corrections that need to be made.

The threats to the Palestinian culture are immense and difficult and while seeming relatively recent, only beginning in 1948, actually draw from the thousands of years of occupation undergone by these people and their ancestors. The problem of the numbers of Palestinians inside and outside of Palestine is becoming overwhelming and cannot continue in its present state. The future of the Palestinians as a culture is unsure, but it must be handled delicately to ensure its endurance.

Questions

1. Can Palestinian refugees ever integrate into their host societies? If they do, would they be compromising their Palestinian-ness?
2. Does the United Kingdom, because of the long-term effects of the mandate period on Palestine, have any responsibility toward the Palestinians and the protection of their culture? What about the international community in general?
3. What kinds of measures can be taken to ensure that Palestinian culture is not erased from world records and to enhance and develop it?
4. What issues deserve priority in terms of their being addressed at the next round of "peace talks" between the PNA and Israel?
5. What could the governments in the region, international agencies, and nongovernment organizations do to help heal the physical and psychological wounds suffered by Palestinians and Israelis as a result of the Intifada?

NOTES

1. John Quigley, *Legal Consequences of the Demolition of Houses by Israel in the West Bank and Gaza Strip* (Ramalla, West Bank: Al-Haq, 1994); Amnesty

International, *Israel and the Occupied Territories. Demolition and Dispossession: The Destruction of Palestinian Homes* (Washington, DC, and New York: Amnesty International, AI Index: MDE 15/59/99, www.amnesty.org).

2. Harold Dichter, "The Legal Status of Israel's Water Policies in the Occupied Territories," *Harvard International Law Journal*, vol. 35, no. 2 (1994); Sharif El-musa, "Dividing Common Water Resources According to International Water Law: The Case of the Palestinian Israeli Waters," *Natural Resources Journal*, vol. 5, no. 1 (1995); Rosina Hassoun, "Water Between Arabs and Israelis: Researching Twice-Promised Resources," in *Water, Culture, and Power: Local Struggles in a Global Context*, ed. John M. Donahue and Barbara Rose Johnston (Covelo, CA: Island Press, 1998), 313–338; Sharif Elmusa, *Water Conflict: Economics, Politics, Law, and the Palestinian-Israel Water Resources* (Washington, DC: Institute for Palestine Studies, 1997); Lema Bashir, "Murky Waters: The Palestinian-Israeli Battle for the West Bank Aquifer," Honors Thesis, University of Nebraska–Lincoln (Lincoln: University of Nebraska, 2001).

3. For discussions of Palestinian rights including prisoners in Israeli prisons, see Ann Elizabeth Mayer, *Islam and Human Rights: Tradition and Politics* (Boulder: Westview Press, 1995); Ilan Peleg, *Human Rights in the West Bank and Gaza: Legacy and Politics* (Syracuse: Syracuse University Press, 1995); Mula Mazzai, *Palestine and the Law* (Beirut, Lebanon: Ithaca Press, 1997); Fiona McKay, *The Palestinian Minority in Israel: Economic, Social and Cultural Rights* (Nazareth, Israel: The Arab Association for Human Rights, 1998); Simona Sharoni and Mohammed Abu-Nimer, "The Israeli-Palestinian Conflict," in *Understanding the Contemporary Middle East*, ed. Deborah J. Gerner (Boulder, CO: Lynne Rienner Publishers, 2000), 161–200.

4. Maureen Meehan, "Palestinian Police Undergo Human Rights Training to Curb Brutality They Learned in Israeli Prisons," *The Washington Report on Middle East Affairs* (October/November 1999), 25.

5. For discussions of Palestinian society and perceptions of Palestinians, see J. Migdal, *Palestinian Society and Politics* (Princeton: Princeton University Press, 1980); Judith Miller, *God Has Ninety Nine Names: Reporting from a Militant Middle East* (New York: Touchstone, 1996); M. Muslih, *The Origins of Palestinian Nationalism* (New York: Columbia University Press, 1988).

RESOURCE GUIDE

Published Literature

Bowen, Stephen, ed. *Human Rights, Self-Determination, and Political Change in the Occupied Palestinian Territories*. The Hague: Martinus Nijhoff Publishers, 1997.

Busool, Assad Nimer. *Palestine: Whose Land Is It?* Palos Hills: Islamic Association for Palestine, 1998.

Dumper, Michael. *The Politics of Sacred Space: The Old City of Jerusalem in the Middle East Conflict*. Boulder, CO: Lynne Rienner Publishers, 2002.

Gerner, Deborah J. *One Land, Two Peoples: The Conflict Over Palestine*. Second edition. Boulder, CO: Westview Press, 1994.

Hassoun, Rosina. "Water between Arabs and Israelis: Researching Twice-Promised Resources." In *Water, Culture, and Power: Local Struggles in a Global Context*, ed. John M. Donahue and Barbara Rose Johnston. Covelo, CA: Island Press, 1998. 313–38.

Kimmerling, Baruch, and Joel S. Migdal. *The Palestinians: The Making of a People.* Cambridge, MA: Harvard University Press, 1993.

Kretzmer, David. *The Legal Status of Arabs in Israel.* Boulder, CO: Westview Press, 1990.

Lewis, Bernard. *The Middle East: A Brief History of the Last 2,000 Years.* New York: Touchstone, 1995.

McKay, Fiona. *The Palestinian Minority in Israel: Economic, Social and Cultural Rights.* Nazareth, Israel: Arab Association for Human Rights, 1998.

Peretz, Don. *Palestinian Refugees and the Middle East Peace Process.* Washington, DC: U.S. Institute of Peace Press, 1993.

Rice, Kenneth A. *The Middle East since 1900.* New York: Longman, 1993.

Tessler, M. *A History of the Israeli-Palestinian Conflict.* Bloomington: Indiana University Press, 1994.

Wolf, Aaron T. *Hydropolitics along the Jordan River: Scarce Water and Its Impact on the Arab-Israeli Conflict.* Tokyo: United Nations University Press, 1995.

Films and Videos

Aqabat Jaber: Peace with No Return. 1995. Film directed by Eyal Sivan. Available from First Run/Icarus Films: http://www.frif.com/ Film about a fifty-year-old refugee camp outside of Jericho.

Daughters of Allah. 2000. Directed by Sigrun Slapgard for NRK. Film about modern Palestinian women.

Encounter in Ramallah. 1997. Produced by Peter Lofgren and Emil Larsson for SVT. Filmakers Library: http://www.filmakers.com/

On Our Land. 1981. A film by Antonia Caccia. Available from First Run/Icarus Films: http://www.frif.com/ A discussion of the treatment of Palestinians in Israel who farm land that is no longer there, centering on Umm el-Fahm, the largest Arab village in Israel.

Our Honor and His Glory: Honor Killing in the Palestinian Zone. 1999. Produced by Sigrun Slapgard for NRK.

The Road to Palestine. 2000. Films for the Humanities and Sciences http://www.films.com/

WWW Sites

Al-Haq, West Bank affiliate of the International Commission of Jurists
http://www.alhaq.org

Arab-American Anti-Discrimination Council
http://www.adc.org

Arab Association for Human Rights
http://www.arabhra.org

Association of Forty
http://www.assoc40.org

The CIA World Factbook
http://www.odci.gov/cia/publications/factbook

Institute for Palestine Studies
http://www.ipsjps.org

Israeli Coalition against House Demolitions
http://www.ariga.com

Law Society
http://www.lawsociety.org

The Palestinian Diaspora and Refugee Center, Shaml
http://www.shaml.org

Palestinian Information Center
http://www.palestine-info.net

Palestinian National Authority
http://www.pna.org

Palestinian Return Center, London, United Kingdom
http://www.prc.org.uk

The Palestinian Society for the Protection of Human Rights and the Environment
http://www.lawsociety.org/pa.html

United Nations Relief and Works Agency
http://www.UNRWA.org

Organizations

Al-Haq
P.O. Box 1413
Ramallah, Palestine
Telephone: (972) 2–295–4646
Fax: (972) 2–295–4903
Email: haq@alhaq.org
Web site: http://www.alhaq.org

Bat Shalom
P.O. Box 8083
Jerusalem 91080, Israel

B'Tselem, Israeli Information Center for Human Rights in the Occupied Territories
43 Emek Refaim Street
Jerusalem 93141, Israel
Telephone: (972) 2–561–7271

Fax: (972) 2–561–0756
Email: mail@btselem.org

Institute for Palestine Studies
3501 M Street, NW
Washington, DC 20007
Telephone: (800) 874–3614
Web site: http://www.ipsjps.org

Israeli Committee against House Demolitions (ICAHD)
Rehov Tiveria 37
Jerusalem, Israel
Telephone: (972) 5–065–1425
Fax: (972) 2–623–2310
Web site: http://www/net-a.org/hdemol

Israeli Council for Israeli-Palestinian Peace
P.O. Box 2542, Holon 58125, Israel
Telephone/Fax: (972)-23–556–5804
Web site: http://www.members.tripod.com/-other_israel/

LAW
The Palestinian Society for the Protection of Human Rights and the Environment
P.O. Box 20873
Jerusalem, Israel
Telephone: (972) 2–583–3430
Fax: (972) 2–583–3317
Email: law@lawsociety.org
Web site: http://www.lawsociety.org/

One World Action
59 Hatton Garden
London EC1 United Kingdom

Palestine Academic Society for the Study of International Affairs (PASSIA)
18 Halem At-Ta'i Street, Wadi Al-Joz
P.O. Box 19545
Jerusalem, Israel
Telephone: 02–6264426
Fax: 02–6282819
Email: passia@palnet.com
Web site: http://www.passia.org

Palestine Human Rights Information Center
4201 Connecticut Avenue, NW, Suite 500
Washington, DC 20008

Palestinian American Research Center (PARC)
% Randolph-Macon College
P.O. Box 5005

Ashland, VA 23005
Telephone: (804) 752–3790
Fax: (804) 752–7231
Email: parc@rmc.edu
Web site: http://www.parcenter.org

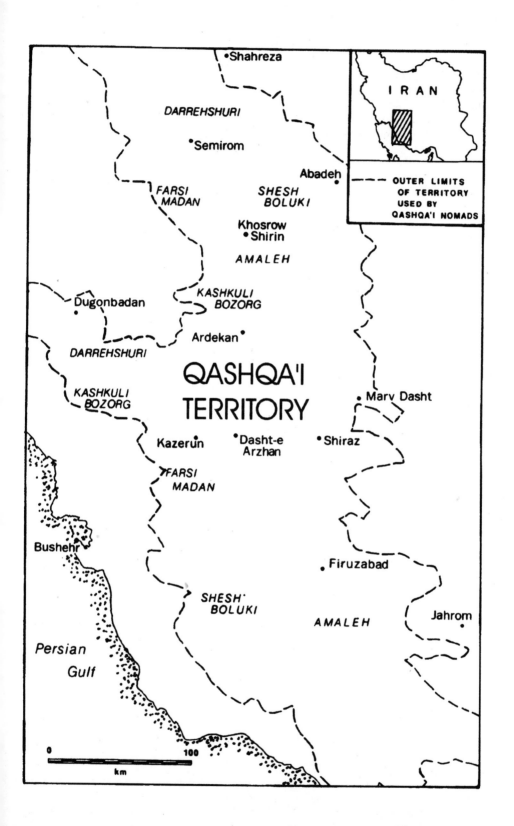

Shahreza

DARREHSHURI

Semirom

Abadeh

SHESH
BOLUKI

FARSI
MADAN

Khosrow
Shirin

AMALEH

Dugonbadan

KASHKULI
BOZORG

Ardekan

DARREHSHURI

QASHQA'I
TERRITORY

KASHKULI
BOZORG

Marv Dasht

Kazerun

Dasht-e
Arzhan

Shiraz

FARSI
MADAN

Busher

Firuzabad

SHESH
BOLUKI

AMALEH

Jahrom

Persian
Gulf

0   100
km

I R A N

OUTER LIMITS
OF TERRITORY
USED BY
QASHQA'I NOMADS

Chapter 10

The Qashqa'i of Iran

Lois Beck

CULTURAL OVERVIEW

The People

Nomadic, seminomadic, and settled residents of the plateaus and valleys of the Zagros Mountains of southwestern Iran, the Qashqa'i people are members of a tribal confederacy of some 800,000 individuals. They are Shi'i Muslims, Turkish speakers, and one of Iran's many ethnic and national minorities. Persian is the official language of Iran.

The Qashqa'i tribal confederacy was formed over several centuries by culturally diverse people, Turks primarily but also Lurs, Kurds, Arabs, Persians, Baluch, gypsies, and others, who were joined together in southwestern Iran, beginning in the eighteenth century, by an elite tribal family functioning as agents of state rulers. The ruling family and many components of the confederacy originated in what are today Central Asia, Afghanistan, Caucasia, Turkey, Iraq, and the vast territory of Iran. In the past 200 years, the paramount leaders of the confederacy participated politically in a wider Iranian and sometimes international context, which affected the ways central and local governments dealt with the tribespeople.

The Setting

The Qashqa'i people resided primarily in and adjacent to the semiarid, steppe, and mountainous lands of Fars Province in southwestern Iran. During winter and summer, Qashqa'i nomads lived in small tent encampments in their seasonal pastures; during spring and autumn, they used pack ani-

Qashq'ai woman during migration, 1979. (N. Keddie/Anthro-Photo)

mals to migrate from one seasonal territory to the other. In the 1990s and early 2000s, many nomads lived in huts or small, rudimentary houses in their seasonal pastures and transported their household goods by motorized vehicles. Most Qashqa'i nomads who settled in villages chose locations in or near their winter or summer pastures, and many continued to practice pastoralism. Some Qashqa'i also resided in towns and cities throughout southwestern Iran in order to engage in wage labor and salaried jobs.

Traditional Subsistence Strategies

Until the 1970s most Qashqa'i people were nomadic pastoralists who migrated with their sheep, goats, and camels as many as 400 miles semi-annually between their winter pastures in the foothills near the Persian Gulf and summer pastures high in the mountains to the north and east. Since the 1970s some Qashqa'i people have settled in villages and towns, although still often maintaining animal husbandry as a means of livelihood, while others have adapted their customary patterns of nomadic pastoralism to include changes such as motorized transportation and dwellings more substantial than goat-hair tents.

The vast majority of the Qashqa'i people subsisted on a mixed pastoral-agricultural economy in the 1990s and early 2000s. They consumed their own products and sold the surplus in order to buy necessary commodities. The nomads depended more on sheep and goats, while the villagers relied more on agriculture. In the spring and summer, the nomads and villagers sold live animals and dairy products in villages, town markets, and urban centers. Women wove blankets, saddlebags, and other utilitarian items from the yarn they spun from sheep wool and goat hair, including the knotted pile carpets for which the Qashqa'i have been internationally renowned since the nineteenth century. Many Qashqa'i cultivated fodder crops for their animals and grain for human consumption.

Since the 1960s some planted orchards of fruit and nut trees and sold the produce commercially. Increasing numbers of Qashqa'i, primarily men, have taken on wage labor and salaried jobs in tribal territory and its periphery and in towns and cities. Because of the continuing success of an innovative program for the formal education of tribal children begun in the 1950s, some Qashqa'i have found jobs in teaching, governmental administration, and other urban-related professional occupations. By 2001, the members of any given extended family were often engaged in a variety of livelihoods, from customary nomadic pastoralism to urban office jobs, and each relied on the others for pastoral and agricultural products, cash, and urban services.

Social and Political Organization

Every Qashqa'i person was a member of a set of sociopolitical groups: a nuclear or extended family, a patrilineage, a subtribe, a tribe, and the confederacy. Members of the same lineages and subtribes tended to live together, share in economic pursuits, intermarry, and celebrate rituals communally.

Qashqa'i nomads lived in small tent encampments in winter and summer pastures. During the long migrations of spring and autumn, they traveled in larger groups for purposes of defense and security. Their social ties at the local level were based primarily on patrilineal ties, but bonds of economics, social compatibility, and politics were also considered relevant. Qashqa'i villagers lived in similarly constituted but larger social groups, and they lost the flexibility and the seasonal social changes that the nomads appreciated. The Qashqa'i people in towns and cities often resided in the same neighborhoods together and kept close social ties with one another. These dwellers of villages, towns, and cities often enjoyed visiting their nomadic kinspeople in seasonal pastures, and the nomads relied on their settled kin for help in handling governmental affairs and market contacts.

The Qashqa'i tribal confederacy consisted of a ruling dynasty of hereditary leaders (the Janikhani family), five large tribes (Amaleh, Darrehshuri, Kashkuli Bozorg, Farsi Madan, and Shish Boluki), some smaller tribes, and specialized occupational groups (such as camel drivers, musicians, and ritual specialists). The leader of the confederacy was the *ilkhani*, or paramount khan (chief), a member of the Janikhani family and a direct descendant of the first Qashqa'i *ilkhani*. He was assisted by an *ilbegi*, also a Janikhani. Each tribe except for the Amaleh had its own ruling family of khans. The *ilkhani* appointed one khan from each tribe as *kalantar*, a leading khan, who was responsible for liaison with the *ilkhani*. The last functioning *ilkhani*, Khosrow Khan Qashqa'i, was captured and executed by military forces of the Islamic Republic in 1982, at the end of a tribal insurgency that he had led after he was expelled from his duly elected seat in the national parliament. Since then, other members of the Janikhani family who could possibly succeed Khosrow Khan have been under political restrictions in Iran or in involuntary exile abroad. Many of the khans of the component Qashqa'i tribes were still living in Qashqa'i territory in 2001, but the government restricted their political activities, and they were no longer the tribespeople's mediators in the ways they had been before the Islamic Republic's formation in 1979.

Each Qashqa'i tribe consisted of many subtribes, each of which was headed by a *kadkhuda*, a headman, until 1980. These men were appointed by the khans of their tribes, who usually recognized the men whom the people themselves had selected as headmen. They were confirmed in their positions by Iranian governmental officials. Local Qashqa'i groups also fell under the authority of the rural police and were held under surveillance by the secret police. In the Islamic Republic they were subject to the control of revolutionary guards and committees and newly reorganized security forces. Since 1980 the government has encouraged Qashqa'i nomads to form Islamic councils, which were intended to assist the people in their relationships with the new Islamic government. In 1999 Qashqa'i villagers and town dwellers were also allowed to vote for their own Islamic councils, and many Qashqa'i candidates successfully ran for election.

Religion and World View

The Qashqa'i are Shi'ite Muslims, as are 90 percent of Iran's population. Another 6 percent are Sunni Muslims, Sunni Islam being the dominant form of Islam in the world. Being Shi'ite Muslims in an Islamic Republic dominated by Shi'ite Muslims, the Qashqa'i escaped some of the problems experienced by many of Iran's other tribal peoples who are Sunni Muslims (such as the Baluch, Turkman, many of the Kurds, and some of the Arabs) and by Iran's religious minorities (Christians, Jews, and Zorostrians, Bahais, and others). Most Qashqa'i people were not as dedicated as many other Muslim Iranians to performing the rites of daily prayer, fasting during the month of Ramazan, and pilgrimage to Mecca in Saudi Arabia. By 1999, primarily because of religious instruction in state-run schools and increased exposure to religious information in the state-controlled media, a greater percentage of the Qashqa'i people participated in Islamic rituals than in the past.

THREATS TO SURVIVAL

Environmental Problems

The struggle of the Qashqa'i people for access to, and control over, the land they needed for their livelihoods stood at the center of their difficulties in 1999. Although some nomads held governmental permits to exploit certain sections of pastureland in winter and/or summer territories, these permits were temporary and sometimes contested. Governmental officials had promised to provide thirty-year leases for exclusive pasture use but had not done so in most areas by 1999.[1] The nomads constantly faced encroachers on their land, usually Persian and Lur villagers who wanted to expand their own agricultural land. Because the nomads occupied any specific territory for only part of the year, they were often victimized by encroachers who came during their absence to convert pastureland to cultivation. The issue of water was central in these disputes, for most agriculturalists needed a permanent, reliable source of water and often acquired the technology and financial resources to exploit it, at the expense of the nomads who were now denied access. Qashqa'i nomads and villagers who decided to begin or expand their own cultivation experienced difficulty in securing long-term rights to the land. Since the national land reforms of the 1960s, rights over communally and privately owned or controlled land have not been adequately clarified and legalized in most areas. Those individuals, especially the settled Persians and Lurs, who had ties to governmental officials were advantaged over those who did not, such as many nomads.

Expanding populations, overexploitation of land, and degradation and scarcity of resources were troubling environmental problems for all Qashqa'i people. Competition over land and resources was great throughout most of Qashqa'i territory and the periphery in the 1990s. Natural pastures were not adequate for the numbers of people and animals present. Cultivable land, especially with dependable supplies of water, was growing increasingly scarce. The land that was cultivated was less productive than in the past when farmers more frequently rotated crops and allowed land periodically to lie fallow. Those cultivators with the means to dig deep wells and install motorized pumps lowered the water table not only for the surrounding inhabitants but also for themselves. The routes of passage used in the past for the nomads' migrations were increasingly encroached upon by urban sprawl, expanding agricultural settlements and cultivation, irrigation works, and roads. These problems were not easy to solve, especially by a government that was experiencing major, multiple economic problems in all parts of Iran.

Soon after the Islamic Republic's formation, governmental officials created the Ministry of Rural Reconstruction, whose aim was to help improve the lives of rural peoples. It contained a special division, the Organization of Nomadic Affairs, to address the nomads' specific problems, and many of its agents were themselves of tribal, nomadic backgrounds who tended to be sympathetic to those they served.

Economic Problems

The main economic problem for most Qashqa'i people in 1999 was finding adequate, reliable sources of income. Those households with diverse economic activities tended to be more fortunate than those who continued to rely on one source of income, such as sheep and goats. With Iran's national economy under stress, especially in terms of the high rates of annual inflation, all citizens experienced problems. Many Qashqa'i people appeared to be more adaptive than many other Iranians in villages, towns, and cities who struggled to survive on single sources of income, such as monocrop cultivation, teaching jobs, or factory labor. The prices of items needed to improve the standard of living, as well as those necessary for subsistence, rose rapidly. Those Qashqa'i who moved to urban areas to seek cash income from wage labor and salaried jobs found escalating living expenses there to be burdensome.

Political Problems

Ruling from 1941 until his forced ouster in 1979, Mohammad Reza Shah Pahlavi attempted to modernize Iran and centralize his government. In both these projects he confronted resistance from many of the ethnic, tribal, and other minority peoples living within Iranian borders. Viewing many of these people as obstacles to his efforts, he sought to pacify them militarily and politically and then integrate them into a unified Iran. In the case of the Qashqa'i, he attempted to disarm them, eliminate or control their tribal leaders, end their nomadism, settle them in villages and towns, and assimilate them into the wider Persian-dominated society and culture. He employed military, political, economic, and social means to achieve these ends.

Sociocultural Problems

Mohammad Reza Shah was especially annoyed by the presence of people in Iran who appeared to him to be backward and primitive.[2] Their existence was an affront to his efforts to create a modern society, and he attempted by various means to blend them into the wider fabric of a modernizing, urban-connected, Persian society and culture. The very features that marked the Qashqa'i people as distinct from other Iranians were often those that raised his ire. Their Turkish language being a special target, he instigated governmental programs to teach them the Persian language and make them adjust to a wider Persian-speaking society. He supported an educational program for Qashqa'i children by training Qashqa'i teachers and sending them back to their own or others' tribal groups. The language of instruction was supposed to be exclusively Persian. Once the children completed the five years of elementary school, they were expected to further their education in town schools, enter the national labor force, and eventually assimilate to Persian society and culture.

At the same time that the shah was instigating programs for the military and political pacification of the Qashqa'i, he and other governmental agents were also aware of the tourist appeal of so-called exotic peoples to foreigners as well as urban middle-class Iranians. The Qashqa'i especially drew outside attention because of their lengthy and dramatic semiannual migrations, traditional livelihoods and lifestyles, unique and colorful clothes and ceremonies, and relative autonomy. With camels heavily laden with household goods, vast numbers of Qashqa'i nomads migrated by Shiraz, the largest urban area of southwestern Iran, on their travels between winter and summer pastures. Foreign observers in particular marveled at what they considered to be an amazing spectacle. Some Qashqa'i territories were also conveniently located near this urban center, unlike the territories of many of Iran's other ethnic and tribal minorities who lived in isolated and/or mountainous areas near international borders. Hence, once the shah and his military officers deemed the Qashqa'i people to be pacified militarily and politically, his regime instigated programs to exploit their appeal for an audience consisting of foreigners and urban Iranians. Many Qashqa'i people took advantage of this situation by maintaining and enhancing their customary practices. In this way, the shah's policies did not have all the results he expected. He somehow supposed that the Qashqa'i could maintain their exotic appearance while at the same time joining the wider Persian-dominated society.

The Qashqa'i people experienced a short-lived period of cultural freedom during the revolutionary overthrow of the shah and his government in 1978–1979 by the followers of the Ayatolla Khomeini. Not all people were able to participate fully, given the political turmoil of the time. Once the Islamic Republic of Iran was declared in 1979, circumstances changed rapidly, and within a year or two, governmental officials banned or restricted many cultural activities throughout the country for ostensibly "Islamic" reasons, following the Quran (Islam's holy book) in its strictest interpretations. They declared that all females from the age of nine must observe standardized Islamic codes of dress by wearing head-to-toe veil wraps or hair-concealing head scarves and loose overcoats, all unadorned in somber, solid colors.

Officials forbade the Qashqa'i people to participate in some of their traditional customs, particularly musical performances, dancing, and a competitive stick-fighting sport conducted to music, all of which had played vital parts in Qashqa'i weddings and other festive occasions and had helped to define them as a unique people. Declaring that music and dance inspired lewd thoughts possibly leading to immoral actions, the state's religious leaders condemned the musicians and the participants. Among the Qashqa'i the full measure of these severe restrictions was never apparent, given the difficult and tragic circumstances of the Iraq–Iran War (1980–1988) that resulted nationally in hundreds of thousands of deaths. Out of respect for their own casualties—the killed, the missing in action, and the prisoners of war—and their grieving survivors, all Qashqa'i people restricted their cultural performances during weddings and other social occasions. Several years after the war ended, the government began to relax some of its restrictions concerning dress and entertainment.

Unlike the shah's regime, the rulers of the Islamic Republic did not seem particularly threatened by some other aspects of Qashqa'i cultural identity. They placed no restrictions on the use of the Turkish language. Ethnic dress per se, unless certain items of attire were perceived to violate Islamic standards of modesty, raised no problems. Even the possession of firearms—a crucial symbol of autonomy for the Qashqa'i but forbidden by the shah for military reasons—was allowed and even encouraged through easily acquired gun permits, inexpensive and government-provided ammunition, and government-sponsored shooting contests.

RESPONSE: STRUGGLES TO SURVIVE CULTURALLY

The ability to adjust to changing political and economic circumstances has been essential to the survival of the Qashqa'i as a distinctive people in Iran for the more than 200 years of their existence as a sociopolitical group.

Economic Diversification

In environmental and economic matters, the Qashqa'i people have adjusted their livelihoods to confront changes in the government, new market demands, inflation, and increased pressures on land and other natural resources. Many Qashqa'i families adopted diverse sources of income to spread out their risks. Few nomadic pastoralists relied solely on animal husbandry anymore. The rapid spread of formal education allowed many young Qashqa'i men, and small numbers of women, to find new kinds of occupations, often outside tribal territory.

Tribal Affiliation and Identity

Since the beginning of the Qashqa'i tribal confederacy as a significant sociopolitical entity in southwestern Iran in the eighteenth century, its various political institutions adapted well to political vicissitudes in the region and the state. The confederacy emerged in response to political pressure, largely issuing from the state, and continued to adapt to the wider political climate. Hence, despite military and political attacks against Qashqa'i leaders soon after the revolution in 1978–1979 and the Islamic Republic's formation, other levels of the political hierarchy were still able to respond to some of the people's needs. In the context of frequent political discord in Iran over the past two centuries, the Qashqa'i people had developed institutions (such as a hierarchy of political leaders and a high degree of local-level political autonomy) that could adjust to the needs of the tribespeople according to changing circumstances. In the 1990s Qashqa'i tribal identity remained as strong as in earlier decades, if not stronger.

Cultural Revival

Since the forced ouster of Mohammad Reza Shah in 1979, many Qashqa'i people have a renewed, revitalized sense of their distinctiveness as a people in Iran. Even under the shah, some Qashqa'i had paid increasing attention to their cultural uniqueness and attempted to communicate their enthusiasm to others. Designed to integrate Qashqa'i children into a wider Persian-controlled state but staffed entirely by young Qashqa'i men and women who stressed their own ethnic and linguistic identity, the tribal schools helped to make the children proud of their unique cultural heritage. The war with Iraq, following soon after the Islamic Republic's formation, caused its own disruptions among the Qashqa'i people and within the wider society, but once the war was over, many Qashqa'i people were able to turn their attention again to the many cultural expressions that were meaningful to them.

Given the loss of some significant features of their society because of modernizing processes and political control, such as migrating by camels and attending large tribal gatherings at the khans' encampments, many people began to stress other features, including the more intangible ones. An example from summer pastures in 1996 demonstrates this point: Sitting by the open fire at night, listening to the distant wolves howl and the camp dogs respond, and preparing to roast the wild partridges he had struggled to hunt that day, a Qashqa'i man commented wistfully as he gazed into the starry night, "Isn't this how it used to be?"[3] He would not have thought to utter such a remark twenty years earlier.

Just as was the case before the revolution, many Qashqa'i people remained sheltered and insulated in 1999 by their family and kinship groups, the tribal system, and the relative physical isolation of most of their territories. They enjoyed a barrier of protection that many other Iranians lacked. The apparent hands-off policy of state authorities had allowed the tribal people to exercise autonomy in many aspects of their lives. Other than for increasing concern about the inflationary national economy and the scarcity of some consumer goods, people tended to hold different, less critical attitudes toward the new government than many other Iranians, a circumstance explained by their supportive kinship and tribal networks and the extent of their political autonomy. Less affected by restrictive new policies than many urban and rural peoples, they were less disapproving of the government.

Writers on Iran often stress the extensive transformations occurring there because of the revolution and the new Islamic government. They tend to ignore the ways that life also continues in well-established patterns. And they tend to disregard, or be uninformed about, sectors of Iranian society that are outside Tehran, distant from other metropolitan centers, or perceived to be politically unimportant. If for this reason only, it is important for outsiders to know about the Qashqa'i people.

Since the revolution in 1979, continuities are demonstrated in their society and culture. Despite some of the possibly superficial trappings of change—such as motorized vehicles, permanent houses (humble as they are), and new material goods—the people still seemed to be governed by the same societal and cultural norms and expectations as thirty years ago.

Of primary importance to the people were the institutions, political and social organizations, norms, and values of tribally organized society. The tribal groups with which they identified, the leaders they still respected (despite their being in involuntary exile abroad or under surveillance and control), and the rules they tried to live by stood at the center of their lives. Their notions of kinship, family, and gender relationships were similar to what they had been in the past. They continued to live within and rely upon the types of social groups that they had formed many decades and more before.

Expressions of Qashqa'i culture, especially the notions of identity that the people held about themselves, were significant factors in their survival as a distinctive group. The Qashqa'i people lived within a culturally diverse nation-state where linguistic, ethnic, religious, tribal, and regional distinctions figured prominently in people's interrelationships. The Qashqa'i expressed their culture in many ways, and together these expressions formed a unique cultural unit unlike any other in Iran. Where change had occurred, it was in the increasingly proud and assertive nature of people's awareness. Their consciousness of themselves as Qashqa'i and the ways they marked this identity were much more explicit in 1999 than in 1970 and before.

Many Qashqa'i individuals having special interests in Qashqa'i music, dance, painting, poetry, oral history, and traditional technologies (such as weaving and tent construction) emerged after the revolution as authorities on the culture that most or all Qashqa'i people in the past had shared and participated in. A photography book displaying the rich diversity of Qashqa'i weavings drew the avid interest of many, not just weavers. A posthumously published memoir of a Qashqa'i *ilkhani* drew positive attention from many, including those who disapproved of the hierarchy of khans. Qashqa'i women and girls increased their efforts to style their clothes, especially those worn for ceremonial purposes, in the manner of the past and often ignored the state's regulations about modest Islamic dress.

Many individuals recorded the music performed at weddings and other ceremonial gatherings and played the audiocassettes at home for their families' enjoyment. Wealthy families videotaped their elaborate wedding celebrations. Fathers taught their sons the strategies of the stick-fighting game and encouraged their children to recite poetry and sing traditional songs. Becoming aware of the many Persian words and phrases that had entered their everyday language, people increasingly strove to eliminate them and to return to their native Turkish terms. For instance, a father was overheard questioning his daughter when she asked him about a school lesson. "Are you speaking to me? I can't understand those strange words you are babbling."[4] Of course, he was fluent in both Turkish and Persian, but he wanted to make sure she understood the importance of the Turkish language to her cultural heritage. Speaking Persian in school was required, but speaking Persian at home was another matter altogether.

Another factor, the livelihood and lifestyle itself, helped to perpetuate certain aspects of society and culture for many Qashqa'i people. Nomadic pastoralism in remote mountainous plateaus and valleys, linked with a high degree of individualism in political and economic activities, led to a retention of the supporting social and cultural systems. The relative physical isolation of many locations and the people's physical separation from non-Qashqa'i society are related factors. For example, many Qashqa'i women did not need to abide by new national (especially urban) standards of modest Islamic dress in the 1980s and 1990s because most of them lived within their own kinship groups. They were freer to behave in customary ways than they might have been, had they resided in towns and cities and fallen under the constant, critical gaze of enforcers and supporters of governmental regulations.

FOOD FOR THOUGHT

Few Iranians or outsiders had predicted the revolution that quickly brought down the shah and his repressive government. Fewer yet had predicted the formation of an Islamic government in a country that had appeared to be well along the path of modernization, Westernization, and secularization. Now, twenty years since these events, people within Iran and around the world are still surprised that this form of government has persisted. It is clear that the situation for the Qashqa'i people is in flux, and none of them know what the far or even immediate future will bring.

Questions

1. By what diverse means have the Qashqa'i people been able to modify and yet perpetuate their society and culture?

2. What does the future hold in store for the Qashqa'i as a distinctive people in Iran? Will they be able to continue their unique livelihoods and lifestyles, or will they become increasingly similar to other citizens of Iran who live in villages and small towns?

3. Will those individuals who choose a new life in the cities, surrounded by non-Qashqa'i people, be able to retain their Qashqa'i identity? And what will become of their children, the next generation, who will probably seek out livelihoods and lifestyles notably different from those of their grandparents?

4. Will the current efforts of those Qashqa'i individuals to communicate the idea of a distinctive culture through many expressive forms (such as music, dance, painting, fiction and nonfiction writing, poetry, oral history, photography, and weaving, and other customary technologies) be adequate to pass on Qashqa'i culture?

5. Will these increasingly stylized forms of expression be seen as realistic representations of life, as models for the new generations to follow, or only as symbols of a bygone era seen nostalgically?

NOTES

1. Qashqa'i informant, field notes of Lois Beck, Fars Province, Iran, July 1999.
2. Ervand Abrahahamian, *Iran Between Two Revolutions* (Princeton: Princeton University Press, 1982); Eric Hoogland, *Land and Revolution in Iran, 1960–1980* (Austin: University of Texas Press, 1982); Lois Beck, *The Qashqa'i of Iran* (New Haven: Yale University Press, 1986); Lois Beck, *Nomad: A Year in the Life of a Qashqa'i Tribesman in Iran* (Berkeley: University of California Press, 1991).
3. Field notes of Lois Beck, Fars Province, Iran, July 1999.
4. Qashqa'i informant, field notes of Lois Beck, Fars Province, Iran, July 1999.

RESOURCE GUIDE

Published Literature

Beck, Lois. *Nomad: A Year in the Life of a Qashqa'i Tribesman in Iran.* Berkeley: University of California Press, 1991.

———. *The Qashqa'i of Iran.* New Haven, CT: Yale University Press, 1986.

———. "Women among Qashqa'i Nomadic Pastoralists in Iran." In *Women in the Muslim World*, ed. Lois Beck and Nikkie Keddie. Cambridge, MA: Harvard University Press, 1978. 351–73.

De Schooren Ullens, Marie Therese. *Lords of the Mountains: Southern Persia and the Kashkai Tribe.* London: Chatto and Windus, 1956.

Khoury, Philip, and Joseph Kostiner, eds. *Tribes and State Formation in the Middle East.* Berkeley: University of California Press, 1990.

Kiyani, Manuchehr. *Departing for the Love of Anemone: Art in the Qashqa'i Tribe.* Shiraz, Iran: Kian Nashr Publishers, 1999.

Oberling, Pierre. *The Qashqa'i Nomads of Fars.* The Hague: Mouton, 1974.

Films and Videos

Iran: A Revolution Betrayed. 1984. Directed by Ahsan Adib. British Broadcasting Corporation, London.

Woven Gardens (Tribal Eye). 1976. British Broadcasting Corporation, London. Film examines the woven rugs of the Qashqa'i tribe of Iran and explains how the rugs are made, what functions they serve, and the significance of the traditional symbols used in their design.

WWW Sites

Ghashghai (Qashqa'i) Nomads of Iran Development Project
http://www.ghashghai.bigstep.com

Iranian Cultural Organization. (Contains a study of Iran that discusses the Qashqa'i)
http://itsa.ucsf.edu/~ico/history/2societyandenvironment.html#peoples and languages

Iransaga: Iran (Persia): The Country. The land, people, and maps of Iran.
http://www.artarena.force9.co.uk/country.htm

Organization

Public Affairs Committee for Shi'a Muslims
Stone Hall, Chevening Road
London NW6 6TN,
United Kingdom

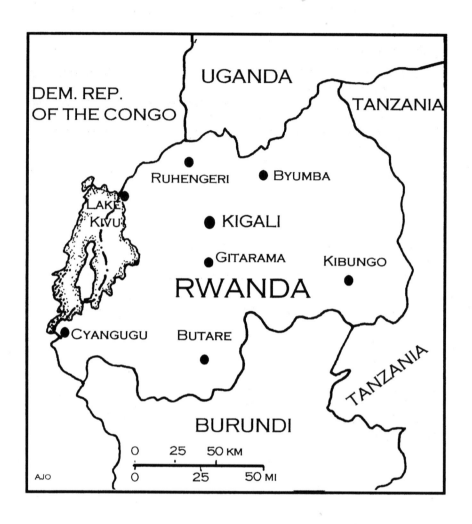

Chapter 11

The Rwandese

Clea Msindo Koff and Ralph J. Hartley

CULTURAL OVERVIEW

The People

The Rwandese[2]1 are a set of peoples who live in the country of Rwanda in eastern central Africa who today number an estimated 7.9 million.[2] Rwanda is a small country that has the highest population density (numbers of people per square-mile) in Africa. All Rwandese speak Rwanda (Kinyarwanda), and some speak French, Swahili, or English. Rwandese identify with three population groups called Hutu, Tutsi, and Twa. Today, these labels are used as ethnic identifiers; however, in the past they designated an individual's occupation.

It is not clear if the words *Hutu*, *Tutsi*, and *Twa* existed in ancient times when people from surrounding regions began migrating to Rwanda in greater number. But by the end of the nineteenth century, most agriculturists were known as Hutu, most pastoralists as Tutsi, and those who primarily hunted and gathered were known as Twa. This system of classification was not hierarchical in its earliest usage, and Rwandese could be classified differently throughout their lives if their mode of production changed.

The labels have become more rigid over time, and a hierarchy was introduced in the classification scheme. This transformation of the meaning of group identities began in the late nineteenth century as a complex state system grew in Rwanda. The labels were solidified during the period of European colonial rule that commenced in 1899 with a German protectorate. Tutsi became the elite, Hutu were treated as subjects, and Twa were marginalized.

The labels *Hutu, Tutsi,* and *Twa* were inherited through the father's lineage or, if a child was born to an unmarried mother, through the mother's lineage. The labels no longer indicated an individual's mode of production, could not be altered during the course of a person's life, and were concretized by being added to the mandatory identity cards all Rwandese began to carry. This last practice was introduced in the 1930s by the Belgian colonial administration (1915–1962) and persisted until 1994 despite the end of colonial rule in 1962. Prior to 1994, it was estimated that 85 percent of the population held an identity card that designated their ethnicity as Hutu, 14 percent were labeled as Tutsi, and 1 percent of the population was recognized as Twa.

The Setting

The nation of Rwanda, which covers an area of 10,169 square miles, is about the size of the state of Maryland. The Rwandese live in a country known both as the Switzerland of Africa and as the Land of a Thousand Hills. Both titles refer to Rwanda's mixture of grasslands, rolling hills, and volcanic mountain ranges. In addition, waterfalls can be seen in the crevices of some mountainsides. Rwanda sits just south of the equator, yet it experiences a range in daily temperatures, creating a lush tropical climate with an average temperature of 73°F. There are two rainy seasons, from February to May and from September to December, characterized by heavy daily downpours separated by brilliant sunshine.

Both the topography and climate of Rwanda can be differentiated between the eastern and western portions of the country, as measured from the ridge line of the Congo-Nile Divide, the mountain range that runs from north to south in western Rwanda. The eastern portion is characterized by open pastures, low hills, and less rainfall during the rainy seasons. In addition, when it is hot in Rwanda, the eastern region is always hotter and drier than the west, particularly as one approaches the border with Tanzania where temperatures can reach 90°F.

In contrast, the western side of the Congo-Nile Divide presents a steep descent to Lake Kivu and the Ruzizi River Valley. Temperatures in western Rwanda are lower on average than those in the east and are accompanied by more rainfall year-round. Despite the slope of the land in western Rwanda, Rwandese farmers have cultivated most hillsides for agriculture. The difference in topography between western and eastern Rwanda is so marked that as one begins to descend from the Congo-Nile Divide by car toward the central plateau, one will have a bird's eye view of a great expanse of land stretching out far below that resembles a quilt due to the

Young boys at Lake Kivunear, Kibuye, Rwanda. (Courtesy Ralph J. Hartley)

multihued rectangular agricultural fields and grazing lands that cover the landscape.

The ridge lines of the mountains in Rwanda present yet another climate. The volcanic Virunga mountain range in northwestern Rwanda borders both Uganda and the Democratic Republic of Congo (former Zaire) and contains the National Park of the Volcanoes. The highest peak here rises to 14,870 feet above sea level and is snow capped. The vegetation is that of a tropical forest, and the mountains are home to, among other animal species, the last bands of endangered mountain gorillas studied by primatologist Dian Fossey and the subject of the film *Gorillas in the Mist*. The higher elevations of the Congo-Nile Divide itself, such as above 9,000 feet, experience overnight temperatures below freezing, and scrub forests abound.

Traditional Subsistence Strategies

Due to the presence of fertile soil and dependable rainfall on the slopes and crests of hills, agriculture has been a steady feature of Rwandese subsistence. In addition, most cultivators raise some cattle, and some pastoralists rely on larger herds of cattle alone. The primary subsistence crops are beans, peas, sorghum, cassava, sweet potatoes, maize, and bananas. Bananas are an important crop to the Rwandese: Not only are they a year-round staple, but they are also used to brew banana beer—a drink served in formal social interactions. In addition to various kinds of bananas, the Rwandese consume more sweet potatoes and beans than any other food product.

Traditionally, shifting cultivation was employed whereby new areas were farmed when the soil in older plots of land was exhausted. Population growth, however, has rendered opportunistic migration impossible; therefore, settled agriculture is now practiced, and the same plots of land are reused, employing crop rotation or a fallow period under ideal conditions. Farming is undertaken by small-scale family units who attempt to cultivate plots at diverse elevations to reduce the risk of food shortages due to inadequate rainfall or extreme erosion. The slope of most plots makes mechanized agriculture difficult, if not impossible; so the traditional hand-farming tools of hoes and machetes have continued as the primary subsistence implements.

The goal of each family unit is to provide food for the family. Thus the raising of cash crops is of secondary importance even though cash crops are the main source of income for individuals. The primary cash crop for export to the world market is coffee, but tea and pyrethrum, a flower used in insecticides, are also grown. On the local level, bananas are the main cash crop. Some Rwandese also raise goats, sheep, and chickens, and younger men fish with nets along the coast of Lake Kivu. Many Rwandese supplement their incomes through engaging in rural industries, including craft production and sale, and through migrating to the major towns and cities for purposes of work. In the new millennium, there is still a fairly sizable number of Rwandese whose subsistence base is provided by relief agencies and nongovernment organizations.

Social and Political Organization

Precolonial Rwandese society was made up of about thirteen *ubwoko*, or clans (groups whose members assume they have a common ancestor but cannot precisely trace their relationship to each other), and are further divided into patriclans (*imiryango*) (kinship groups where ancestral linkages are traced through males). Descent is normally traced patrilineally, that is, through the male line, but women did not take their husband's name upon marrying. People of the same clan were very close and helped each other. Each clan was represented by a specific totem, usually an animal, bird or reptile. While certain clans produced kings, others provided functions that supported the monarchy. The king (*mwami*) and queen-mother (*umugabekazi*) had political power, supported by a royal council (*abiru*) that provided advice. The social and economic system of Rwanda was characterized by *ubuhake*, which entailed that people with less wealth and power would become clients to the wealthy, in exchange for protection and cows—one of the most valued commodities in traditional Rwandan society.

In the late nineteenth century, the region that is now Rwanda was occupied by several small kingdoms, many of which were often at war with each other. The largest kingdom, the Abanyiginya dynasty, expanded its power and influence and eventually controlled all the land in Rwanda's current boundaries. The leader of the Abanyiginya kingdom was attributed divine power and dominated the people with his chiefs. For many years several smaller kingdoms in the northwest part of the country resisted this control, but by World War I, the new German colonial administration (1890–1916) helped incorporate these kingdoms into the evolving social and political organization. After 1916, near the end of World War I, the Belgians gained control of Rwanda and began exercising greater control over the primarily Tutsi central aristocracy. The Belgian colonists empowered the king and his administrative rulers with enhanced economic and social control over the people. These rulers were essentially subject to Belgian authority. The people were obligated to grow cash crops to pay high taxes to the ruling government, while the Tutsi monarchy maintained access to land—reserving much of it for pasture for their cattle. This political and social system, in which wealth and strength were established by cattle ownership, reinforced the Tutsi king's power and, in turn, maintained Belgian control. The divisions between Tutsi and Hutu were codified and institutionalized by the Belgian colonial administrators. They ensured educational and employment opportunities for Tutsi, causing entrenched resentment among many Hutu, some of whom were relegated to forced labor. Only Tutsi boys were selected for training as chiefs, positions that amounted to being administrative officials of Belgian authority and that were rewarded according to the amount of taxes chiefs collected.

Rwanda gained independence in 1962. The constitution, passed by the National Assembly, permitted the election of a president as head of state and head of the army. The country was divided into ten administrative regions, known as prefectures, and 141 communes, representatives of which were elected in obligatory elections.

Religion and World View

Several religions are followed in Rwanda. The majority of the population of the country—perhaps 80 percent—is Catholic, with the remaining 20 percent of the population equally divided between Muslims and traditionalists (those who practice indigenous religions). Despite the apparent Christianization of most Rwandese, it is likely that many practice a blend between traditional Rwandese beliefs and Christian dogma.

Traditional Rwandese religious beliefs center around Imana, a Supreme Being who is considered the Original being, the Creator, and the great Provider. Worship of Imana does not involve ritual so much as prayer, oaths, blessings invoking Imana's name, and naming of children after Imana. Rituals are associated with supernatural forces that are believed to inhabit all things and with the unhappy spirits of ancestors who live in the underworld. Both small offerings, such as a few drops of milk, and large offerings, such as a goat, are provided to placate these spirits at periodic intervals.

Catholicism arrived in Rwanda as part of the intense and sustained Christian missionization of East Africa. Missionization had commenced in Tanzania in the mid-nineteenth century, then expanded into Uganda and southeastern Kenya, all neighboring countries to Rwanda. The turn of the century brought a particular order of French Roman Catholics—the White Fathers—from Uganda into Rwanda. They built their first mission at Save in 1899 just as the country became part of German East Africa. By 1919, the White Fathers had established at least sixteen missions throughout the country where they provided education and wage labor opportunities. Conversion by Rwandese was slow at first, but the period from 1927 to 1935 saw an enormous conversion to Roman Catholicism, from 36,978 to 202,732. Today, most primary and secondary education in Rwanda is still provided by the Catholic Church.

There was some initial resistance to Catholicism because Rwandese were following the example of the king, Musinga (1896–1931), who refused to convert. Organized resistance came most strikingly in the form of the Ny-abingi cult of northern Rwanda. The Nyabingi cult was multiethnic and multiregional; its adherents lived in Uganda, northwestern Tanzania, and it surfaced in southern and central Rwanda under the name Ryangombe or Kubandwa. The cult is named for the hero goddess of fertility, health, and prosperity, and its followers believed that Nyabingi's power, among other capabilities, could melt European bullets. Both the German and Belgian colonial administrations had difficulty in suppressing the cult, which protested against missionaries and colonialists several times before it was sent completely underground in 1934.

Whether a given person follows Christianity, Islam, or traditional beliefs, all Rwandese emphasize the importance of family and believe that children have particular value because children are the link between life and death. Oral tradition provides guidelines for living through stories, myths, and aphorisms.

THREATS TO SURVIVAL

Demographic Trends

The population of Rwanda has steadily grown due to improved nutrition and health programs enacted during colonialism and decreased infant mortality. The population density, therefore, has increased; the number of persons per square mile was approximately 700 in 1990, and it was nearly 990 persons per square mile of arable land (i.e., roughly 71 percent of the country). By comparison, the population density of the state of Maryland (a comparable size) is approximately 470 persons per square mile. Rural resident projections (made before the 1994 genocide) estimated that Rwanda's population density in 2025 would exceed 1,300 persons per square mile. Rwanda currently has one of the highest population densities in Sub-Saharan Africa and one of the highest birthrates. In juxtaposition to the high birthrate, the fast-growing AIDS epidemic will take the life of 1 person out of 10 in the coming decade.[3]

Current Events and Conditions

Two major threats face the Rwandese today: environmental degradation and internal violent conflict. The first threat stems from a food need and the second from resource competition. Both these sources, however, are related to the high—and increasing—population density in Rwanda. This relationship can be visualized in the following manner: Population growth leads to resource competition, which, in turn, contributes to internal violent conflict and increased food needs, which, in turn, leads to agricultural intensification (more labor and energy invested) and the expansion of agricultural activities in marginal lands. Eventually, these processes result in deforestation, environmental degradation, soil erosion, and encroachment on park land, including areas where there are endangered species, notably the mountain gorilla, a number of whom have been killed over the past several years in spite of concerned efforts to conserve them.

The second threat, internal violent conflict, stems from the competition for natural and material resources. Competition between people can take place at both the political and personal levels, and that competition is associated with violent conflict.

Environmental Crisis

Although Rwanda encompasses land that is highly fertile, such as that found in the numerous river valleys and the volcanic soils in the northwest, only 70 percent of Rwanda's total land is suitable for farming or grazing because of the amount of hilly and mountainous terrain. Some percentage of the suitable land is still further unexploitable due to waterways, unpredictable climate, or because it is reserved for industrial use. The limited amount of ideal and available agricultural land has led the Rwandese to employ some practices aimed at increasing food production that have detrimental effects on the land. These practices include moving into marginal lands, intensive cropping, overgrazing, and encroaching on forest and parkland.

Marginal land refers to those lands that do not provide ideal conditions for agriculture. In Rwanda, this means the steeper slopes. Steep slopes require a barrier in the form of a terrace, drainage ditch, or vegetation to keep soil from washing down during rains. Rwandese farmers using the steepest slopes are often younger and only cultivating the marginal slopes because all the "good" ridge line plots are taken by older family members. The younger farmers feel pressure to maximize the amount of ground dedicated to crops; therefore, erosion control in the form of additional plantings are rarely used, and the slopes both lose soil and create a landslide danger. In addition, the plots on the steepest slopes are often planted with crops that grow well in poor soils but still have a high calorie level, such as manioc, maize, or tubers, but these crops have no inherent erosion control features—that is, they do not provide cover for the soil from rain. When soil loss does occur on hills, the runoff becomes sedimentation in the valleys, and this increases potential for flooding.

There has been intensive cropping in both the marginal lands and those areas that are well suited to agriculture. Intensive cropping encompasses the planting of crops one after another without employing a fallow period that allows the soil to "rest" and rebuild its nutrients. By shortening or eliminating a fallow period, a Rwandese farmer can, in the short term, increase the probability of producing food year-round. In the long term, however, intensive cropping removes the natural nutrients from the soil that allow crops to thrive. Without the addition of fertilizer, crops grown in depleted soil are weak and therefore more vulnerable to unfavorable conditions, such as erratic rainfall. Many Rwandese farmers cannot afford chemical fertilizers, and the use of natural fertilizers, such as manure, is limited to bananas, beans, and other important crops located close to the family compound. Eventually, soil planted under these conditions will not be able to support a crop at all. The same is true in pasture areas that have been overgrazed; here, vegetation is no longer able to regenerate itself over time.

Much of the land now used for farming was originally part of Rwanda's natural forests. It is estimated that less than 600 square miles of forest remain. Deforestation reduces soil stability and leads to deterioration in the density or structure of vegetation cover, a phenomenon known as degradation.

The end result of weak crops is lower yield; in turn, low yield leads to food shortage, which in its extreme form is famine. In Rwanda, the very efforts employed to meet the food need are increasing the inability to provide food.

Sociocultural Crisis

No one has anything. So that creates competition between groups. If someone has no work, he says it's the other group that has all the work.[4]

The second threat facing the Rwandese is internal violent conflict. Civil wars, in 1959, 1963, and 1972, caused many Rwandese to flee to neighboring countries where they lived as refugees until the wars ended. When they tried to return to Rwanda, however, the government would not readily allow them to do so. The justification given for the "closed border" policy was that there was not enough land for all the people already in Rwanda and letting the refugees back would only compound the problem—especially because 90 percent of Rwandese depend on agriculture for their livelihood. In 1990, the Rwandan Patriotic Front (RPF), an army made up of Rwandese living in Uganda, attacked Rwanda's government army, from the north. The RPF goal was to defeat the army, overthrow the standing government, and let the refugees return to Rwanda. They did not succeed, and in the following three years, defenses against the RPF grew: Organized militias in Rwanda were armed, and the army was strengthened under President Juvenal Habyarimana. Many resident Tutsi were categorized as being potential accomplices to the RPF—a Tutsi-led army—and were murdered.

In conjunction with the refugee issue, Rwanda's economy was under stress. During the 1950s, the world's market for coffee, Rwanda's main export, had fluctuated wildly. By 1989, the price Rwanda received per kilo of coffee had dropped almost 50 percent. As a result, the income of people living in rural areas was drastically reduced. In addition, a disease that affects coffee trees reduced yields in some areas, and a serious famine racked the south and southwest parts of the country in the fall of 1989. Farmers needed to cut down coffee trees to make the land available for food production, but this made it difficult for them to pay increased taxes used to support school education, health care, water supply, and distribution networks. Moreover, rising costs of fuel and military demands put families in stressful situations.

By the late 1980s, the average family had little more than two acres on which to grow crops, while some of the more wealthy and powerful people in the country were increasing their landholdings. Poverty was increasing while divisions between social classes grew wider. The future appeared bleak for many, especially for young men who were required to have a house before getting married, but most had no access to land and little education, and there were few available jobs.

Into this climate of concern for the future, one radio station in Kigali, the capital of Rwanda, poured fuel for hate: Radio Milles Collines included daily speeches by extremist political leaders that identified the RPF—and by extension, all Tutsi—as the source of Rwanda's problems and a threat to Rwanda's future. The leaders behind the hate speech were therefore distressed when President Habyarimana responded to another unsuccessful attack by the RPF in 1993 with a meeting to discuss peace. This meeting led to a peace negotiation that called for President Habyarimana to share power with RPF leaders; the negotiations took place in neighboring Arusha, Tanzania, and became known as the Arusha Accords.

The government stipulated by this peace agreement was not fully implemented when, on April 6, 1994, a plane carrying President Habyarimana was shot down over Rwanda. The next day, the extremist wing of the then-ruling party initiated the systematic murder of over 500,000 men, women, and children. Tutsi were targeted specifically. Identity cards, required of all Rwandese, became a distinguishing label of those who were to die and those who were to live. The majority of those killed were noncombatants and not associated with the RPF. In the first few days, gangs of militia (*Interahamwe*) went from house to house, killing Tutsi and Hutu residents who had opposed extremist political and social positions. Within a week of the beginning of the killing, thousands of victims were herded to churches, schools, stadiums, and other public areas where they were subsequently massacred with machetes, hoes, clubs, spears, bullets, and grenades, sometimes over the course of several days. This mass murder lasted from April through June of 1994 and is identified as the first legally defined genocide in Africa. The massacres ended with the advance of the RPF into Rwanda and their takeover of the government.[5]

Yet another threat facing Rwanda and other central and southern African countries is the HIV/AIDS crisis. Like other Sub-Saharan African countries, Rwanda has a substantial number of people who have HIV/AIDS, and there are hundreds of thousands of orphans in Rwanda whose parents have either died from AIDS or other diseases or who have lost their lives in the violence that has wracked the country.

RESPONSE: STRUGGLES TO SURVIVE CULTURALLY

The relationship between environmental degradation and food shortage is recognized by the Rwandese. The attention paid to it has been particularly acute during the famines Rwanda has suffered. The Rwandese response has taken several forms, but the 1994 genocide has severely constrained large-scale mitigation efforts as the focus has turned to the healing of the population. Between the colonial era and the 1990s, a number of government-sponsored efforts to mitigate environmental degradation were launched throughout Rwanda. In some cases, these efforts were well received by Rwandese farmers and are credited with improving conditions; in others, however, the mitigation methods had degradation outcomes of their own. For example, the largest government effort to mitigate the shortage of land was the relocation of families from around the country to planned agricultural settlements, primarily in the northwest. These government-sponsored cooperatives were called *paysannats*, and the crops grown were for export: coffee, tea, pyrethrum, wheat, and potatoes. The *paysannat* plan, in effect during the 1960s and 1970s, was successful in easing the population density of some rural areas; however, the land cleared for these cash crops was often natural forests—further damaging the overall environmental condition through deforestation.

Numerous mitigation methods were introduced to rural farmers, and they were adopted to various degrees. Erosion was combated with a hedge-planting campaign and some small terrace building on the steeper fields. Soil conservation measures were encouraged, including mulching of crops, digging of drainage ditches, and intercropping. Two new crops, rice and soybeans, were introduced because they are high-yield crops and were expected to decrease food shortages. Deforestation was addressed through planting of fast-growing trees, such as cypress and eucalyptus, in communal forests or along roadsides. As for grazing lands, pastoralists were encouraged to plant foraging crops for their herds.

Since 1994, however, most of these efforts have been deemphasized or diminished entirely due to the social disruption from the genocide. Rwandese in the north and northwest of the country have been particularly hard-hit because this region was heavily mined during the conflict and continues to experience violence. Farmers from this region have been reluctant to cultivate fields that have not been cleared of mines, and many Rwandese are concerned about the overall insecurity of the region. In addition, Virunga National Park and its neighbor, Akagera National Park, are no longer protected because the government has little control in the area, making them vulnerable to further deforestation as local residents look for wood, the main source of fuel for most Rwandese. Indeed, deforestation has greatly increased since the genocide as camps for internally displaced people lead to the total removal of all trees and small vegetation in the immediate area—usually encompassing several miles. The vegetation is initially removed to make room for tents or lean-tos, and then the remaining wood is rapidly consumed as firewood.

Although it is estimated that 20 percent of land in Rwanda was not cultivated directly after the genocide, the new government is aware that land and food shortages continue to pose a threat, particularly as the population now holds not only 2 million returnees from the genocide but nearly 800,000 refugees who have returned from decades in effective exile. All of the returnees vie for land rights with the survivors of the genocide. To address this, the government has attempted to increase arable land by converting swampland into farms, promoting resettlement, and distributing seeds to those farmers who already have land. Resettlement consists of providing families with housing and several acres of land, primarily in the eastern region—the last less populated region of Rwanda but also the drier and less fertile region.

Churches, women's organizations, and some international aid agencies are promoting efforts to heal emotional wounds resulting from the 1994 genocide. Vice President Paul Kagame emphasized in 1996 in an interview, "People think it is a matter that we should have got over with and forgotten. But, no, no, no, no. We are dealing with human beings here."[6] The government has attempted to improve the cohesiveness of all Rwandese by eliminating reference to ethnicity on identity cards, eradicating reference to ethnicity in speeches or public documents, and ceasing gathering of data on ethnicity in education and government. It has established the National Reconciliation Commission to promote a common history by removing myths for all Rwandese while monitoring government programs to confront bigotry and promote national unity. Tens of thousands of people are imprisoned for allegedly participating in the genocide; however, many of them are in overcrowded jails without having been formally charged. The government is attempting to rebuild the judicial system so these prisoners can be brought to trial.

Attempts are also being made to decentralize decision-making power and lay the groundwork for some kind of multiparty democratic political system. The outlawing of ethnically based political parties is a major element of this effort. Social and economic support for villages in Rwanda is a key to assuring greater stability. Enforcing security for village residents in the face of revenge killings, coercion, and extortion is an ongoing challenge to political and civic leaders. Improving the material well-being of families is integral to rebuilding the social system of Rwanda and constitutes the most significant challenge to the country's leaders as well as their most valuable legacy.

Along with efforts to promote conflict resolution by international agencies, nongovernment organizations, and community-based organizations in Rwanda, there are substantial investments being made in promoting the health, education, and welfare of the Rwandese. Some of the investments are being made in HIV/AIDS education and treatment programs and the reconstruction of the social and physical infrastructure of the country relating to health and educational services. In some cases, excombatants are working together to promote development and peace initiatives at the local level in Rwanda.

FOOD FOR THOUGHT

The sources of threats to the Rwandese are interconnected. The environmental crisis stems from a lack of sustainable agriculture in a country that depends on agriculture for its subsistence yet lacks the economy to support an import/export system. The degradation of the environment, coupled with a growing population, leaves the Rwandese people vulnerable not only to severe and ongoing food shortages but also to the potential coercive tactics of politicians whose agenda for power consists of the literal elimination of their enemies—as was the case in 1994. The genocide radically altered the emotional, economic, and social lives of the nearly 8 million people now living in Rwanda. Postgenocide reconstruction is aimed at reconciling all Rwandese, for the key to their long-term cultural survival lies with finding a balance among population growth, food production, and social and material well-being. Finding this balance can reduce future threats to the social system of Rwanda that center around the potential for competition that in the past has been labeled "ethnic conflict"—a phrase that does not describe the struggle for survival by Rwandese both today and in the past.

Questions

1. What are the factors that led Rwanda to have such a high density of population?

2. Why is sustainable agriculture so important for Rwandese survival?

3. What are the legacies of colonialism for Rwandese social and political organization?

4. The 1994 genocide in Rwanda is often explained as a result of "ethnic conflict." What are some of the alternative explanations for why some Rwandese would choose to participate in genocidal violence?

5. What can the rest of the world do to help the Rwandese reconcile their differences and stabilize their social and economic system?

NOTES

1. We have defined the Rwandese here as the people of the country of Rwanda. The population of Rwanda consists of three major peoples, all of whom are considered endangered: the Hutu (89 percent), Tutsi (10 percent), and Twa (1 percent). The three groups speak Ruanda (Rwanda, Kinyarwanda, Orunyarwanda). There are intermarriages among the Hutu and Tutsi, blurring social, ethnic, and linguistic distinctions. The Hutu and Tutsi also have a common heritage and had a long history of coexistence, much of it peaceful.

2. The Rwandese as a group are some of the most endangered peoples in Africa. Not only were there between 500,000 and 800,000 Tutsi, Hutu, and Twa murdered systematically in 100 days in April–July, 1994, but there have been thousands of retaliatory killings since 1994, not only in Rwanda but also surrounding countries, including the Congo, Burundi, Tanzania, and Uganda. In the eastern Congo, which has seen over 2.7 million deaths in the past two decades of struggle, there have been tens of thousands of Rwandese who have been killed or who have disappeared, including Hutu, Tutsis, and Twa, among other groups.

3. Data on AIDS are from the World Health Organization and United Nations AIDS (UNAIDS).

4. Quote by Alexi Kayitsinga in Jeff Drumtra, *Life after Death: Suspicion and Reintegration in Post-Genocide Rwanda* (Washington, DC: U.S. Committee for Refugees, 1998), 37.

5. Alison des Forges, *Leave None to Tell the Story: Genocide in Rwanda* (New York: Human Rights Watch, 1999), 37–38; United Nations, *The United Nations and Rwanda 1993–1996* (New York: United Nations, Department of Public Information, 1996), 8.

6. Paul Kgame in Philip Gourevitch, "After Genocide—A Conversation with Paul Kagame," *Transition* 6, no. 4 (1996): 162–84.

RESOURCE GUIDE

Published Literature

Des Forges, Alison. *Leave None to Tell the Story: Genocide in Rwanda.* New York: Human Rights Watch, 1999.

Drumtra, Jeff. *Life after Death: Suspicion and Reintegration in Post-Genocide Rwanda.* Washington, DC: U.S. Committee for Refugees, 1998.

Keane, Fergal. *Season of Blood—A Rwandan Journey.* London: Viking, 1995.

Newbury, Catherine. *The Cohesion of Oppression: Clientship and Ethnicity in Rwanda, 1860–1960.* New York: Columbia University Press, 1998.

Preunier, Gerard. *The Rwanda Crisis—History of a Genocide.* New York: Columbia University Press, 1995.

Scherrer, Christian P. *Genocide and Crisis in Central Africa: Conflict Roots, Mass Violence, and Regional War.* Westport, CT: Praeger, 2001.

Rwandese

Taylor, Christopher. *Milk, Money, and Honey: Changing Concepts in Rwandan Healing.* Washington, DC: Smithsonian University Press, 1992.

Uvin, Peter. *Aiding Violence—The Development Enterprise in Rwanda.* West Hartford, CT: Kumarian Press, 1998.

Waller, David. *Rwanda—Which Way Now?* An Oxfam Country Profile. Oxford, United Kingdom: Oxfam, 1993.

Films and Videos

AIDS in Africa. 1990. Roger Pyke Productions. Filmmakers Library, 124 East 40th Street, New York, NY 10016. Telephone: (212) 808–4980. Fax: (212) 808–4983. Email: info@filmakers.com. Web site: www.filmakers.com.

Chronicle of a Genocide Foretold. 1996. 3 volumes. Directed by Danièle Lacourse and Yvan Patry. For more information, contact Alter-Ciné, 5371 Avenue de L'Esplanade, Montréal, Québec, Canada H2T 2Z8. Film about the genocide in Rwanda in 1994, shot over three years.

Forsaken Cries—The Story of Rwanda. 1997. 35 minutes. Amnesty International USA.

A Republic Gone Mad, Rwanda 1894–1994. 1996. Directed by Luc de Heusch. Available from First Run/Icarus Films, 32 Court Street, 21st Floor, Brooklyn, NY 11201. Telephone: (800) 876–1710. A film about the history of Rwanda from German rule in 1885 to the genocide in 1994.

Rwandan Nightmare. 1994. Directed by Simon Gallimore. Available from First Run/Icarus Films, 32 Court Street, 21st Floor, Brooklyn, NY 11201. Telephone: (800) 876–1710. Film about the genocide in Rwanda and how political struggle, not ethnic hatreds, led to it.

"Valentina's Nightmare." 1997. *Frontline*, April 1, 1997. Produced by Mike Robinson. Fergal Keane, Correspondent. Corporation for Public Broadcasting.

WWW Sites

Africa News Web Site
http://www.africanews.org/east/rwanda/

NetAid
http://www.netaid.com/survival project

Rwanda Hope Society
http://www.rwandahope.com

Rwanda Page
http://www.sas.upenn.edu/African_Studies/Country_Specific/Rwanda.html

United Nations Office for the Coordination of Humanitarian Affairs, Integrated Regional Information Networks (IRIN). Humanitarian information newsletter. http://www.reliefweb.int/IRIN/index.phtml

Organizations

African Rights
11 Marshallsea Road
London, SE1 1EP, United Kingdom
Telephone: (44) 171–717–1224
Fax: (44) 171–717–1240

Association for the Promotion of the Batwa
BP 2472
Kigali, Rwanda
Telephone/Fax: (250) 74761.

CAURWA (Communaute des Autochtones Rwandais) (Association for the Pro-
motion of the Batwa and the Association for the Global Development of the
Batwa of Rwanda).
P.O.Box 3809
Kigali, Rwanda
Telephone/Fax: (011) 250–776–40

Physicians for Human Rights
100 Broylston Street, Suite 702
Boston, MA 02116
Telephone: (671) 695–0041
Fax: (617) 695–0307
Email: phrusa@phrusa.org
Web site: http://www.phrus.org

Rwanda Hope Society,
206–207 West Hastings,
Vancouver, BC V6B 1H7, Canada
Telephone: (604) 488–0860
Fax: (604) 684–1296
Email: info@rwandahope.com
Web site: http://www.rwandahope.com

Chapter 12

The Somali of the Horn of Africa

Virginia Luling

CULTURAL OVERVIEW

The People

The Somali, who number an estimated 9.2 million, inhabit northeast Africa, the so-called Horn of Africa, where evidence suggests that their ancestors have lived for 2,000 or more years. Somali share physical and linguistic affinities with other northeastern Africans, including Ethiopians. Located as they are at the crossroads between Africa and the Middle East, the Somali have traces of Arab ancestry, though they tend to be taller and darker than most Arabs.[1]

The consensus among scholars is that what became the Somali people originated in what is now southern Ethiopia and from there gradually occupied most of the Horn of Africa, carrying with them the Somali language, which in the process evolved into its various dialects. The Somali displaced, mixed with, or incorporated other peoples, some of whom were hunter-gatherers, who were in the region already. Though there are varying theories about its timing, this process was evidently complete by the end of the first millennium A.D., by which time the Red Sea coast of Africa was Somali territory.

From there, beginning in the tenth century, some sections from two of the great branches of the Somali people, the Isaaq and the Daarood, gradually moved southward again, through the farming lands of the two major rivers, the Jubba and the Shabeelle, only reaching the present northeastern part of what is now Kenya in the nineteenth century, just before the British

arrived. There are now also Somali communities in many other parts of the world.

Until a generation ago, Somali was not a written language. The use of the Roman alphabet and the spelling system of the Somali language was made official by Siyad Barre's government in 1972.

In traditional society education was Islamic, and those who could read and write did so in Arabic. However, there is a rich tradition of poems and songs, composed and passed on orally.

The Setting

Contemporary Somalia is a large country of 257,773 square miles bordering the Indian Ocean and the Gulf of Aden and the Red Sea. The north of the Somali territory is mostly arid, having no permanent rivers. There are mountains along the Gulf of Aden, but the Indian Ocean coast is low lying, while the country inland rises toward the highlands of Ethiopia. In the south, along the two rivers Shabeelle and Jubba and in the plain between them, the land is more fertile, while further south still the country is once more arid.

To understand the present-day map of that part of the world it is necessary to go back to the colonial era. The country inhabited by the Somali was divided between four colonial powers: The northwest became the British protectorate of Somaliland, the center and the more fertile southern plain round the two rivers was an Italian colony, while the territory further to the south became part of British Kenya. In the extreme north, the French acquired a small enclave round the port of Djibouti, while much of the west of the territory inhabited by Somalis was incorporated into the Ethiopian Empire.

In 1961, both British Somaliland and the Italian Somalia gained their independence and amalgamated to form the Republic of Somalia. In spite of the desire among many Somalis to unite all their territories, the other three have remained separate: French Somaliland became (after various name changes) the ministate of Djibouti, independent but closely linked to France. The other ethnic group living in Djiboui are the Afar, a pastoral (herding) people related to the Somali. The western Somali territory remains under the control of Ethiopia, and the far south is part of the modern nation of Kenya. The borders of the Somali territory have been the subject of conflicts, something that has contributed to the current state of Somalia's political and territorial uncertainty.

Traditional Subsistence Strategies

Along the Jubba and Shabeelle rivers most of the people are farmers, living in villages and growing maize, sorghum, and various kinds of vegetables and in modern times also bananas, sugar, and cotton. Traditional cultivation is done with the hoe, and an ingenious system of intercropping (mixing of crops in the same plots) is used. In the plain between the rivers, cattle herding is combined with farming.

In the riverless north, however, as in the plains of northeast Kenya, the environment does not allow farming except in a few places. Here the typical strategy is nomadic herding, and the most valued animals are not cattle but camels, which can go for long periods without water. Small groups of related families camp together. Each group moves over a wide territory that they know well, but their movements are flexible, since they must follow the grass, which in turn depends on the sparse and unpredictable rainfall. Generally, families with children stay near a well or other water source with the sheep and goats, while the camels, since they need to be watered only rarely, are herded far off by the young men and boys, who grow to manhood in this tough school. Herding and farming are still the basis of most people's lives, even though nowadays about 22 percent of Somali are town dwellers.[2]

Although up to the colonial period the basic economy was subsistence based, trade in livestock and grain has been going on for centuries, both within Somalia and with the Arab lands. Caravan routes to Ethiopia and the African interior passed through the Somali country from the trading cities on the coast. It was the Italian colonists who created the banana plantations along the Jubba and Shabeelle rivers; these, together with livestock, became the country's principal export.

Social and Political Organization

These two ways of life, pastoral nomadism and farming, correspond to a fundamental division within the Somali people. The two groups show many differences of culture and speak markedly different dialects, which can even be described as separate languages.

In their own tradition, the two communities are seen as the descendants of two brothers, Samaale and Sab; Samaale is the ancestor of the pastoralists, Sab of the farmers. This system follows from the Somali method of tracing descent through the father's line. A Somali person, if asked his or her name, will give first his/her own name, followed by the names of his/her father and grandfather, for example, "Farah Mohamed Ali" or "Faduma Mohamed Ali." Many people can continue and name their great-grandfather, his father, and so on, backward for twenty generations to the founders of the Somali nation. So the whole of Somali society is plotted on the diagram of one immense family tree (though there can be disagreement over where particular groups fit in).

The "Sab" and "Samaale" are divided into six large groups. Those in the Samaale division are the 'Iise, Isaaq, Daarood, and Haawiye. Those

Potter in Buur-Heybe, Somalia. (Courtesy Dee Aker)

deriving from Sab are the Digil and Rahanweyn (or Reewiin). These groups are often referred to as clans, though they are more properly called groups of clans or clan-families. Each is made up of numerous clans, which in turn divide into subclans and major and minor lineages, down to the level of the extended family.

223

The system makes more sense if it is seen not so much as large groups that split into smaller ones but rather as small family groups that amalgamate into ever larger alliances according to their need. As one well-known modern Somali politician put it:

The extended family in the Somali case is the basic economic unit, adopted and adapted throughout the ages for the survival of its members. One family member may be a skilled worker in town, another a merchant, a third abroad in Europe or oil-rich Arabia, and another left to tend livestock in the hinterland. All their incomes buttress one another. As such the Somali extended family is a versatile system that is self-reliant . . . [but] . . . sometimes the extended family system may not have the carrying capacity to fully provide for the needs of its members.[2]

Then the larger groups, the upper levels of the system, come into play. As Somali intellectual Ibrahim Meygag Samatar put it in his reflections on the Somali struggle, "The more difficult the problem to be solved in extent and intensity, the higher the level called upon."[3]

Thus, lineages are combined into larger units (on the basis of sharing a more remote ancestor), and those into larger ones again, in a pyramidal structure. However, these larger groupings will fall apart into their constituents when the situation that led them to unite alters. Order and security are thus only achieved through the balance of opposing groups, and the effort to achieve this balance leads to the shifting political alliances that are a common feature of Somali politics. It is when the balance breaks down that conflict follows.

Though clan membership is determined by descent, strangers can be adopted, either as individuals or as groups, and their descendants will continue to live with the adopting clan. Among the Digil and Rahanweyn in the south this happens so often that most people belong, in effect, to two different clans at once, original and adoptive. It has been suggested that this contributes to the more peaceful society of the farming areas, since people of different origins have to learn to cooperate.

Somali pastoral society by tradition had no rulers—the "kings" or "sultans" of certain clans held positions of honor rather than power. Government was by the consultation and agreement of all the adult men of a group, with special consideration given to elders. Among the farming populations the local rulers had more real power, but here, too, they governed only in consultation with the elders and other adult men.

Religion and World View

The Somali lands lie near to those of the Arabs, and cultural contact between them goes back into prehistory. It is not surprising, therefore, that Somalis were among the first people to become converted to Islam, beginning in about the ninth century of the common era. The Somalis are orthodox Sunni; Islam is deeply embedded in their culture and is an essential part of their identity. In recent centuries, the influence of the Sufi orders, with their mysticism and ecstatic communal chanting, and their emphasis on brotherhood, has been very strong.

Within the overarching unity of Islam, and the idea of their shared ancestry, the division between pastoralists, on the one hand, and farmers and townspeople, on the other, is reflected in their cultures and attitudes toward life. The pastoral Somali have a strong warrior tradition and value toughness and independence; people from the farming areas are more peaceable and have a greater respect for authority. Pastoralists tend to see farmers as feeble and narrow in outlook; farmers see pastoralists as lawless and uncivilized. This is an intensely patriarchal (male-dominated) culture; yet women have often exercised much informal influence. Though Muslim, most Somali women have never gone veiled.

THREATS TO SURVIVAL

At the time of independence in the 1960s, there were great hopes of merging all clans in a united Somali identity; but competition for resources has continued to lead to disunity, which still goes along clan lines. The system of clans and lineages grew up in a traditional political environment, and it continues to operate in "modern" contexts, probably because it is, from the point of view of the individual, an effective method of organizing in a situation of competition. In traditional society, people used the descent system to compete for pasture and land and the control of trade routes. In the modern world they compete for governmental power and the wealth that goes with it. To quote one Somali commentator:

Because of the strong belief of almost the entire population in clanism as a necessary and inevitable political regime, no political organization with an open-door non-clan-based membership has yet appeared in the political landscape. Any member of the Somali society who aims for an active political participation is required to present himself as a clan member who plans to foster his clan interest. The notion of politics outside clan affiliations has no roots in our minds.[4]

Between 1969 and 1990, Somalia was under the dictatorship of President Mohamed Siyad Barre, who came to power in a coup in 1969. A number of opposition groups were formed, but though several of these organizations had started with a genuine attempt to start a non-clan-based movement, they ended by dividing along clan lines. However, they adopted ideological titles in English, shortened to sets of initials. For instance, the USC (United Somali Congress) represents the Haawiye clan-family, the SSDF (Somali Salvation Democratic Front) the Majeerteen clan, and the SPM (Somali Patriotic

Movement) the Ogaadeen clan. After Siyad Barre's fall, these organizations, which had little in common but their hostility to his rule, turned on one another. Somalia became a chaos of competing clan-based militias. The notorious intervention of the U.S.-led United Nations force UNOSOM (United Nations Operation in Somalia) in 1992 failed to achieve peace.

The principal prizes for which they fought were the control of the former capital Mogadishu and the rich productive land along the two rivers with their banana plantations. This "land grab" is nothing new. Large areas of agricultural land, originally mainly in the hands of small subsistence farmers, had been taken over for plantation agriculture by the Italian colonists. After independence, the existing plantations increasingly came into the hands of Somali entrepreneurs. At the same time, the expropriation of land from small farmers continued. Under Siyad Barre, plantation land was held mainly by his fellow clansmen and protégés; with his fall, "liberators" from other clans took them over. Either way, the earlier inhabitants of the land have lost out.

The fighting has mainly been between Samaale clans from the pastoral tradition (though many of the individuals concerned were from urban backgrounds). The Sab farmers and the minority populations, having no militia of their own, initially figured mainly as victims, though it was their land that was being fought over. They have been subject to plunder, massacre, and rape. It was not until the mid-1990s that the Digil and Rahanweyn formed their own militia and began to fight back and not until 1999 that they were backed by Ethiopia and gained real military successes.

Those who suffered worst were the minorities, whom the aggressors despised as not proper Somali. The part-Arab city populations were targeted for their real or supposed wealth, and the Jareer made easy victims because of their low status.

Current Events and Conditions

The Djibouti Peace Conference of 2000 succeeded in setting up a provisional national government (see below), but throughout the 1990s Somalia remained disunited, and episodic violence continued. The entry into the conflict in 1998 of Ethiopia and Eritrea altered the balance of forces.

One of the most dangerous factors in this civil conflict, with which any new government will have to deal, are the young men, urban unemployed or from a pastoral background, who have learned to live by the gun, finding it more profitable and more fun than herding camels. Rather than being at the service of their supposed commanders, they simply operate as bandits, for instance, extorting protection money from farmers and traders or taking control of water reservoirs and charging high sums to people who need to water their animals. Education has broken down, and a generation of teenagers is growing up who know no other life. Another set of people who, while they need peace, have reason to fear what a rule of law might bring are those who have taken over property—whether real estate in Mogadishu, pasture lands, or plantations. Those who have profited do not want the process reversed.

A significant, though not dominant, element in the Somali political scene are the Islamic "fundamentalist" movements, which have succeeded in setting up courts administering the Sharia law (formal Islamic law) in several areas. They appeal to those who see submission to the Islamic law in its fullness, as they understand it, as the solution to the lawlessness of the country. There is no dispute that where the Islamic courts rule, there is a measure of peace and security, and hence they enjoy much public support. Punishments such as amputation and stoning to death, though they may outrage opinion in Europe and America, are not unpopular with the Somali public, since they are seen as bringing safety to the streets. There are several such movements, all of them receiving funds from overseas but differing in their programs and objectives and in their degree of acceptance by the people. Al-Itihad Al-Islam, funded from Saudi Arabia, is the most prominent. As well as controlling parts of Somalia, its adherents have been active in Ethiopia, where they are an antigovernment force. This has led to the intervention of Ethiopia in Somalia.

Other States

In the Ethiopian region of the Ogaden (named after the Somali Ogaadeen clan who live there) the Ogaadeen National Liberation Front, which aims at secession, is keeping up a guerrilla campaign. In northeast Kenya the troubled relations of the Somali clans with one another, with other pastoral peoples, and with the Kenyan government are further exacerbated by armed militias raiding across the Somali border and by the large influx of refugees.

Diaspora

There has long been a Somali diaspora (the settling of people far from their homelands) of small overseas communities, especially in East Africa and the oil-rich Arab countries where people go in search of work. As a result of the civil war they have been joined by a great flood of refugees. An estimated 500,000 of these people are living in harsh conditions in refugee camps in Kenya and Ethiopia.

As well as in Africa and Arabia, there are now large Somali communities in the United States, Canada, Australia, Britain, Italy, and other European countries. For those who, escaping bullets and hunger, have succeeded in reaching Western countries, there are more subtle threats: the isolation, the difficulty of adjusting to an alien culture and a foreign language, the endless uncertainty of whether or not one will be allowed to stay, and the demoralization of not finding work and living on welfare. There are many women bringing up children alone, because their husbands are dead, or left behind, or have abandoned them in the new country. They cannot call on their own extended family for support, as they would at home. Alcohol and substance abuse have become problems, and there are cases of suicide, which in Somalia is almost unheard of. Children can grow up, lose their mother tongue language, and become alienated from their culture.

Environmental Crisis

The hardships of life in a war-torn country are made worse when the rains fail or are insufficient, leading to poor harvests and the death of livestock. The pastoral areas have always been subject to drought, which can sometimes be disastrous. The terrible famine of 1992, however, affected the most fertile part of Somalia, the two rivers and the plain between them. That was a man-made disaster; warring armies had robbed the farmers of their grain stores and drove them from their homes, preventing them from sowing a crop for the next season. When international agencies delivered relief grain, the misery was compounded because armed groups stole relief supplies or demanded high payments before they would allow them to reach their destinations.

Drought, aggravated by the violence, continues to be a threat, as does flooding in the river valleys. In 2000, it was estimated that at least 600,000 Somalis were affected by drought, while 600 to 700 families were made homeless by floods.

RESPONSE: STRUGGLES TO SURVIVE CULTURALLY

After 1991, Somalia became a "collapsed state." Could it ever, the Somalis asked, be put together again as one nation, and was it really worth trying? Was it the fate of Somalis to live instead in several tiny clan-based states?

If the region was to enjoy peace, it did not seem likely to come from agreement between the so-called warlords, the generals (mostly from Siyad Barre's army) and their clan-based militias. Ever since 1993 they had held repeated peace conferences, encouraged by the United Nations and other international bodies. These conferences passed many resolutions, but few were kept.

One view was that peace must come, if at all, from the grassroots, and indeed there have been many peace-making initiatives among those who do not wield the guns. There has, for instance, been an important resurgence of traditional political forms. Clan elders and "sultans," whose political role was devalued under the centralized state, are showing that they can still play an important part, negotiating with armed groups and acting as peacemakers. Women and women's groups are prominent among those working for peace, both within Somali and in the diaspora.

Both in Somalia and in the diaspora, the despised "Jareer" people and other minorities are showing a new political consciousness and militancy. An area of relative peace and stability is the northwest, the land inhabited mainly by the Isaaq pastoral clans, which was formerly the British Protectorate of Somaliland. This area suffered terribly when its people rebelled against Siyad Barre's rule in the 1980s, and the capital Hargeisa was flattened and thousands of the population fled. In 1991, after Siyad's fall, it declared itself an independent republic, readopting the frontiers and the name of the old Somaliland. Even though the Somaliland Republic has not been granted international recognition, it has achieved a remarkable degree of reconstruction and prosperity and has established a working administration, including police and defense forces, a judiciary, and a parliament incorporating the traditional elders as an upper house.

Another more peaceful area is the northeast, which in 1999 declared itself an autonomous region under the name of "Puntland" (the ancient Egyptian name for the land that is generally identified as Somalia), though with the declared aim of uniting with the rest of Somalia if ever a stable government was achieved. The port of Bosaso enjoys a boom economy, based on export of livestock. It remains to be seen, however, how long this stability will last.

In June–August 2000, the Somali National Peace Conference brought together more than 2,000 participants based on clan representation in Djibouti. It was the first conference where the warlords did not have control of the conference agenda, and it set up a Transitional National Assembly (TNA), attempting a balanced representation of all the main clan groups including Jareer and minority groups, with a special provision for women representatives. Abdiqasim Salad Hasan was elected by the TNA as president and announced his decision to embark on national reconstruction. The conference and the TNA, however, have been rejected by Somaliland and Puntland and by elements in the rest of the country as insufficiently representative. The future will show whether this fragile structure will succeed in restoring peace to the nation.

Meanwhile, among the Somali communities abroad, many people have established themselves in work or business and settled down to become productive members of their host nations. Such people are generally contributing generously to their relatives at home, and the economy in Somalia is boosted by remittances from abroad.

Cultural Life

In spite of the violence, economic life goes on and even thrives. The center of Mogadishu may be bombed out, but the markets on the outskirts are busy; with a well-functioning, privately run satellite service, it is far easier to telephone Somalia than it was before the war.

Community-based organizations and human rights organizations are active. Somali cultural life is very much alive. Poems and songs are composed and circulated on cassette. All over Somalia, there are local newspapers; even in war-torn Mogadishu, there are several daily papers, produced on photocopiers. In the Somali diaspora newspapers, magazines, and books are being published, and there are a number of Somali Web sites. Among Somali communities abroad, plays and musical performances are popular.

An important new departure in the diaspora is the growth of writing by and about minority groups, often in their languages. The Somali language was first given an official written form under the Siyad Barre government. This was an important forward step; but it was inevitably a form of the dialect of the pastoral Samaale' that became the "standard" Somali language. The dialect of the Digil and Rahanweyn was neglected. However, there are now publications in the language. Exiles from the city of Brava have begun to publish records of their distinctive culture, history, and language.

FOOD FOR THOUGHT

Somalia has come to be seen as a prime example of a "collapsed state." And yet this is what was previously hailed as the most "unified" state in Africa, with a single culture, language, and religion. It is easy to talk as though people fight one another "because" they have different religions or languages or are of different colors or ethnic groups. None of these differences apply in Somalia. Instead, there are rivalries between clans and alliances of clans. Somalia reminds us to distinguish between the underlying causes of state collapse and the fault lines along which the collapse occurs.

Looking at Somalia can also, however, remind us how, even without anything we would generally recognize as government, people can run their lives and settle their problems and how a lively cultural life can continue even under the shadow of the gun.

Questions

1. What is it about Somali society that makes the formation of a unified state so difficult? Compare what has happened to the Somalis, who were allowed to form an independent nation state, with people such as the Tuareg of the Sahara or the Kurds of the northern Middle East, who have not been able to do so.

2. What does traditional Somali society suggest about the way a society may develop in different environments? Are differences in environment the whole story, or are there other factors?

3. Is it appropriate for the "international community" to intervene to bring peace to a warring state? What are the problems?

4. Think about a young Somali person growing up in a Western city like Seattle, Minneapolis, or Toronto. What sort of problems, conflicts, choices, would he or she face?

5. Discuss the role of Islam in Somali life. How does Somali society compare with other Muslim nations? How would their history be different if they had remained "pagan" up to colonial times?

NOTES

1. The Somali are classified by some anthropologists as Cushites (or "Hamites"), peoples who are located in the northeastern part of Africa and the Horn, including what is now Ethiopia, Somalia, Djibouti, and Eritrea. They speak various languages that are part of the Afro-Asiatic family, and they share some other cultural, physical, and linguistic affinities with the other populations of northeastern Africa. For information on their genetic backgrounds, see L. Luca Cavalli-Sforza, Paolo Menozzi, and Alberto Piazza, *The History and Geography of Human Genes* (Princeton, NJ: Princeton University Press, 1994), 165, 171–74; see also I.M. Lewis, "The Northern Pastoral Somali of the Horn," in *Peoples of Africa: Cultures of Africa South of the Sahara*, ed. James L. Gibbs, Jr. (New York: Holt, Rinehart and Winston, 1965), 321–22.

2. Data obtained from fieldwork in Somalia by the author. See also Harold D. Nelson, ed., *Somalia: A Country Study* (Washington, DC: U.S. Government Printing Office, 1982), 67, and http://www.unsomalia.org.

3. Personal communication by a Somali politician, Mogadishu, Somalia, 1993.

4. Ibrahim Meygag Samatar, "Reflections on the Somali Struggle," in *Mending Rips in the Sky* (Lawrenceville, NJ: Red Sea Press, 1997), 339.

5. John G. Sommer, *Hope Restored? Humanitarian Aid in Somalia, 1990–1994* (Washington, DC: Refugee Policy Group, 1994).

RESOURCE GUIDE

Published Literature

Ahmed, Ali Jimale, ed. *The Invention of Somalia*. Lawrenceville, NJ: Red Sea Press, 1995.

Aman. *Aman: The Story of a Somali Girl*. New York: Vantage Books, 1994.

Besteman, Catherine Lowe and Lee V. Cassanelli, eds. *The Struggle for Land in Southern Somalia: The War Behind the War*. Boulder: Westview Press and Haan Associates, 1996.

Cassanelli, Lee V. *The Shaping of Somali Society: Reconstructing the History of a Pastoral People*. Philadelphia: University of Pennsylvania Press, 1982.

Lewis, I.M. *A Pastoral Democracy: A Study of Pastoralism and Politics among the Northern Somali of the Horn of Africa.* London: Oxford University Press for the International African Institute, 1961.

———. *Saints and Somalis: Popular Islam in a Clan-Based Society.* London: Haan Associates, 1998.

Loughran, Katheryne S., John L. Loughran, John William Johnson, and Said Sheikh Samatar. *Somalia in Word and Image.* Washington, DC: Foundation for Cross Cultural Understanding in Cooperation with Indiana University Press, Bloomington, 1986.

Omar, Mohamed Osman *The Road to Zero: Somalia's Self-Destruction.* London: Haan Associates, 1992.

Samatar, Ahmed I., ed. *The Somali Challenge: From Catastrophe to Renewal.* Boulder: Lynne Rienner Publishers, 1994.

Simons, Anna. *Networks of Dissolution: Somalia Undone.* Boulder, CO: Westview Press, 1995.

Films and Videos

Somalia, a Paradise Destroyed. 1997. Produced by DHM TV Productions, London. The film can be obtained from Abdullahi Dool, 26 Hamilton Way, North Finchley, London N3 1AN, UK.

Somalia: Good Intentions, Deadly Results. 1997. Produced by KR Video and the *Philadelphia Inquirer.* Based on the *Philadelphia Inquirer* newspaper series "Blackhawk Down," 1997.

WWW Sites

BBC Somali Service
http://www.bbc.co.uk/somali/inenglish.shtm/

Somali Net
http://somalinet.com/

Nomad Net
http://www.netnomad.com/

Organizations

Anglo-Somali Society
1 Linkway
London SW20 9AT, United Kingdom
Email: dbrooks@park.demon.co.uk
USA Agent: John W. Johnson
4408 Stephens Drive
Bloomington, IN 47408–2473
Email: johnson@indian.edu
Web site: http://www.zyworld.com/AngloSomaliSociety/Home.htm

Inter-Riverine Studies Association
P.O. Box 1005
Mount Pleasant, MI 48804

Scottish Somali Action
Wilkie House
37 Guthrie Street
Edinburgh EH1 1JG
Telephone: 44–131 650 6315
Fax: 44–131–650 6328
Email: sarah.ssa@btinternet.com

Somali Intellectuals Forum
Totten Hall, Ferdinand Street
London NW1 8EX, United Kingdom
Telephone: 44–171 916 6854
Fax: 44–171 916 6859
Email: Maxamed@aol.com

Somali Voice of Women for Peace, Reconciliation and Political Rights
790 Eglinton Avenue W, # 205
Toronto, Ontario, N5N 1G2, Canada
Telephone/Fax: 001 4326 783 3269
Email: bodaye@sprint.ca

Survival International
11–15 Emerald Street
London WC1N 3QL, United Kingdom
Telephone: (44) (0)20 7242 1441
Fax: (44) (0)20 7242 1771
Email: info@survival-international.org
Web site: http://www.survival-international.org

Chapter 13

The Tuareg

Susan J. Rasmussen

CULTURAL OVERVIEW

The People

The Tuareg, a seminomadic, Islamic people who speak Tamajaq, a language in the Berber family of Afro-Asiatic languages, live in the contemporary African nation–states of Niger, Mali, Algeria, Libya, and Burkina Faso. The aristocratic Tuareg are believed to be descendants of North African Berbers who originated in the Fezzan region of Libya. They later migrated across the Sahara Desert and into border areas.

Their traditional society was stratified (divided into social categories or "strata" that were ranked or arranged hierarchically), each having a specialized, inherited occupation. Gradually, the nobles absorbed the sedentary (settled) farming peoples from south of the Sahara Desert into their society through processes of trade and conquest, including slavery. Many former slaves eventually became integrated into Tuareg culture and society through upward socioeconomic mobility, inheritance of property from their aristocratic owners, and intermarriage.

The term *Tuareg*, of Arabic origin, is the most commonly used name for this culture/ethnic group today. They are also called Kel Tamajaq ("People who speak Tamajaq") and Kel Tagelmust ("People with the custom of the men's face-veil/turban"), the latter referring to the important practice of men wearing a distinctive headdress partially veiling the face, a sign of modesty and respect. Tuareg women, on the other hand, do not wear a veil. Within their home regions, Tuareg are known by more specific names designating their different political and social groupings of regional confederations and clans. In the countryside today, Tuareg are sometimes identified by reference to their membership in stratified groups or social strata, for example, *ima-jeghen*, denoting "nobles/aristocrats," or *inadan*, denoting "smith/artisan." These social categories or strata are similar, though not identical, to the Hindu castes of India. Contemporary Tuareg society therefore comprises speakers of Tamajaq and related dialects who are of diverse social origins but feel a unity through their common language and culture.

The Setting

The Saharan regions where Tuareg originated—southern Algeria, western Libya, eastern Mali, and northern Niger—are still the areas where they predominate today. In the latter part of the twentieth century, many Tuareg migrated to rural and urban areas farther south—into the Sahel, the semi-arid areas bordering the Sahara Desert, and toward the West African coast—due to drought, famine, and political tensions with the central state governments of Mali and Niger. A few Tuareg have immigrated to France, the former colonial power in these regions.

The Saharan and Sahelian regions, where most Tuareg still live, are therefore the principal "biomes" or climate zones to which their culture has adapted. The terrain includes volcanic mountains, flat desert plains, rugged savanna or grasslands, desert-edge borderlands, and desert oases of date palms, other fruit trees, and cereal crops where agriculture is possible only with daily irrigation. The major mountain ranges are the Ahaggar Mountains in Algeria and the Air Mountains in Niger. Temperatures range from 39°F at night in the brief cold season, with high winds and sandstorms from December to March, to upward of 129°F during the day in the hot season. There is a short and unreliable rainy season between June and September; annual precipitation often amounts to less than ten inches.

Pastures for livestock animal herds have been shrinking, due in part to what has become known as "desertification," degradation of habitats as a result of population growth, land use intensification, and droughts, as was seen most recently in 1969–1973 and 1984. Droughts brought much suffering to many Tuareg, who lost animal herds. Some people had to sell their possessions and migrate to places in search of food and work and were forced to compete for a dwindling number of jobs.

Before French military conquest of the Sahara, Tuareg communities were predominantly rural and nomadic, with a few urban centers of trade and Islamic scholarship such as Agadez (in contemporary Niger) and Timbuktu (in contemporary Mali). The Tuareg, traditionally nomadic stock breeders who raised camels, goats, sheep, donkeys, and in some areas, cattle, came to prominence in the fourteenth century as caravan traders when routes to salt, gold, ivory, and slave markets in Africa, Europe, and the Middle East sprang up through their lands. Today most Tuareg are seminomadic and

tices. For example, they did not seclude or veil women, men and women interacted with considerable freedom in public, and allegedly, they did not always perform ritual washing ablutions before praying. Local tradition did not require female chastity before marriage, women could visit and receive male visitors after marriage, and women could initiate divorce. While female chastity before marriage appears now to be more important, particularly in some clans of Islamic scholars, women still own property, visit and travel freely, and inherit and manage property. But, as previously mentioned, some inheritance is disputed when some men attempt to impose Koranic law. In Islamic observances, men are more consistent about saying all the prescribed prayers. Men also use more Arabic loan words, whereas women tend to use Tamajaq terms. Both sexes report that women are "afraid" to touch the Koran.[2] But there is no formal restriction against women becoming practicing Islamic scholars.

Many rituals combine pre-Islamic and Islamic symbols. For example, in many rites of passage such as babies' name-days and weddings, there are references to ancient female ancestresses. Many myths and folktales refer to spirits, important culture heroes/heroines from before Islam, and the important relationship between brothers and sisters in ancient matrilineal (female-ancestry) clans, as well as those from Koranic legends about Islamic heroes. Spirits are mentioned in both the Koran and in pre-Islamic mythology and world view. There is the belief that people can become possessed by an occupying spirit of either type; each requires healing by a different means. Prominent healing specialists are also religious specialists. Islamic scholars heal with verses from the Koran. Herbal medicine healing specialists, predominantly elderly women, give ritual offerings to tree spirits before gathering their medicinal barks and leaves. There are also references to pre-Islamic beliefs in the local art: For example, many silver jewelry pendants made by smith/artisans are decorated with designs representing natural environmental features of mythical and historical importance, such as the triangular shapes representing fertility figures and etchings representing various animal footprints. These symbols recur throughout Tuareg oral history, poetry, and songs.

THREATS TO SURVIVAL

Demographic Trends

The total population of Tamajaq speakers who identify themselves culturally as Tuareg has been estimated at between 750,000 and 1.2 million. Tuareg constitute about 8 percent each of the populations of the countries of Niger and Mali. In nations where the Tuareg live, the different cultural/ethnic groups tend to be distributed unevenly, and the regions where they reside have contrasting resources. In many cases, these regions received less attention from colonial and postcolonial powers than other, more densely populated, areas.

Much conflict between Tuareg and their neighboring peoples is demographic and regional in basis. For example, in Niger the total population is approximately 8,702,800 (1994 estimate), and the total area is 489, 191 square miles, with a population density of 17.8 persons per square mile. This population is distributed unevenly, and it increases gradually from a density of less than one per square mile in the northern Agadez Department or province to thirty-three per square mile in the southern Maradi Department or near the border with Nigeria. Niger's populations of diverse cultural/ethnic groups, in addition to the Tuareg, include the Zarma-Songhay; Hausa; Peul (also called Fulani), Kanuri (also known as Beri-Beri and Manga); Tubu; and Arab peoples. The Hausa predominate numerically, making up approximately 53 percent of the population, followed by the Zarma-Songhay (21 percent), the Peul or Fulani (10 percent), the Tuareg (8–10 percent), the Kanuri or Beri-Beri (4.4 percent), and then Arab, Tubu, and a few Gourmantche who together constitute approximately 1.6 percent of the total population.[1] While many of these groups, like the Tuareg, have migrated into all regions of the country, traditionally the more pastoral nomadic and seminomadic Tuareg and Peul have predominated in the north; and the others, many of whom are sedentary agriculturalists like the Zarma-Songhay, Hausa, and Kanuri, have predominated in the southwest, south, and southeast, respectively.

What is striking in the contemporary Tuareg cultural predicament are several conditions or current "realities" of life at the beginning of the twenty-first century. First, census reports between 1987 and 1996 indicate that the Tuareg population has actually declined, thereby suggesting that Tuareg constitute an "endangered" people and culture, in that their physical existence is threatened.[3] Second, while their culture remains vital and dynamic, their political influence has diminished and their autonomy (capacity for self-determination) has been threatened in recent nation–state politics. Third, Tuareg constitute a cultural/ethnic minority in all the nation–states where they reside today. They are not only a minority in terms of their population size but also with respect to their lower degree of power, access to economic resources, and control over their own destiny.

The cultural, economic, and political predicaments intensified in recent years, especially during the Tuareg nationalist/separatist armed rebellion against the governments of Mali and Niger from 1990 to 1995. The immediate catalyst for this movement was a massacre of Tuareg civilians by some militia at the village of Tchin Tabaradan in central Niger in 1990. Its roots, however, are more complex and involve longer-term processes.

In precolonial eras, Niger included regions of several traditional Sudanic African polities—kingdoms, empires, or "traditional states," including Mali, Songhay, Kanem, Bornu, and the Hausa-Fulani emirate states. These were characterized by varying degrees of centralization: The Tuareg system fell between the extremes of decentralized lineage (clan)-based local bureaucracies under the Songhay and the more centralized Hausa emirate system. All of these polities were stratified or subdivided into ranked, hereditary occupational groups who were supposed to marry within their own social strata groupings.

Tuareg society cannot be treated in isolation, for there has been long-standing contact between Tuareg with other populations of North and West Africa for many centuries. The Tuareg obtained some grain and dates by taxing sedentary oases peoples. They also traded for well over half of their food and material requirements as they moved through the Sudan and Sahel region along the Saharan frontier. The Tuareg invested in diverse activities, ranging from stock breeding to transport, landownership, and commercial brokerage investments that crossed cultural boundaries, however defined. Commercial networks that united the desert and savanna areas assumed a particularly critical importance in disasters such as drought. These economic ties provided "safety valves" for migrating desert Tuareg in their efforts to cope with an environment that was temporarily unable to support them. Even in prosperous years, however, people of the desert and savanna were usually bound together through mutually beneficial transactions. The Tuareg and their neighbors have interacted within a large, composite society and economy in which cultural distinctions often reflected degrees of economic specialization. There has been much movement across borders during periods of interdependence and peaceful trade, as well as during times of tension and armed conflict.

In the past, the Tuareg sometimes raided and enslaved sedentary settled peoples, although the dominant mode of interaction was that of cooperation and peaceful trade. Furthermore, the communities where Tuareg raided for slaves also had slaves themselves. For example, at the time of the French colonial military conquest, Zarma-Songhay society was made up of approximately two-thirds slaves who were predominantly war-captives. Evidence suggests that raiding of populations may have occurred more frequently on the eastern and western fringes of the desert than in the central Sudanic region to the south. In the eastern and western peripheral areas, economic interaction between nomadic pastoralists and settled farming people was less intense than in the central area. As a consequence, the Tuareg had less of a stake in the welfare of their western sedentary Songhay neighbors than they did in the case of more central Sudanic neighbors such as the Hausa.

The Tuareg traded intensively with the Hausa, with whom they resided for longer periods on trading expeditions into (present-day) southern Niger and Nigeria. Yet the Tuareg often promoted their interests by alliances with the Songhay as well. For example, as allies in the salt trade, some Tuareg chiefs were given daughters of the *askiya* (the ruling dynasty of the Songhay empire) in marriage. Furthermore, religion was not a serious source of conflict; for despite intermittent military expansion from Islamic puritanical movements like the one headed by the Hausa-Fulani reformer Ousmane Dan Fodio in the nineteenth century, the Tuareg and their neighbors remained Muslim. The population of Niger is well over 95 percent Muslim, across all geographic regions. Nonetheless, the Tuareg historically often clashed with the Songhay and other groups, in precolonial as well as colonial and postcolonial times.

The precolonial African Sudanese empires like the Songhay, at the crossroads of the Sahara and Sahel, attempted to exercise some control over trade throughout the desert itself in order to shift economic relationships in their favor. Their military concerns were reflected in the recurrent pattern of expansion by strong states on the desert fringe. A sedentary farming-based state near the desert would sometimes seek to control the desert ports and long sections of the desert-savanna frontier. Political control throughout history has tended to oscillate between the nomads of the desert and the kingdoms/empires of the Sudanic areas south of the desert.

Whenever these latter states controlled the southern termini of the Saharan trading network, they extended their influence into the Sahara. The nomads, by their own choice, became incorporated into this hegemonic state at times. When the state's power declined and it was no longer able to protect trade in the desert-Sahel interface, the nomads pressed south into the Sahel border zone. Military invasion into the desert was almost impossible since the Sudanese troops were no match for the Tuareg camelry. On the other hand, the Tuareg camels became ineffective in the more humid climates in the south. Thus there was a delicate military balance, in precolonial times, between the Tuareg and the Songhay, since each side had a distinct advantage within its own ecological zone.

Environmental and Sociocultural Crises

Ecology, economics, and demography have caused some of these conflicts that have had a regional rather than solely an "ethnic" basis. Historical and political processes have further contributed to these conflicts, shaping ecology, economics, and demography, on the one hand, and on the other, also being shaped by them. Thus, the many reasons for threat to Tuareg survival must be considered within a more interconnected network. Oversimplified explanations such as a "single cause" or biased assumptions such as "racism" or "colonial exploitation" are inadequate for understanding their predicament.

Niger is one of the poorest countries in the world, with a GNP (gross national product) per capita of U.S.$220 (1995). Annual rainfall varies greatly and is irregular. The northern zone of Niger is devoted primarily to pastoral nomadism with some oasis gardening. As one moves from north to south, the population density increases, camels decrease, cattle increase, and the southern zone is devoted more to agropastoralism. Farther south the economy becomes essentially agricultural. Niger is mostly a flat country, except for the few Saharan mountain ranges situated in the North. It is also landlocked and lacks ocean ports. Minerals such as uranium and phosphates, now mined in the northern region around the town of Arlit, were discovered only recently.

The predominantly peaceful trading networks across the Sahara and Sahel between the Tuareg and their neighbors first became disrupted when the centers of African trading began to shift during the fifteenth century. Along the west coast of West Africa, transatlantic trade was dominated by the European colonial powers and slave traders. The interior region and its empires subsequently began a decline because they had been very dependent on trans-Saharan trade. For the Tuareg, this meant a diminishing of their once prominent role in the trans-Saharan trading network. When the French colonized the areas where Tuareg lived in the late nineteenth and early twentieth centuries, their powers were further curtailed by new restrictive policies.

Niger under French colonial rule (from the early twentieth century until 1960) was part of French West Africa or French West Sudan. The French administrators at first believed this area to be lacking in resources. They neglected the country's development, and they treated it solely as a military buffer state to protect their colonial interests from other European colonial powers in Africa. Not a single mile of paved road or railroad was built between 1922 and 1944. No efforts were made to encourage river transportation. Almost no money was spent on social services, and the veterinary service, so vital to livestock, was established only in 1927. The literacy rate remained among the lowest in Africa. The motive that finally prompted the French to build schools was to provide the administration with candidates who could fill minor posts. At first, higher education opportunities were limited for all the peoples of Niger. Nigerois were barred, for example, from attending levels beyond the *école normale* (teaching college). In 1940, there were only 631 African functionaries comprising all categories and grades, and the majority were non-Nigerois. Among the educated Nigerois at the time, the most numerous were from the Zarma-Songhay group.

The Tuareg resisted the French longer than other cultural/ethnic groups in the area. The French found it relatively easy to subdue the Zarma-Songhay of the southwest along the Niger River, given their more accessible geographic location, their more decentralized sociopolitical system, and their large number of slaves. The servile population, however, had less to lose than the aristocratic Zarma-Songhay rulers under the new colonial administration. The capital, previously located in Zinder in the eastern Hausa region, was in 1927 moved to Niamey in the Zarma-Songhay region along the Niger River, and up to the present day this continues to be the capital and seat of government in Niger. Most presidents and government functionaries, until very recently, have also come from the southern and southwestern regions of Niger, as well as from the settled farming Hausa and Zarma-Songhay groups. Ethnicity, therefore, constitutes an important element of recurring disunity and conflict in contemporary Niger. Apart from the intermittent military conflict between the Zarma-Songhay and the Tuareg in the nineteenth century, the peoples of Niger have little historical basis for exclusively ethnically rooted hostility and conflict in their precolonial past. Rather, contemporary cultural/ethnic conflict stems largely from deliberate decisions of Niger's colonial and postcolonial rulers and as the result of different responses by the various groups to colonial economic and educational policies.[4]

It was the pastoral nomadic Tuareg in the north who rebelled against the French in the Senoussi Revolt in 1917. The French squashed the Tuareg with retaliatory massacres and massive population relocation. The French colonial administration thereafter tended to discriminate against the northern, pastoral nomadic Tuareg population. For example, only a few clinics and nomadic boarding schools were established in the northern regions. Coercive methods were used to force children into those schools.[5] This antinomadic, anti-Tuareg, and antinorthern bias was inherited by some, though not all, postcolonial military and government officials, who were predominantly from the Zarma-Songhay and Hausa farming populations to the south and west of the Tuareg core or "home" space. Although all regions in Niger have suffered from poverty and climatic uncertainties, nonetheless, historical factors have produced tensions between the different cultural/ethnic groups and greater marginalization of the Tuareg, particularly those in northern Niger. Southern farmers were gradually forced to settle more in northern border lands near the Tuareg. Their soils had been depleted by cash cropping cotton and peanuts, and the French had imposed heavy taxes. This crowding and quest for new farmlands along the borders of Tuareg lands has caused some tensions between the nomads and the farmers. There was also some bitterness when the freed slaves of the Tuareg, popularly called Buzu in Niger, were given some of these lands in the middle of present-day Niger, on the borderlands between the pastoral nomadic and agricultural zones in the 1920s.

Development agency programs, furthermore, tended to work against the Tuareg needs in their misguided efforts to maximize short-term gains at the expense of long-term benefits. Some French agencies installed gasoline-powered pumps, and nomads clustered their livestock around these water points. This crowding disrupted the delicate ecological balance of water and pasture, increasing the distance between them and bringing about the deaths of many animal herds. Overgrazing of animals and the chopping of trees for firewood also contributed to social tensions, erosion of farmlands, and expansion of the desertlike conditions, thereby diminishing the natural resources and destroying the protective local adaptations that had previously been effective in dealing with the harsh environment. Consequently, Niger's already meager resources were further reduced. Forced sedentarization of nomads also contributed to bitterness. Medical services, for example, often came "with political strings attached." During immunization campaigns and food relief distributions efforts, for example, people were forced to come into settled towns and listen to political speeches in order to receive services and goods. An additional problem was that many medical personnel were, until recently, from distant regions and from other cultural/ethnic groups. Many local patients found these individuals unsympathetic.

In sum, by the twentieth century, the French had brought the Tuareg under their colonial domination. As a result, Tuareg forfeited their rights to tariff collection and protection services for trans-Saharan camel caravans. Also, as already noted, ocean routes had diverted much of the trade to the West African coast. After independence and the establishment of nation–states in their region in the early 1960s, the Tuareg continued to lose economic strength and political power. They had resented first French and later central-state government schools and taxes, suspicious of them as strategies to forcibly make them settle down. Today the Tuareg still tend to be underrepresented in jobs and central government, although since the signing of the Peace Pact between nationalist/separatist rebels and government in April 1995, this situation has been changing.

RESPONSE: STRUGGLES TO SURVIVE CULTURALLY

Human Rights Concerns and the Politics of Rebellion

The early decades of the twentieth century saw a number of rebellions. Even with the approach of independence in West Africa, several important Tuareg chiefs in Niger and Mali attempted to form a federation to keep themselves outside the political control of the southern regions. In Mali in the 1960s, there were several tax revolts, notably around the Kidal region. These were, however, unsuccessful and resulted in massacres of civilians. In Niger, the sultan of Air in Agadez was deposed in favor of his son and exiled to Birni-n-Konni, while another traditional Tuareg leader in Agadez, the *anastafidet*, was likewise deposed and exiled to Tillaberi, replaced by his brother. In Niger, however, in contrast to Mali, such incidents did not lead to further agitation on the part of the Tuareg. During the Hamani Diori regime (1960–1974), which immediately followed Niger's independence from France, the Tuareg were treated with special consideration. One of their traditional chiefs, the *amenukal*, served in the cabinet as a minister of Saharan affairs and was often resident in the northern town of Agadez as well. Free salt, tea, and sugar were distributed to the migrating clans during their annual gathering with their animals at a salt lick near the oasis of In Gall. The northern Saharan Air Mountain region was administered with a gentle hand—part of a general awareness of Tuareg sensitivities and their potential volatility.

Following the 1974 coup d'état by military officers against Diori, the Seyni Kountche regime "regularized" policies toward the Tuareg. Though a number of Tuareg joined President Kountche's cabinet in key posts (including one, Alghabid, as prime minister), many Tuareg chiefs tended to look back with nostalgia to the Diori days when Air was, in many ways, free from southern interference. In 1980, Libya allegedly tried to foment the growth of separatist nationalism among Niger's Tuareg following the break in diplomatic relations with Niamey.[6] A number of Tuareg civil servants were enticed by Libyan blandishments and left for Tripoli, the Libyan capital. On at least three occasions Diori's self-exiled son, with Libyan support, led groups of Tuareg in assaults against some Nigerois military installations in the Air region in an effort to attain a comeback for his father. After one armed incident in 1985, Kountche expelled from Niger tens of thousands of "non-Nigerois" Tuareg (difficult to distinguish in reality, because of their nomadism). This action indirectly set the stage for the five-year Tuareg nationalist/separatist rebellion, which broke out between 1990 and 1991.

In Mali, in contrast to Niger, until recent "democratization," the Tuareg were severely repressed, and incidents of political violence against them were frequent. Indeed, to some extent the recent rebellion in Niger had its origins in events earlier in Mali, such as the tax revolts and reprisals for them, as well as in the 1990 Tchin Tabaradan massacre in Niger. In the 1970s, there were allegations that the government of Mali prevented food from being distributed to Tuareg.[7] There have been attacks in Tuareg-owned businesses in towns in Mali, particularly in Timbuktu.

In northern Niger, grievances against Niamey began to increase in the 1970s with the greater intrusion of central government into Air, as the uranium and other mining enterprises were set up in and around Arlit, northwest of Agadez. Much of the workforce in these mines was Tuareg. Although employment provided an invaluable source of income, their cultural alienation and marginalization from cherished values were problematic. For example, Tuareg men had to remove their face-veils in the mine pits, something that males also had to do in schools when they were photographed for identification cards. This produced a kind of "love/hate" relationship between Tuareg and these institutions. Furthermore, the influx of tourists, while an important source of income, nonetheless irritated many Tuareg who resented that the tourists wandered around "without respect" in the region immodestly dressed, discarded their garbage in the environment, and sometimes desecrated Islamic tombs and prayer grounds.[8]

In the 1980s, a bout of further repression in neighboring Mali and

Kountche's expulsion of tens of thousands of Tuareg from Niger after the armed incident solidified a desire to attain their former autonomy. Tuareg expressed this desire in a variety of ways, including the emergence of the nationalist/separatist liberation movements at the onset in Mali and later in Niger. The goal was to establish a "Saharan Republic," or an autonomous Azawak (a region of nomadic migrations stretching across central Niger and into Mali). Although not all Tuareg supported the rebellion—indeed, some opposed it and favored compromise—it was a powerful political movement and still retains strong support in some regions, with sporadic continued armed conflicts even after the 1995 Peace Pact.

The nationalist/separatist rebellion had its immediate origins during the 1984 drought, when some Tuareg men, calling themselves *ichumar* ("an unemployed person"), left for Libya, where they received military training and weapons. In the early 1990s they returned to their homes and demanded autonomy. The 1990 Tchin Tabaradan massacre led many more Tuareg to take up armed resistance against the governments of Mali and Niger. The 1990 massacre took place against a broader background of simmering conflicts that included an assault by a small number of Tuareg to capture arms and the return to Niger of tens of thousands of Tuareg who were expelled by Mali. These Tuareg held grievances against Niamey's failure to fulfill government promises to assist in their resettlement. Funds earmarked for Tuareg assistance allegedly were stolen by local officials.[9] Many young Tuareg men had become resentful toward the central government over the past several decades.

There had been growing discussion in Tuareg political and intellectual circles of their marginalization and the sidelining of their interests. There were repression, massacres, and attempts to stamp out Tuareg expressions of identity and desire for greater political participation, culminating in the massacre by Nigerois militia of reportedly several thousand Tuareg civilians. This massacre finally ignited a full-scale Tuareg rebellion.

This rebellion, which eventually included as many as a dozen liberation movements, ended in 1995, with the signing of a Peace Pact in Ouagadougou, the capital of Burkina Faso. Although there are still occasional outbreaks of guerrilla activity, the Tuareg and the government of Niger maintain relatively amicable relations, in spite of the fact that the Tuareg continue to feel that their needs are not being met as much as they would like.

Tuareg Cultural Revitalization

There have also been various ways of expressing Tuareg identity, nationalism, and cultural revitalization that do not involve armed conflict. For example, Temoust, established in the 1980s, is an organization designed to promote Tuareg cultural revitalization and autonomy. It has offices in France as well as Niger that seek to educate the public about Tuareg culture, society, and history. This organization, and others like it, offers classes in Tamajaq. Tifinagh, the Tamajaq alphabet, is currently being revived and adopted for use in computers and printing. The director of Temoust has initiated dialogues with French politicians and the United Nations about Tuareg cultural and political concerns such as refugee and political asylum issues. Currently there are a number of Tuareg in France, Belgium, and the United States, most of whom are there as political exiles, migrant laborers, engaged in the sale of Tuareg art objects, or doing university studies, some of whom seek to promote awareness of the situations facing the Tuareg.

There has emerged a large body of oral and written literature—poetry, music, and song—that began as political and social commentary in songs of the Tuareg rebels, accompanied by guitar, called *ichumar* music. This music has now become popularized, called simply *guitar*, and is performed at dances and festivals. There are also international cultural revitalization organizations for peoples who speak other languages in the Berber family, related to Tamajaq: For example, there is an association called Amazigh, established in the 1970s, that denotes "Berber" in many of these dialects.

FOOD FOR THOUGHT

The question now arises, Exactly how effective have recent Tuareg efforts toward cultural survival been? Was the armed rebellion successful in winning any legal, economic, and more generally, human rights reforms beneficial to the Tuareg? What were the results of these efforts, and their wider implications, and how do they contribute to the understanding of cultural identity and human rights?

The terms of the 1995 Peace Pact included central government programs to further develop the northern regions of Azawak and Air. These were initiated by paving roads near the Agadez markets. There were also a few more mobile medical units sent into the Air countryside. There was a staffing of local Air clinics with more local Tuareg nurses. The former rebel fronts have been organized into regional peacekeeping police forces, who shortly after the Peace Pact began disarming and explaining the terms of the pact to local residents. They also began to work with local councils' traditional chiefs, Islamic scholars, and elders in adjudicating local disputes and administering justice in rural courts. Several Tuareg have been integrated into the central government and its military, and more Tuareg attend the University of Niamey. One former leader in the rebellion, Rhissa Boula, was appointed minister of tourism.

There remain, however, problems of economic crisis and political uncertainty throughout Niger. Since the early 1990s, there have been two coups d'états, and Niger has alternated between transitional governments that attempt to move toward parliamentary democracy and reversion to military governments. Unemployment and shortages persist. There have also been droughts in the western regions of the country that have driven up prices of millet, an important staple cereal for many people. There has also been armed conflict in the eastern, Kanuri-dominated region. Nevertheless, there is a tradition of religious and ethnic tolerance on the part of most Nigeriens, despite intermittent tensions.

Official attitudes and policies toward the Tuareg are therefore difficult to assess, and future trends are uncertain. One must be cautious about making generalizations since local opinions are varied, and they often diverge from official government policies and perspectives. The important point is that it is an oversimplification to define these problems as "ethnic" when additional, finer nuances are at play. Many Tuareg have absorbed ethnic outsiders into their communities through such processes as specialized work, intermarriage, and political alliances. Tuareg have also integrated foreign customs and ideas into their society. Many individuals have indicated that anyone is welcome in their community "if they like the region and live and work here."[10] Even those from outside Niger who conduct business there are not necessarily resented, provided they respect the local culture. Non-Tuareg have learned Tamacheq, and they have themselves adopted Tuareg dress, customs, and identity.

Thus there is much flexibility in local cultural identity and tolerance for cultural pluralism alongside pride in Tuareg culture, traditions, and the Tamajaq language. These sentiments are not contradictory. While local autonomy and representation in the northern regions have been important goals of many leaders in the Tuareg nationalist and cultural revitalization movements, "outsiders" are not all defined solely on the basis of rigid ethnic criteria. Indeed, in the American and European popular media, such emphases are misleading and distorting. It is important to recognize that they are the product of Euro-American beliefs about people's identity, and they do not always apply to African situations. The Tuareg case underscores the importance of cultural and economic diversity and the processes that shape the formation of complex societies that see themselves not so much as an ethnic unit but as a set of peoples seeking respect, rights, and justice.

Questions

1. What were some of the characteristics of precolonial Tuareg society that have been powerful in shaping recent Tuareg responses to threats to their cultural survival?

2. Compare and contrast the Tuareg cultural predicament with the predicament of some other group that you have studied.

3. Discuss the combination of conditions, in the natural environment and ecology and in the human environment of economic activity, social organization, and

cultural beliefs, that have shaped contemporary Tuareg society and also its relationship to the larger nation–estate of Niger.

4. Discuss the problem of trying to understand a different culture through the categories of thinking we use in our own culture, for example, our own language, in order to view that culture and language. In your opinion, can distortions be avoided or minimized? How?

5. What lessons for Americans can be learned from the Tuareg experience in Niger? How can our own State Department better understand other peoples' problems? In this discussion, imagine that you are an anthropologist who studies a different culture and speaks their local language. How would you advise the State Department in the area of human rights concerns? For example, do you believe "democracy" is always necessarily the best form of government for all peoples, everywhere, or not? Your reasons?

NOTES

1. Summer Institute of Linguistics, *Ethnologue* (Dallas: SIL International, 2000).
2. Per statements made to the author during the course of ethnographic field work.
3. The census data on Tuareg from 1987 through 1996 are available from the various government archives of the countries in which the Tuareg are found, including Algeria, Chad, Libya, Mali, Mauritania, and Niger.
4. See Jeremy Keenan, *Sahara Man: Traveling with the Tuaregs* (London: John Murray, 2002), 131–132.
5. Susan J. Rasmussen, *The Poetics and Politics of Tuareg Aging: Life Course and Personal Destiny in Niger* (DeKalb: Northern Illinois University Press, 1997), 107.
6. Ibid., 56.
7. Johannes Nicolaisen and Ida Nicolaisen, *The Pastoral Tuareg: Ecology, Culture, and Society* (New York and London: Thames and Hudson, 1997), II: 765; A. Campbell, personal communication, 2001.
8. Statements to the author by Tuareg informants. See also Jeremy Keenan, "The Sahara's Indigenous Peoples, the Tuareg, Fear Environmental Catastrophe," *Indigenous Affairs* 4/01 (2002): 50–57.
9. Statement to the author by Tuareg informants.
10. Statement to the author by a Taureg informant.

RESOURCE GUIDE

Published Literature

Baier, Steven, and Paul Lovejoy. "The Desert-Side Economy of the Central Sudan." In *The Politics of Natural Disaster: The Case of the Sahel Drought*, ed. Michael H. Glantz. New York: Praeger Publishers, 1976. 144–75.

Decalo, Samuel. *Historical Dictionary of Niger*. 3rd ed. Lanham, MD: Scarecrow Press, 1996.

Nicolaisen, Johannes, and Ida Nicolaisen. *The Pastoral Tuareg: Ecology, Culture, and Society*. New York: Thames and Hudson, 1997.

Norris, Harry Thirlwall. *Sufi Mystics of the Niger Desert*. Oxford: Clarendon Press, 1990.

Rasmussen, Susan J. *The Poetics and Politics of Tuareg Aging: Life Course and Personal Destiny in Niger*. DeKalb: Northern Illinois University Press, 1997.

———. *Spirit Possession and Personhood among the Kel Ewey Tuareg*. Cambridge: Cambridge University Press, 1995.

Films and Videos

African Drought—Nomadic Peoples. 1974. American Broadcasting Corporation (ABC), New York. A study of the nomadic Tuareg people.

The Salt Road. 1989. Ambrise Video Publishing, New York. Film that examines the role of the Tuareg in the salt trade between Morocco and Niger.

The Tuareg. 1972. Disappearing World Series. Films Incorporated Video, 5547 N. Ravenswood Avenue, Chicago, IL 60640–1199. Telephone: (800) 323–4222, ext. 43.

Women of the Sahel. 1995. Directed by Paolo Quaregna and Mahamane Souleymane. 1995. First Run Icarus Films, 32 Court Street, 21st Floor, Brooklyn, New York 11201. Telephone: (800) 876–1710.

WWW Sites

Art & Life in Africa. "Tuareg Information"
http://www.uiowa.edu/~africart/toc/people/Tuareg.html

Beloit College, Logan Museum of Anthropology, Tuareg Artifacts
http://www.beloit.edu/~museum/logan/catalog/africa/north/tuareg/index.htm

"Touring with the Tuareg"
http://www.geographical.co.uk/geographical/features/nov_2000_tuareg.html

Organizations

The Amazigh Voice
P.0 Box 1774
Hyattsville, MD 20788

Association Culturelle Amajeghen en Amerique (Amajir or Berber Association in America)
P.0. Box 58502, Penn Center Station
Philadelphia, PA 19102–8502
or
442 Route 206 North, Suite 163
Bedminster, NJ 07921
Telephone: (205) 592–7492

Association de Partenaires des Artisans du Sahel (APAS)
83 Bis Rue Jolist Curie
69005 Lyon, France

Temoust: Survie Touaregue—TEMOOUST
7, Rue Major Martin
69001 Lyon, France
Telephone: 0033–72–33–51–87

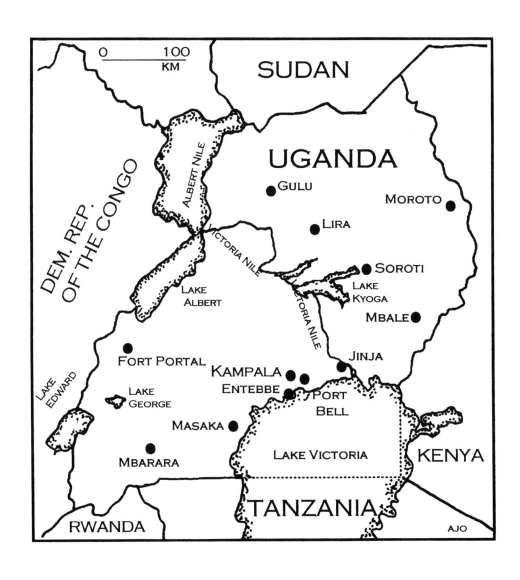

Chapter 14

The Ugandans

Dee Aker

CULTURAL OVERVIEW

[I]f we accept that the building blocks of the physical universe in which we live are particles of matter too small to be seen by the naked eye, we must surely realize that the fate of our community of nations could be accurately measured by what happens to small Third World nations like Uganda.[1]

Over the last millennium, trade, war, marriage, migrant labor, flight from famine, and colonial adventurism have all played roles in bringing peoples from a variety of backgrounds to what has been called "the Pearl of Africa." This is the story of the Ugandans and their rich cultural heritage that almost self-destructed. The women and men of Uganda have been key to the survival and recovery from complex ethnic, religious, and political struggles in their country. They have been instrumental in transforming, incorporating, and adapting strategies that both saved and united Uganda's diverse people and cultures, many of which were nearly devastated by genocidal civil wars following independence from British rule in 1962.

The People

The people of Uganda fall into four linguistic categories, reflecting the major migrations of early people: Bantu, Nilotic, Nilo-Hamites, and Sudanic peoples. Intermarriage, territorial security, trade, and finally, the British invasion encouraged alliances among the pre-Uganda peoples in the region. While empires rose and fell, nomadic cattle-herding groups in the north and settled agrarian communities in the south established different economies and lifestyles, but there is no reason to believe that relations among the pre-Uganda peoples were perpetually antagonistic and irreconcilable.

Tribal identities were the principal social and organizational factors used by the British colonialists to manipulate the behavior of people when they took control in the late 1800s. Ethnic pride was used to undermine possible unity against colonialists and became the base of new political identities that prevented national cohesion.

In the 1840s Arab traders introduced international commercial ties and Islam to the Buganda kingdom, a well-organized power in the southern region of the country. The English adventurer John Hanning Speke arrived in 1862, followed by British and French missionaries in the 1870s. At this point the pillars of the great Buganda kingdom became shaky. Loyalties were suddenly divided by external powers and competing new religions, as well as old tribal rivalries.

In addition to European colonialists, laborers from India had come at the turn of the century to build the Uganda Railway. By the time of Uganda's independence in 1962, this group played a major role in commerce and industry. Although three generations call Uganda home, the Ugandan Indians' distinct ethnic identity led to their expulsion in 1972 by a notoriously vicious Ugandan leader named Idi Amin. Rwandan and Burundian migrant laborers married into southern Ugandan communities in the 1940s and 1950s. The 1990s civil wars have brought Rwandan, Sudanese, and Congolese refugees.

About fifty different ethnic groups speaking forty-five languages can be identified within Uganda's borders today. The largest of these groups is the Buganda, who comprise about 19 percent of the total population of the country, followed by the Banyanhole at 9 percent, and the Bakiga and Basoga with about 8 percent each. The Langi make up about 7 percent of the total population and the Acholi approximately 6 percent.[2] The smallest group is the Batwa, or Pygmies, who are fewer than 1,500, or .0001 percent of the population of Uganda.

The Setting

Uganda is a small landlocked country, 91,135 square miles in size, straddling the equator in the Nile Basin of eastern Africa. Many Ugandans call their country "the green land." British Prime Minister Winston Churchill called it the "Pearl of Africa" because of its stunning beauty. The small country stretches from huge Lake Victoria on the eastern border, across the 3,300- to 4,600-feet-high plateau of central Uganda, to the "Mountains of the Moon," the Rewnzoris, in the west. Land accounts for 82 percent of Uganda's total surface. The rest is made up of great lakes, swamps and rivers. Most rivers and streams flow into the River Nile, which begins its 3,728-mile journey to the Mediterranean Sea from Uganda.

The diverse landscape accommodated nomadic herders, settled farmers, and forest hunters. While Uganda has far less mineral wealth than some of its neighbors, it has hydropower and cash crops for export. This lush, gorgeous land, as well as the industrious, friendly people, has drawn many people to it, for better and worse. During peaceful times today it brings ecotourists from around the world to its national parks, beautiful great lakes, white water rivers, and sparkling Murchison Falls. Unfortunately, Uganda also serves as a crossroads or site for the misadventures of much larger neighbors, too. This has had profound political, economic, and more recently, health and security consequences.

The Democratic Republic of the Congo (DRC), until 1997 called Zaire, lies to the west and is nearly ten times the size of Uganda. It is rich in minerals and political chaos. Uganda has long served as an illegal trade route for its gems and coffee.

Another insecure border for Uganda now exists in the southwest with Rwanda, a tiny, but recently lethal, neighbor. Raids and refugees from Rwanda are complicating Uganda's security. The southwest region is now threatened by Hutu rebel-exiles from Rwanda's 1994 civil wars between the Hutu and Tutsi people. Tragically, this region is home to one of the last two stands of mountain gorillas. Uganda had successfully established its sanctuary for the 300 remaining mountain gorillas in Uganda in 1994, and the sanctuary attracted scientists and tourists from all over the world until recently, when attacks by Rwandese rebels led to a cessation of the visits.

Sudan, to the northeast, is the largest country in Africa and perhaps the most troubled. Years of civil—religious—ethnic war in Sudan have contributed significantly to northern Uganda's instability. The Sudanese Muslim government and the Christian animist south have fought against one another for two decades. The Sudanese government has supported Joseph Kony's Lord's Resistance Army (LRA), a northern Ugandan rebel group that operates from bases in Sudan. The LRA, which itself claims to be Christian, helps the Sudanese government fight opposition armies of Sudan's Christian south. The LRA is primarily ethnic Acholi, but it also attacks its own people in northern Uganda. Sudan's support for the rebel group has increased instability and turmoil in northern Uganda.

This political instability in the nations surrounding Uganda encouraged the creation of strong civil society in many regions of the country and resulted in increased collaboration of Ugandan women during the 1990s. Many Acholi and Langi women from the north have joined the constitutional government of Uganda, working with others to seek security and peaceful social change.

Bugandan herd boy in 1992. (Courtesy Dee Aker)

Traditional Subsistence Strategies

Advantaged by the rich lands, human communities have had a wide range of occupations reaching back hundreds of years in Uganda. Adequate rain and fertile soils provide multiple growing seasons and have encouraged agrarian communities in central and southern Uganda. Even as members of these communities moved into modern times and urban settings, their attachment to their pastoral (herding) and agricultural roots as farmers was not lost. Long-horned cattle, a reflection of wealth and status throughout Uganda, are deeply prized. City dwellers, even Ugandan President Yowari Kaguta Museveni, care deeply about their cattle back on their homesteads. Rich growing seasons encourage continuous planting of *matoke*, a green plantain that is a basic staple, and even corn along city roadways, as well as on *shambas* (small farms).

One reason that Uganda may suffer less from massive slums common in developing nations is acceptance of midtown subsistence farming in this perfect climate. Colonists established tea and coffee plantations, along with a few other cash crops, which stratified the peasants as never before but did not essentially redistribute ethnic groups. Ugandans remain agriculturally based, with 90 percent of them farming small landholdings.

Lake Victoria in the east and the Kyoga, Albert, Edward, and George Lake complex in the west gave rise to successful fishing communities long ago, while the north, with less rain and fewer water sources, supported nomadic cattle grazers. But because of ongoing rebel skirmishes in the north, which have moved well beyond the old traditions of cattle rustling, even subsistence traditions are in jeopardy. Women, who have been the traditional subsistence support systems, do not feel secure enough to care for their animals or small plots of land. In some cases, they and their children are being herded into refugee-style camps, away from their homesteads, for security reasons.

Social and Political Organization

In Uganda, community was the prime factor in social organization. Ancestral customs and traditions controlling individual thinking and behavior within distinct ethnic groups were unique. The "African" concept of rights was one that applied more to groups and communities than to individuals. Community was, simply, more important than the individual. The common good was paramount in all decisions; the individual found true dignity within community, not standing out from it.

Certain precolonial freedoms allowed for diversity among tribal cultures to flourish. One was the freedom of religion: Individuals, families, and clans freely subscribed to deities they chose. The second was a right to culture: As tribes were conquered or territories annexed by expansionist kingdoms, local groups were usually left to practice their cultural heritage freely. A third important basis of most Ugandan tribal societies was equality of all before the law. Many cultures had elaborate procedures to assure a just trial, as this was considered a solid foundation for stability and peaceful communal living.

Most precolonial cultures followed humanitarian rules in war: The lives of children, women, the disabled and sick, and the old were spared in intertribal fighting. War was for able-bodied men; women could be taken as loot, but they were seldom killed or maimed. On the other hand, precolonial times saw abuse of some rights generally common today. Freedom of speech, association, assembly, and movement were restricted to maintain political control. Punishment for breaking traditional laws was generally severe and intended to serve as a deterrent. Slavery existed in some cases. Women had few rights and were excluded from landownership, political participation, administration of justice, and leadership. Techniques for controlling women's behavior ranged from female circumcision (or, as some describe it, female genital mutilation) to child marriage arrangements.

261

Tribes experienced different standards of freedom and justice from the colonial authorities. Suspected resisters and rebels suffered punishment with few humanitarian considerations, and there was no equality before the law. Europeans, Asians (as the people from India are called), and the "Natives" had separate courts and could expect different treatment for similar crimes. Detention without trial became common. Freedom of religion, too, was gradually limited. Among the most costly social and politically divisive decisions during the British colonial administration was the exclusive employment of certain southern tribes in civil service while recruiting people from the north primarily for the armed forces. Seeds for a bitter intertribal power struggle were sown.

In precolonial, colonial and postindependence eras, women played significant roles in the agricultural labor base, as lynchpins in intermarriage alliances, and as sources and indications of wealth, but women had little or no influence in political decision making. Even in those few communities where women shared decision making behind the scenes or, occasionally, in public, arriving Europeans dealt only with men. This European bias that ignored women and their rights added to the disintegration of local women's access to community participation. Discrimination by oppressive customs and laws remained the reality of women until recent times. Over the past twenty years, women have again begun to participate in decision making and assumed leadership roles within their ethnic groups and nationally. The challenge to Uganda's people has been to promote diversity and to end the opportunistic and murderous manipulation of ethnic differences, without giving up individual cultures.

The legacy of the colonial rule did in some cases have positive influences in the social and political organization of local tribal life and national development. Colonial administrations established an infrastructure that included civil service, an independent judiciary concept, and a call for leaders to address education and health. It set up the roads and economic connections that would unite tribes, for better or worse. However, tribes and regions experienced these connections to varying degrees and, correspondingly, varied in their trust and support of a national identity.

In spite of the infrastructure left behind, what emerged at independence in 1962 was the lack of cohesion and intertribal trust. The prospect of independence had created wonderful expectations such as redistribution of wealth, equitable development, and the return of land to original owners. but divisions between tribes and inadequate experience in practicing democracy caused these dreams to evaporate. In spite of a 1962 federal government–style constitution that recognized the need for representation from different parts of the country, a gross and horrific abuse of human rights would soon begin.

In the first federalist state, the first president was a Bugandan king from the south, and the first prime minister was a Langi leader from the north.

Both were power hungry, vengeful, and tribally focused, rather than seeing themselves first as Ugandans. Southerners had fared better under colonial rule as civil servants. Northerners had not received equal treatment in most arenas during colonial times, as they had been trained only as soldiers, which led to immediate resentment and conflicts. People in Uganda still viewed themselves as tribesman, not Ugandans, needing to gain spoils for their own group.

Within four years of Uganda's independence in 1962 the constitution was scrapped, the Bugandan president, "King Freddie," was in exile in London, and Langi Prime Minister Milton Obote, with his Langi and Acholi soldiers, had seized power. Obote fell victim to the same revenge and intertribal hatreds when Idi Amin, another military man from a different West Nile region tribe, seized power in a coup in the early 1970s. Amin had feared Obote's Langi and Acholi forces because of his earlier brutalities against them. He led a national reign of terror for eight years. Exiled Ugandans, with help from the Tanzanian army, ended the regime of this man who would be known as "the better devil" among Ugandans as things got worse. The economy of Uganda was devastated, and substantial numbers of Ugandans fled the country. Hope for a new political and social vision was dashed when Milton Obote returned to power through rigged elections in the early 1980s.

Religion and World View

Traditional religious practices varied among the tribes in precolonial times, but all were based in animism (traditional belief systems involving ancestors and spirits). Supernatural powers, which could be good or evil, were to be treated with respect as they could affect both the community and the individual. Legitimate chiefs were assumed to have access to these forces that fostered the well-being of a community; special priests or witches were sought out for specific help with the "powers" for personal solutions to problems.

The religious beliefs among the Acholi are important to their story and a good example of a tribal belief system. Traditional Acholi believe in *jogi*, powers that could act in political and religious spheres. Harnessing *jogi* for the public interest was a responsibility of a chief or priest; using the power of even a single *jok* (political and religious power, singular) for personal gain or destruction constituted witchcraft.

When the Acholi encountered new people and experiences, such as Arabs and Christian missionaries, they assumed there was a *jok* within these forces. As Christianity gained influence, new types of *jogi* emerged such as *Jog Jesus*. Such *jogi* are known as *tipu*, the term for the ghost of a dead relative. Tribal priests and healers associated with Christianity were thought to have access to *tipu*, such as *Tipu Maleng*, the Christian Holy

Spirit. Local healers and priests, using a mixture of European Christianity and traditional beliefs, drew many followers.

A sizable percentage of the Ugandan population is Christian, a third of them Roman Catholic, and a third Protestant. Between 16 and 20 percent of Ugandans are Muslim. Like many Africans, Ugandans sometimes follow several belief systems at the same time, combining traditional or indigenous practices with those of Christianity, Islam, or Baha'i.

THREATS TO SURVIVAL

Uganda's history has brought numerous challenges to its peoples, in spite of success in recent years that quelled much of the past ethnic violence. Global threats to human societies are reflected in some of the threats Uganda faces today: (1) extreme violence and the creation of child soldiers; (2) the spread of HIV/AIDS (human immunodeficiency virus/aquired immunodeficiency syndrome; (3) the struggle for national political stability with a fair representation of a multicultural population; and (4) the struggle of individual cultures to determine what customs can change to help assure their survivals.

Obote and his "bandit soldiers," bent on genocide—the purposeful effort committed with the intent to destroy, in whole or in part, a national, ethnical, racial, or religious group through systematic murder or through deliberately inflicting on the group conditions of life calculated to bring about its physical destruction—were finally brought down in the mid-1980s by the rag-tag soldiers of the National Resistance Movement (NRM), an organization led by now-President Yoweri Museveni. The National Resistance Movement was made up of farmers, professors, students, women of different tribes, and folks from different religions who could no longer abide the killing or living in exile. They joined under the leadership of Museveni, an educated revolutionary leader preaching responsible government, respect, and inclusion of all the peoples of Uganda and an end to the madness tearing the country apart. The leadership and policies of Museveni, the multitribal, multireligious National Resistance Movement, and women willing to step beyond all traditional norms brought a new Ugandan identity to life.

I was a Bishop's daughter, I married a lawyer, I had six children, but I did not know what it meant to be Ugandan, until I went into the bush for the NRM. Here I saw how most Ugandans really live, here I worked side by side with many different people. Now I know what it means to be a "Ugandan."[3]

These words were spoken by Gertrude Njuba, a woman who went to the "bush," the countryside, for five years to organize and educate people that the government was supposed to help people, not kill them. The personal cost was high: five years away from her family and living in the wild, giving up traditional expectations of being a good but unseen wife. At the end of the war, Gertrude Njuba, this simple woman, became the first minister of reconstruction and worked tirelessly among all groups of people to establish a multiethnic base in government and helped set up the first electoral system used to get national involvement in creating a new constitution.

At the end of the civil tribal wars in 1986, Uganda's infrastructure had essentially been destroyed. Many roads were nearly impassible, the country was bankrupt, homesteads were overgrown by the bush, schools had been devastated, hundreds of thousands had been killed or displaced and there were a million war orphans in a population of about 14 million people. The government, limited in how it could respond to the country's devastation and under suspicion for being a "central government," restructured civil society.

Child Soldiers

In the northern part of Uganda, children are taken violently from homes and schools by Joseph Kony's Lord's Resistance Army and used as pack animals on the trek to the rebel base camps in Sudan. A child who stops to help another may be clubbed to death. Other children are forced to participate in the killing and looting that occurs along the way. Once in the base camp, they receive some military training. Boys are expected to become killers like their captors and are tested in killing raids. Girls are given to rebel commanders as "wives" or sold as slaves. Statements from rescued children detail human atrocities beyond comprehension to most of the world, let alone the children's own families in Uganda.

I was abducted while my mother and I were going to the field. . . . One of the other abducted girls tried to escape, but she was caught. The rebels told us that she had tried to escape and must be killed. They made the new children kill her. They told us that if we escaped, they would kill our families. They made us walk for a week. . . . Some of the smaller children could not keep up, as we were walking so far without resting, and they were killed. . . . Some of the children died of hunger. I felt lifeless seeing so many children dying and being killed. I thought I would be killed.[4]

Treatment of the Acholi and other northern tribes in the colonial times and the Acholi religious world view built the platform on which these abhorrent acts are taking place. Acholis, Langis, and other northerners were trained for military service during colonial rule, but discipline was weak. Service in the name of the nation was superseded by tribal competition for spoils and revenge. Milton Obote and Idi Amin, who had taken power in coups, had their soldiers, primarily Acholi and Langi, commit atrocities against tribes in the south and even against fellow northerners.

This was a difficult history to overcome when the "bandit soldiers" from the north lost the civil war in 1986 to Museveni's National Resistance Movement. Another influence was an unusual prophet named Alice Lakwena, with her Holy Spirit Movement. After gaining followers as a healer, Lakwena warned that all male Acholi children would be killed unless they followed her into battle against Museveni and the National Resistance Movement. Magnetic and charismatic, Lakwena had considerable power. Her choice to inflict violence on Acholi civilian populations as well as on the National Resistance Army soldiers was justified as "weeding out the local evil." After a defeat in January 1987, she fled to Kenya, and many of her exhausted followers left the rebel movement. A few, however, turned to twenty-year-old Joseph Kony, who claimed to inherit Lakwena's power.

Kony's Lord's Resistance Army could not recruit enough soldiers for the cause, so they began abducting children to become the frontline soldiers of the LRA. Claiming today's crimes against humanity to be a Christian holy war against both their own nonrebel Acholi people and the multinational government of Uganda, Kony justifies his brutal acts in the name of the Lord and as a descendant of "Alice Lakwena." This abduction, violence, and military use of children in the Lord's Resistance Army represents one of the world's worst examples of a global trend toward increasing reliance on child soldiers in civil ethnic wars. It is devastating the families, especially mothers and women who are the primary providers. Uganda's government has sought to defeat the Lord's Resistance Army but has thus far been unable to put down the rebellion or to capture Joseph Kony. Opposition leaders have been critical of the government's efforts, and some of them have called on President Yuseveni to undertake peace negotiations.[5]

My children, all of them, are gone. They all died of Slims disease [AIDS]. We are trying to raise our grandchildren, but there is no money for school fees. My husband is not well, but we do what we can.[6]

Following the civil war, there were 1 million war orphans in Uganda to be recovered and integrated into society. How to care for the children, how to help them get some sort of education after the destruction of the schools and communities by the "bandit soldiers" and how to help them overcome the scars of civil war was a monumental task in 1986.

AIDS

Within five years it was apparent a new crisis, AIDS, was destroying individuals, families, and communities faster than the postwar problems could be addressed. Trade and smuggling routes ensured the rapid spread

266

of the sexually transmitted disease from its isolated beginnings on the African continent. Uganda was close to ground zero and hardest hit by what has become a global problem.

Long-standing tribal customs encouraged the spread of the disease, especially sexually transmitted diseases (STDs). High rates of prostitution in areas where men away from their families are passing through, such as navy ports of call and trading centers, and the cultural customs in Uganda, which included polygamy and the levirate (the custom of a wife marrying one of the brothers of her deceased husband), contributed to the disease problems, especially HIV/AIDS, which has had devastating effects on the people of central Africa, including Uganda. It is ironic that traditional customs, which once provided labor sources and economic security for women, proved deadly when combined with this plague, killing large numbers of both men and women. In the south, some villages have lost a whole generation of young adults.

On the national level, HIV/AIDS has decreased the labor force and strained medical resources. Local cultures are threatened by another encouragement to change their traditions in addition to caring for the orphans and dealing with the social stigma associated with AIDS. The women, as caregivers and family subsistence providers, are left to carry a huge burden. On the positive side, Uganda has made huge strides in AIDS education, and the rates of infection of Uganda's people appear at present to be on the decline. On the negative side, AIDS continues to exact a terrible toll on Ugandan society.[7]

Civil War

Some statements made at the meeting of political party leaders reported in "Partyists, in Big Meet Vow to Die" are very strong and perhaps undemocratic. It is disheartening to hear someone call on people to shed their blood. Although many people in Uganda long for democracy they have not started thinking democratically.[8]

Uganda's civil wars grew out of inflamed tribal competition and manipulation of different religions. Both tribal and religious power plays were made manifest through political parties (i.e., tribes dressed in political party clothing) to begin their modern wars. People were often coerced into voting a party line by fellow tribe members. Political parties that gained power used their military might to massacre hundreds of thousands of people targeted for their ethnicity or religion. This resulted in horrendous killings during the 1970s and 1980s, leaving fields of skulls and open graves.

The bitter residue was only abated by very serious efforts to form an inclusive, democratic government not based on old tribal party associations. Individuals and groups, such as youth, women, traditional leaders, laborers, and businesspeople, who had an investment in peace because they had been victims of the wars, regardless of their tribe, got a voice. In spite of achieving peace for most of the country and creating a constitution affirming the rights of participation of every segment of society and tribe, today Uganda faces some tough decisions that could turn back the clock.

The new constitution established that political parties, so associated with cultural conflict in the past, would not be the basis for running for government offices in the first election. This nonparty system seemed to work well, initially. Fair elections were held in 1995, and a soundly functioning government has been in place since. As the time has arrived for reconsideration of political parties and their role in this democratic government, however, many are pushing for a return to a political party system. Milton Obote and Idi Amin, still living in self-chosen exile, and their followers in Uganda and Sudan are among those calling for parties. Attempts to destabilize the government by terrorist acts, combined with calls to return to the old party system, are heard frequently now in Uganda. The road ahead may be mined with *tipu* of the past if parties cannot move beyond old religions and tribal identities.

Women's Rights

The patriarchal tradition that denies women land rights must be fought. Most of those women in the villages where land is held by custom already suffer and are chased off their land after a family crisis. Very few of the women-friendly recommendations were incorporated into the Land Act this year, leaving the lion's share of the land affairs to the men. Submissions to include wives of polygamous unions were completely ignored and issues of inheritance and citizenship were left vague. It does not specifically empower the Ugandan woman who is the backbone of agriculture in Uganda.[9]

Cultural issues of land rights, bride price, and divorce rights are emerging in Ugandan parliamentary legislation. Concerns are being raised, as well, about ending the custom of female genital mutilation (FGM), sometimes called female circumcision, and securing the rights of girl children to be educated equally with boys. New internal tensions are appearing in a number of ethnic groups, although the tendency in the beginning of the new democratic government was in favor of sensitivity to religious and tribal customs, with a few major exceptions. The most notable exception the new government made to old tribal and religious customs was the inclusion of women in decision making.

Emboldened by inclusion, increasing numbers of local women began speaking out about customs that limited their rights at home or endangered them and their children. They saw a chance to participate in the decisions affecting their own and their children's security. More than a few, seeking a way to end the endless wars, took leadership roles. Ankole women in western Uganda now object to their treatment in divorce cases. In southwest Uganda, the issue of bride price was put on the discussion agenda, as women believe it has become a limiting factor in marriage, given the economic challenges after long years in war and struggling with AIDS. They say the cost of this marriage custom, too high for many families to meet, increases the number of out-of-wedlock pregnancies. Meanwhile, Bugandan and other tribal women call for equal access to credit and resources, including land.

A backlash at the local level against women, because of their new demands, is much greater than at the national level. As women gain credit, establish new associations, and find ways to bring the needs of their communities forward, there is growing fear among some traditional leaders, local spiritual leaders, and husbands about loss of control. Old authoritarian traditions may have led to wars, but they also created cultural boundaries that gave definition to a community. It takes those who have previously held power over others longer to see that sharing power with others has more potential for lasting influence. Those who gain their power by sharing with other people must face the frustration of older authorities fearing their loss of control.

RESPONSE: STRUGGLES TO SURVIVE CULTURALLY

Uganda's 22 million people and the distinct cultures with whom they identify are trying to survive. The country has had a hard time charting a course that includes all of these people and tribes. The complex task has been how to overcome ethnic competition and animosities encouraged by precolonial, colonial, and postindependence history, while joining the international community of nation–states working toward just and cooperative societies. It means tackling the threats to survival head-on.

During the 30 years of suffering and destruction of everything, the ethical conduct and ethical standards and moral values did not remain intact. Rebuilding a moral character, like rebuilding the infrastructures of government and roads and hospitals, takes time. Now Uganda must face [that] it too has corruption no matter what good intentions exist and, until we fix that, both evil people like Joseph Kony and well-meaning people with real grievances will have cause to remain outside or against a strong national government.[10]

The struggle to address the violence in the north is led by women in government and in civil society. It is not an easy task, when outside aid to support rebels comes from foreign governments and the local people live in terror of reprisal for trying to establish new associations for security. Women of the Acholi and Langi people in the north spearheaded the initial movement from violence to participation in the new national government. These women, long-suffering victims in wars they did not start, had an investment in change. Two such women are Betty Okwir, a Langi, and Betty Bigombe, an Acholi.

When the National Resistance Movement came to power, fighting persisted in the north. Women saw that if traditional life was to be restored and peace was to come to their territory, they must try to give the new government's plan for peace a chance. That was not easy: The men, their husbands, sons, and brothers, now identified with "the fight." One school headmistress, watching her community collapse around her, responded to desperate mothers and women when they came to her for help. Betty Okwir told the women that they had to go tell their husbands that they would cease to be their wives and to sleep with them if they did not cease the fighting. Betty Okwir's advice was followed closely by a group of thirty women, whose husbands came out of the bush. This community took a leading role in assuring representation of the Langi in the new government, and Betty Okwir became deputy speaker of the Parliament in the new constitutional government.

Betty Bigombe, an Acholi, was minister of state for the north in the Office of the Prime Minister in the early 1990s. Many rebels in her region still fought the central government. Previous attempts to get these rebels to lay down their machetes and guns had fallen on deaf ears, in spite of a well-publicized policy of the central government to give amnesty to rebels who ceased fighting. When Bigombe took office and went north to try to engage in peace talks, many thought this was a joke. Acholi tradition did not sanction women in such a role, so no one would listen, least of all rebels so long bent on destruction and filled with hate. Leaflets and cartoons showing a price on Bigombe's head and signed by rebel commanders appeared. No one showed for the talks, as predicted.

Undaunted, she took another route to change the path of her people. She started meeting with the wives, sisters, mothers, and lovers of the rebels in various areas. Working to convince them how things could change and repeating the promise of amnesty, Bigombe opened a new channel of communication. Many rebels did come home and return to their normal lives. This process was essential in preparing for participation in national elections in which northerners had to elect representatives to determine the form of a new constitution.

It is women like these who have formed alliances and encouraged local women to become the strongest voices for dealing with the Lord's Resistance Army (LRA). The price has been high. Many of these women have had their lips cut off by the LRA for speaking against them and their tactics.[11]

The LRA is a rebel group formed after the exile of Alice Lakwena, leader of the Holy Spirit Movement, by her cousin, Joseph Kony. According to interviews of Acholi women, the LRA has systematically attacked them and the guerilla group has abducted more than 10,000 children for use as soldiers and laborers.[12] Mothers of abducted children have organized. The Concerned Parents Association has petitioned the government for stronger action, and they work with international networks like Human Rights Watch, World Vision, and UNICEF (the United Nations Children's Fund) and individuals like Sister Rachele Fassera. After a mass abduction from her school Sister Rachele followed the LRA rebels into the bush. She negotiated the release of 109 girls and has helped organize volunteers and teachers to assist the children who have managed to escape.[13] Such children need dedicated help to overcome their trauma and reintegrate into their society.

Another response to the situations faced by Ugandans was political. Local councils were set up to deal with all sorts of problems that the government could not handle. Nine people were chosen from the community, including a local traditional leader, a member of the NRA (National Resistance Army), a local businessperson, a young person, a woman, and four others from the community. There had to be at least one woman on each council. The councils were sensitive to local tribes and at the same time introduced new players, such as women and youth, into the local governance. These councils develop a sense of local security and national identity from the ground up. The decentralized political system was able to bring about stability and to lay the foundations for economic progress.[14]

We put out the word that we women must take charge and save the orphans left by the horrible wars. They were so many. Women came, lawyers, farmers, mothers,—from all walks of life and rich and nearly starving—they came and we began UWESO [Ugandan Women's Effort to Save Orphans]. Now UWESO must care for these AIDS orphans, too.[15]

The Ugandan Women's Effort to Save Orphans was organized to address the fact that 1 million out of a population of 14 million were war orphans in 1986. Women set up orphan centers where children found wandering in the bush could be brought and identified. Next they established special "households" for the children, in which two adult war survivors would set up a "family" for twenty children of varying ages. All were expected to develop small money-earning projects, gardens, or husbandry projects to learn how to care for themselves and each other.

Action for Development (ACFODE), another women's organization, was formed in 1988 to help women in recovery and development. Women, with babies and food plots to care for, had not been able to escape the war and were left behind in the worst battle zones. They and their daughters were often raped and beaten, but many survived to build a new life at the end of the massacres. ACFODE helped these women rebuild and soon became the primary group educating and preparing women for public service.[16]

Women were instrumental in encouraging the government to face AIDS.

Uganda, unlike every other African nation, faced the epidemic head-on and early. The government allowed international research; it did not try to hide the problem. Surveys of adolescents with HIV/AIDS in Rakai District in southwestern Uganda were done in the early 1990s by Columbia University and Johns Hopkins University. The Ministry of Health of Uganda had HIV/AIDS education programs in place by the late 1980s.[17] The Ugandan government spread word on cultural customs that must be changed to stop the rapid spread of the disease. Advertisements appeared in the news calling for "zero grazing," which meant not having multiple sexual partners, and for the use of condoms. The minister of gender and culture, now the vice president of Uganda, began getting the word out to remote areas that men must not marry the wives of their deceased brothers and called on women to end the custom of female circumcision, as this often left damaged tissue more likely to be receptive to the virus.[18]

Of course, government decrees do not cause custom to change quickly. It is only now, fifteen years later, with greater access to education for girls, ongoing local community education for adults about the disease, and the continued effort to address the problem with every resource it can muster, that Uganda has seen a decline in AIDS. While the number of cases remains the highest proportionally for a single population anywhere in the world, there is a decline in the actual percentage of the population getting the disease. That is not true elsewhere in Africa.[19]

UWESO, ACFODE, and the Ministry for Gender, Labor and Social Development continue to work in association with international groups to address this devastating and costly concern. They are joined by outspoken Vice President Dr. Wandira Kazibewe, herself a physician, who spent four years working with different cultural groups and explaining the importance of rethinking old customs.

To have parties or not to have parties? . . . The bottom line is that parties have to offer more than their plea for the right to exist. They have to offer credible alternatives in policy and leadership. . . . The catch is that if you participate, you have to be as ready to lose as you are to win.[20]

The tension in Uganda over the decision whether to return to political parties is discussed daily in the press. Regardless of the outcome, the hope for continuing peaceful, inclusive political evolution continues to be modeled by the women of very different cultures in Uganda. In developing the current constitution, during the late 1980s and early 1990s, women were the most united national group to participate in the process.[21] They promoted inclusion of and justice for various groups who had not previously had a voice in decision making. Ugandan women illustrate the rise of common-interest associations based on age, kinship, or territory, rather than tribal associations.

Globalization, urbanization, and constitutional governments ruling over extended territories and diverse people continue to be a worldwide reality. The survival of unique cultures requires members of these communities to place themselves in decision-making positions through new associations that will bring stability without the loss of essential, unique ethnic identities. The common goals of Ugandan women—including security, health, food, and family stability—brought them together. Abducted children, war and AIDS orphans, murdered family members, and the overall lack of security were problems women could no longer tolerate, nor could they tackle these problems alone.

A national Women's Caucus was formed in 1986. The idea was to support each other and broaden the base of support for women's concerns. The group realized their need for skills training. They helped each other with everything from understanding the law and writing legislation to understanding distinct tribal issues. The group, today called the Women's Forum for Democracy, formed a good working relationship with the Uganda Women Lawyers Association and nongovernmental groups like ACFODE who worked in grassroots civil education and addressing women's concerns from domestic violence to securing credit.

The women allied their voting power in Parliament with youth, disabled, and labor. All of these groups were allotted seats in Parliament in the new constitution. This model of common-interest association is important in any decision the nation reaches in regard to the political party issue. With or without parties, the public must see there are associations for their well-being that are of greater value than self-interest based on tribe or religion alone. Without that realization, the chance for a return to war, hate, and genocide looms large.

We have gone through a period of wars for more than 30 years. Wars shatter people's values and morals. Ugandans had to drop the values and value systems that they once knew to adopt strategies of survival. Now people must build, even at the very smallest level, from what was good, what is deep in their African culture, and add the new gender sensitivity.[22]

Long-standing customs of tribes are affected by national law, and a group's participation in the transition of the custom or ritual is very important. It is not possible to stop change; it is possible to make the transition more acceptable. The goal of many women in new leadership positions over the last thirteen years has been to promote understanding of changes that can help the community persevere.

The affirmative action constitution of Uganda guarantees rights to women within their own communities. Some traditional leaders and male heads of households fear loss of their control. One of the arguments against women's rights being placed in the constitution was that too much freedom would make them "unruly." Most women, however, have demonstrated an investment in peaceful, reasoned change. Thus far it appears that where "gender sensitivity," a term heard frequently in Uganda, grows, so do democracy and cultural security.

Local arguments can demonstrate the fierce difference in perspective and approach to some issues. While some men advocate lowering the marriage age and defilement age to twelve from fifteen years so that girls who do not go to school can get married and stop burdening their parents, women argue that equal education and preparing to be an income provider will make everyone more secure. In contrast, in the Kumi region women and men agree that the new constitution must set the tone if the highly patriarchal society is to incorporate women in all levels of decision making.

Recent local elections suggest there are varying degrees of acceptance of women. Without a voice in customs by which they must live, women are likely to turn to the national government and advocacy groups for help. It is likely that the increased participation of women in local decision making will continue. Maintaining cultural identity and security in the long run depends on balance with and within the dominant national culture.

FOOD FOR THOUGHT

The struggle for national political stability with fair representation of a multicultural population is not unique to Uganda. This culturally rich country, after suffering twenty-five years of ethnic and religious civil wars, demonstrates a number of important ways to overcome violence and intolerance. Knowing what caused the problems is only part of the issue; identifying what factors helped address problems is the other. We have focused on the role of women in addressing the problems.

The women of Uganda, from distinct tribal and religious backgrounds, have accommodated a key cultural survival technique: the capacity to change selectively. Women had been caught in genocidal disputes within the modern boundaries of this nation-state. They had been held back by traditional societal positions that did not give them a voice in alternative resolutions to arguments and power plays. In great frustration, they formed new associations outside traditional cultures, while they continued to satisfy basic roles of providing for their families and communities. But new roles involved participating in the planning and transition of their local social groups and working to achieve self-interests as part of a larger society.

There is no option for the Buganda, Acholi, and other women to live in a society untouched by rapid global change. The chaos that led to horrifying civil wars, with the attempted genocide of some tribes, left women as victims, trying to protect and feed their children. When they discovered other women had the same concerns, it gave them a sense of unity. They are attempting to save their diverse cultures and their families through this unity. A change in one part of a culture will affect many other parts dramatically, however. This story is ongoing.

Questions

1. What cultural factor(s) did the foreign powers manipulate to get and maintain control over indigenous people living in Uganda? How did that undermine the social relations that existed?

2. How did religion get tied to killing and intercultural intolerance in Uganda? Does that happen elsewhere in the world?

3. What is the relationship of political parties to special tribal interests in Uganda? Can Uganda be called democratic without parties? And can an individual culture have influence without parties?

4. What primary role of women changed, aiding in the transition of local cultures caught up in intertribal wars? When and how did a true national identity begin to emerge? Why is it important?

5. How could it come to pass that subordinate women from many distinct ethnic groups—women who struggled with access to education, credit, land, employment, custody rights to their children, and a sense of self-worth—have come to play important roles in local decision making?

NOTES

1. Ugandan President Yoweri Museveni in an address to the United Nations General Assembly, New York, October 21, 1987.

2. Summer Institute of Linguistics. *Ethnologue.* (Dallas: SIL International, 2000).

3. Gertrude Njuba, in an interview with Dee Aker, 1986.

4. Sharon, thirteen, one of many Ugandan children interviewed by Human Rights Watch, for *The Scars of Death: Children Abducted by the Lord's Resistance Army in Uganda* (New York: Human Rights Watch, 1997).

5. Human Rights Watch, *Children in Combat* (New York: Human Rights Watch, 1996).

6. Mother of seven deceased children, grandmother of fourteen children, ages one to eleven, in interview in single-room, dirt-floor home in a tiny town in southern Uganda in an interview with Dee Aker, 1990.

7. Data from UNAIDS.

8. Father Paschal Kabura, in a letter to the editor of *The Monitor*, one of two major Uganda daily papers, February 10, 1999.

9. Honorable Maria Matembe, Minister of Ethnics and Integrity, interview with Dee Aker, Kampala, Uganda, February 1999.

10. Ibid.

11. Human Rights Watch, *The Scars of Death*; Human Rights Watch, *Children in Combat*; C. Dodge, *War, Violence, and Children in Uganda* (Oxford: Oxford University Press, 1987).

12. See African Rights, *Year 2000 Report* (London: African Rights, 2000), 54–60.

13. Information obtained during the course of interviews with Dee Aker in the mid-1990s.

14. The information on the political changes that occurred in the period when the National Resistance Movement/NRM was operating in Uganda came from informants interviewed by Dee Aker, the author, in the mid- to late 1980s and the early to mid-1990s in a series of visits to Uganda. See also NRM Secretarian, *The Achievements of the National Resistance Movement, 1986–1990* (Kampala, Uganda: The Directorate of Information and Mass Mobilization, NRM Secretariat, 1991); M. Louise Pirouet, *Historical Dictionary of Uganda* (Metuchen, NJ and London: The Scarecrow Press, 1995).

In 1986 Yoweri Museveni took over the Ugandan government and established a no-party system and a multi-cultural constitution. Interviews were done of women in the Ugandan Government in the 1980s and 1990s.

15. Janet Museveni, First Lady of Uganda, interview with Dee Aker, 1990.

16. Information on women in Uganda was obtained from UNICEF, *Children and Women in Uganda: A Situation Report* (Kampala, Uganda: United Nations Childrens Fund, 1989).

17. (World Health Organization representative, Kampala, Uganda, personal communication to Dee Aker, 1998. For further information on AIDS in Africa, see Tony Barnett and Piers M. Blaikie, *AIDS in Africa* (New York: Guilford Press, 1992); Edward C. Green, *AIDS and STDs in Africa: Bridging the Gap Between Traditional Healing and Modern Medicine* (Boulder, CO: Westview Press, 1996); Carole Campbell, *Women, Families and HIV/AIDS* (Cambridge: Cambridge University Press, 1999). Uganda is home to over 150 non-governmental organizations that are in some way providing relief resources to orphans, since Uganda has the largest number of AIDS orphans of any country on the African continent. See WHO, *The World Health Report 1998* (Geneva: World Health Organization, 1998). Uganda has been recognized for the progress it has made in fighting the AIDS epidemic by the United Nations, the World Health Organization, the World Bank, and the Centers for Disease Control (CDC).

18. Statement by Minister of Gender and Culture, government of Uganda, now the Vice President, to Dee Aker.

19. The statistics for these statements were obtained from UN AIDS, the United Nations AIDS program, 2000.

20. Conrad Nkutu (journalist), *Sunday Vision*, February 14, 1999. *The Vision* is one of two major papers in Uganda.

21. The statements about women being the most united national group to participate in the process were obtained from Ugandan women in government and in civil society by Dee Aker during a series of visits made between the early 1980s and, most recently, in 2002.

22. Matembe, interview with Aker, February 1999.

RESOURCE GUIDE

Published Literature

Baker, Wairama G. *Uganda: The Marginalization of Minorities*. London: Minority Rights Group International, 2001.

Dodge, C. *War, Violence, and Children in Uganda*. Oxford: Oxford University Press, 1987.

Human Rights Watch. *Children in Combat*. New York: Human Rights Watch, 1996.

———. *The Scars of Death: Children Abducted by the Lord's Resistance Army in Uganda*. New York: Human Rights Watch, 1997.

Kasozi, A.B.K. *The Social Origins of Violence in Uganda, 1964–1985*. Montreal, Ontario, Canada: McGill-Queens University Press, 1994.

Mutibwa, Phares. *Uganda since Independence: A Story of Unfulfilled Hopes*. London: Hurst, 1992.

Ofcansky, Thomas P. *Uganda: Tarnished Pearl of Africa*. Boulder, CO: Westview Press, 1996.

Films and Videos

AIDS in Africa. 1990. Roger Pyke Productions. Filmmakers Library, 124 East 40th Street, New York, NY 10016. Telephone: (212) 808–4980. Fax: (212) 808–4983. Email: info@filmakers.com. Web site: www.filmakers.com/.

Mountains of the Moon. 1990. Directed by Bob Rafelfon. Film based on the journals of Richard Francis Burton and Harry John Speke.

Raid on Entebbe. 1977. Directed by Irvin Kersner. Story of the Israeli raid to rescue passengers from a high-jacked airliner in Uganda.

Uganda: The War of the Children. 1999. Films for the Humanities and Sciences, No. EKM 10540. P.O. Box 2053, Princeton, NJ 08543–2053. Web site: http://www.films.com

Uganda Women's Efforts to Save the Orphans. 1990. Directed by Dee Aker. KUSI-TV, San Diego, CA. Film on the role of women in assisting Uganda's orphaned children.

Women Take Post War Leadership. 1991. Directed by Dee Aker. KUSI-TV, San Diego, CA. Film on the role of women in leadership in contemporary Uganda.

WWW Sites

Buganda Home Page
http://www.buganda.com

Children and Armed Conflict around the World
http://www.un.org/special-rep/children-armed-conflict

Forum for Women in Democracy
http://www.nlc.ug/fowode

Foundation for Human Rights Initiative, Kampala
http://www.hri.ca/partners/fhri

Government of Uganda
http://www.government.go.ug

Human Rights Network of Uganda (HURINET)
http://www.uganda.co.ug/hurinet

Human Rights Watch
http://www.hrw.org

Joint United Nations Programme on HIV/AIDS
http://www.unaids.org

Minority Rights Group
http://www.minorityrights.org

National Association of Women's Organizations in Uganda (NAWOU)
http://www.nawou.or.ug

Uganda AIDS Commission
http://www.aidsuganda.org

Ugandan Women's Effort to Save Orphans
http://www.uweso.com

United Nations Children's Fund
http://www.unicef.org

United Nations Development Fund for Women Working for Women's Empowerment and Gender Equity
http://www.unifem.undp.org

United Nations Educational, Scientific and Cultural Organization
http://www.unesco.org/

United Nations High Commissioner for Human Rights
http://www.unhchr.ch/

Women of Uganda Network
http://www.wougnet.org

Organizations

ACFODE (Action for Development)
ACFODE House, Plot 623/624, Bukoto
P.O. Box 16729
Kampala, Uganda
Telephone: (256) 41–530412
Fax: (256) 41–530412
Email: acfode@starcom.co.ug
Web site: www.acfode.or.ug

AWEPON (African Women's Economic Policy Network)
Suite 2.3 Twese Building, Plot 14, Wilson Road
P.O. Box 23425
Kampala, Uganda
Telephone: (256) 41–348868

CEEWA (Council for Economic Empowerment of Women in Africa)—Uganda
P.O. Box 9063, Kampala, Uganda
Telephone: (256) 41–348896
Fax: (256) 41–230990
Email: ceewaug@infocom.co.ug

Foundation for Human Rights Initiative (FHRI)
P.O. Box 11027
Kampala, Uganda
Telephone: (256) 41–530095
Fax: (256) 41–540561

FOWODE (Forum for Women in Democracy)
Plot 5, Dewinton Road
P.O. Box 7176
Kampala, Uganda
Telephone: (256) 41–342130
Email: fowode@starcom.co.ug
Web site: http://www.nicoug/fowode

Human Rights and Peace Center
c/o Faculty of Law
Makerere University
P.O. Box 7062
Kampala, Uganda
Fax: (256) 41–245580

Isis WICCE (Women's International Cross Cultural Exchange)
P.O. Box 4934
East Africa
Telephone: (256) 41–543953
Email: isis@starcom.co.ug

Save SubSaharan African Orphans Organization (SSSO)
c/o Nelson Okuku Miruka
Department of Political Science
University of Nebraska–Lincoln
Lincoln, NE 68588–0328
Telephone: (402) 472–2343
Fax: (402) 472–8192
Email: okukumiruka@hotmail.com
Web site: www.savetheorphans.org

Uganda Women's Network
P.O. Box 27991
Kampala, Uganda
Telephone: (256) 41–543968
Fax: (256) 41–543968
Email: uwonet@starcom.co.ug

UWESO (Uganda Women's Effort to Save Orphans)
P.O. Box 8419
Kampala, Uganda
Telephone: (256) 41–532394
Email: info@uweso.com
Web site: http://www.uweso.com

Women Studies
Makerere University
45 Pool Road
P.O. Box 7062
Kampala, Uganda
Telephone: (256) 41–531484
Email: womenmuk@starcom.co.ug
Web site: http://www.makerere.ac.ug

Glossary

Acculturation. The process of extensive borrowing of aspects of culture in the context of super-ordinate-subordinate relations between societies; sometimes this concept is equated with "Westernization."

Agropastoralism. The combination of crop agriculture and livestock keeping, an adaptation common in many parts of the world.

Animism. A term used by anthropologist Edward Tylor to describe a belief in a dual existence of all things, both physical, visible body and a psychic, invisible soul; in Africa, this term is often used to describe religious beliefs that are indigenous.

Apartheid. A term meaning "apartness" in Afrikaans, the language spoken by the descendants of the Dutch who settled in South Africa in the period after 1652; the term also means "separate development," part of a policy that institutionalized the racial separation system in South Africa, with unequal access to power and resources established by a white minority population.

Assimilation. The process whereby the traditions, customs, and values of peoples are incorporated into other, often dominant, cultures, and the modification of cultures.

Association. An organized group that is not based on either kinship or territory; this group has a number of characteristic features including membership exclusivity, shared interests, and group consciousness of identity.

Autonomy. The right to preserve, protect, and promote values that are different from the rest of society.

Bride price (bride wealth). A gift of goods or money given to the bride's kin by the groom and/or the groom's kin that signifies the bond between two families and serves to symbolize the relationship; in Africa, this custom is often associated with the transfer of cattle by the groom's family in exchange for the wife's services.

Civilization. A cultural entity, a society with a common set of values, attitudes, beliefs, traditions, history, usually consisting of two or more states, the most enduring of human associations.

Clan. A set of people related through kinship whose members believe themselves to be descended from a common ancestor or ancestress; clans are often associated with totems, a means of group identification that sometimes are in the forms of animals or plants that group members are supposed to honor.

Class. A category of persons who have approximately the same opportunity to obtain economic resources, power, and prestige; a cross-cutting segment of a society.

Compensation. The restitution of all losses sustained by individuals, households, communities, and groups as a result of the imposition of policies such as resettlement or dam project implementation, usually in the form either of cash or payment in kind (e.g., land for land, fodder for loss of grazing resources).

Complex humanitarian emergency. Those emergencies that affect sizable numbers of people and require multi-pronged intervention in order to alleviate them.

Cultural relativism. The thesis that other cultures should be assessed on their own terms and not evaluated using the standards of another culture.

Culture. Socially acquired traditions, including patterned, repetitive, and symbolic ways of thinking, feeling, and acting.

Demographic transition. The process of change in fertility and mortality rates that occurred around the time of the Industrial Revolution in which there was a shift from high birth and death rates to low birth and death rates; overall, the result was a lowering of population growth rates.

Desertification. The process of land degradation caused by a combination of human and natural (including climatic) factors in the arid, semi-arid, and sub-humid areas of the world in which vegetation cover is reduced or transformed and soil erosion occurs, with an overall loss of biological productivity, which leads to the land taking on the characteristics of a desert.

Development. The process whereby a nation or agency attempts to raise the living standards of its citizens or members, to enhance their well-being, and to meet their basic needs; as Gandhi put it, "the maximization of the human potential."

Development refugees ("oustees"). People who have been forced from their homes due to a development project such as a dam, road, or agricultural project.

Diaspora. The settling of people outside of their countries of origin such as the Jews outside of Palestine during the period of Babylonian rule and the migration of people such as the Somalis from their ancestral homelands in the Horn of Africa.

Glossary

Disaster. a process or event involving a combination of a potentially destructive agent(s) from the natural and/or social environment that results in damage, loss, or destruction; an actual historical event which results in problems for a society, community, or individual.

Drought. A deficiency of precipitation that results in water shortage for some activity (e.g., plant growth) or for some group (e.g., a farmer); a rainfall-induced shortage of some economic good (e.g., grazing for livestock) brought about by inadequate or badly timed rainfall.

Ecocide. The purposeful destruction of the environment or habitat by a state, agency, or group, done especially as a means of depriving a group of its means of sustenance and/or socially, economically, or ideologically significant resources.

Enculturation. The process whereby a child learns his or her cultural traditions; generational transmission of societal customs and rules.

Endogamy. The rule specifying marriage to a person within one's own (kin, caste, community) group.

Environmental justice. A social movement that links human rights, environment, and social justice and that assesses the effects of policies and programs on diversity, gender and class; it aims at fairness in the distribution of costs and benefits of polies that affect the environment and people.

Environmental refugee. A person who has had to flee his or her home because of stress caused by environmental factors (floods, droughts, environmental disasters).

Ethnic cleansing. The planned, deliberate removal of a population from a specific territory; this process, which is usually done in the pursuit of political or military aims, can range from genocide through deportation and expulsion through population transfers and the encouragement of emigration of groups considered "undesirable."

Ethnocentrism. The belief that one's own cultural values are superior to others; the tendency to judge other cultures by one's own standards.

Ethnocide. The destruction of the culture of a group; a process whereby a people loses their customs, values, beliefs, and traditions as a result of concerted actions by a state, an institution, or another group.

Exogamy. The rule specifying marriage to a person from outside one's own (kin or community) group.

Famine. Severe shortage or inaccessibility of appropriate food (including water) along with related threats to survival, affecting major parts of a population caused by disruptions in supply or decline in food production.

Foraging. The process of collecting wild plant and animal foods and other materials (e.g., stone for making tools, ochre for decoration); also referred to as hunting and gathering.

Genocide. Any of the following acts committed with the intent to destroy, in whole or in part, a national, ethnical, racial, or religious group, such as: (1) killing members of the group, (2) causing serious bodily or mental harm to members of the group, (3) deliberately inflicting on the group conditions of life calculated to bring about its physical destruction in whole or in part, (4) imposing measures intended to prevent births within the group, (5) forcibly transferring children of the group to another group.

Humanitarian assistance. Food, goods, and other resources as well as technical advice that are provided to populations, communities, and nation-states that are under stress either from conflict or environmentally induced factors (e.g., disasters such as earthquakes, drought, hurricanes).

Human rights. Those rights to which all individuals and groups are entitled, including the rights to life, liberty, equality, political participation, fair treatment, and freedom of cultural, social, and religious expression; these rights are outlined in the Universal Declaration of Human Rights (UDHR) of 1948.

Indigenous peoples. Those people who are aboriginal or native to the countries in which they reside; sometimes called Fourth World peoples or "First Nations," these peoples, who number some 450 to 550 million (4 percent of the world's population), have long-standing customary rights to large areas of the world but often those rights are not recognized by the states in which they reside; they tend to have the lowest living standards, the highest rates of mortality and morbidity (sickness), and least access to land and natural resources of all of the world's peoples.

Internally displaced person (IDP). Those individuals who have been displaced within the states in which they live; this displacement can be due to a variety of forces, including conflict, drought, involuntary resettlement, or development projects; an IDP has not crossed an internationally recognized border and must rely on his or her government to provide services and assistance (as opposed to official refugees, who have rights under international law).

Intifada. The term given to the outbreak of violence in Israel and Palestine, sometimes viewed as the "Great Uprising" by Palestinians. In Arabic it is characterized as the "shaking off" of the occupation by Israel of what are seen by some as Palestinian territories. It is also described as an effort to seek self-determination on the part of the Palestinians.

Involuntary resettlement. The resettlement of persons or communities without their permission, often done as a result of development projects.

Islam. The religious faith of Muslims which includes belief in Allah as the high god and Mohammed as his prophet. The term "Islam" means "submission," submission to the will of God. The holy cities of Islam, Mecca and Medina, are in western Saudi Arabia, while the Al-Aqsa Mosque in Jerusalem on the Temple Mount is also an important Muslim religious site. Arabs comprise only about a fifth of the world's Muslims, who number today over 1.2 billion people. One of the world's major religious, it is expanding rapidly in many parts of the world, including the United States, which has 7 million Muslims. Islam is sub-divided into Sunni Muslims and Shi'ite Muslims, among other sections. The differences between these groups have to do in part with interpretations of the Quran (Koran), which is seen as the word of God by many Muslims.

Jihad. A term meaning "to exert oneself" or the exercise of "independent judgement" in Islam's holy book, the Quran; it is sometimes translated as "holy war" although many Muslim clerics reject this characterization.

Levirate. A custom whereby a man is obliged to marry his brother's widow.

Lineage. A set of kin who can trace their ancestry back to a known ancestor through genealogically defined links.

Matrilineality. The tracing of descent through the female line; a matrilineage is a lineage that traces descent through females.

Matrilocality. A social rule that specifies that the couple must live with or near the family of the bride.

Minority. A group numerically inferior to the rest of the population of a state, in a non-dominant position, whose members possess ethnic, religious, or linguistic characteristics differing from those of the rest of the population and show, if only implicitly, a sense of solidarity, directed towards preserving their culture, traditions, religions, or language.

Monogamy. Marriage between only one man and one woman at one time; marriage between two individuals.

Nation. A group of communities or individuals that identifies itself as "one people" on the basis of common ancestry, history, social institutions, ideology, language, territory, and, in some cases, religion.

Nilotic. A term given to those Africans whose ancestral territories are in the Nile Basin in northeastern Africa and who speak Nilo-Saharan languages. Some Nilotic people are pastoralists such as the Dinka, Nuer, and Shilluk in southern Sudan and the Maasai in Kenya and Tanzania while others are farmers such as the Sara of Chad.

Nuclear family. A family consisting of a married couple and their children.

Out-migration. The act of moving out of one's territory or country by an individual or group.

Pastoralism. An adaptation in which human groups depend primarily upon domestic animals for subsistence and income.

Patriarchy. A social system that is marked by the supremacy of males or the father in the family or social unit; the legal dependence of wives and children on the father or male family members; often associated with patrilineality, or the reckoning of descent and inheritance through the male line.

Patriclan. A clan tracing descent through the male line (i.e., patrilineal descent reckoning).

Glossary

Patrilineality. Tracing ancestry, reckoning of descent, and organizing inheritance through the male line.

Patrilocality. A social rule that specifies that a married couple lives with or near the husband's parents.

Peacekeeping. A form of social control practiced by the United Nations, regional organizations (e.g., the Organization of African Unity), and nation-state militaries (e.g., the Canadians) in which military force is used to alleviate conflict and, in some cases, to monitor and report on a cease-fire; these operations are seen as temporary and do not aim to replace the voluntary settlement of disputes through negotiation by parties involved in the conflict.

Peasant. A rural food-producing person who is engaged in subsistence production but who also must contribute some of his or her surpluses (or sell those surpluses on the market) to others who do not produce their own food.

Polygamy. A marriage pattern in which a either the male or female has two or more (multiple) spouses.

Polygany. The marital custom whereby a male has several spouses.

Polytheism. The belief in a multiplicity of gods.

Population density. A measure of the number of individuals per unit area.

Refugee. A person who owing to well-founded fear of being persecuted for reasons of race, religion, nationality, membership of a particular social group or political opinion, is outside the country of his or her nationality; there are also "environmental refugees," people who have had to flee their homes because of environmental stress (drought, disasters); and "oustees" or "development refugees," people who have been forced from their homes due to a development project such as a dam, road, or agricultural project.

Repatriation. A term used to refer to the return of refugees to their home countries.

Safe havens and zones. Areas established under protection by institutions such as international organizations, militaries, peace keeping units, police, or national guards; they are established by organizations to ensure the well-being of the population inside these areas.

Sedentism (sedentarization). The process whereby a group settles down and remains residentially stationary year-round; the process of mobility reduction and the establishment of villages or towns.

Shaman. A religious intermediary, usually part-time, whose primary function is to cure people through various means (e.g., through laying on of hands, application of medicinal herbs [in which case s/he is an herbalist], prayer, divination [foretelling the future], or going into trance); sometimes called a "traditional healer" by Westerners.

Slavery. The situation in which a class of persons does not have rights over their own labor or the products of their labor.

Glossary

Society. A group of people who occupy a particular territory and who speak a common language that is not generally understood by neighboring peoples.

Sorcery. The use by a person or persons of materials or other means (e.g., incantations) in which the supernatural world is invoked in order to bring harm to another person or group; also known as witchcraft or negative magic.

State. A political unit with centralized decision-making which has a governmental monopoly on the use of force and which defines its membership; states are characterized by the possession of armies, police, and the judiciary.

Structural adjustment program (SAP). A set of policies of the International Monetary Fund (IMF) and the World Bank that promote changes in the economies of countries, including privatization, cutting back on domestic expenditures, reduction of the size of the civil service (the public sector), and shifting economies more into foreign exchange–earning, export-oriented systems.

Subsistence economy. A term given to economies that are not market-oriented and are based on reciprocal exchanges between persons that are non-monetary in nature (i.e., not based on money).

Taboo. A cultural prohibition that, if it is violated, is said to bring supernatural punishment (e.g., from the ancestors or spirits).

Third World. The developing nations, the South; those countries other than the First World (Western Europe, Canada, the United States, Australia, and New Zealand) and what used to be the Second World (the former Soviet Union and its allies in Eastern Europe), which include countries in Latin America, Africa, Asia, and the Pacific.

Totem. A plant, animal, or other object that is associated with a clan or other kind of social unit that is a symbol of that group and which may, in some cases, not be consumed by the members of that group (i.e., it is taboo to eat that animal or plant).

Transnational corporations (TNCs). Companies that do business in two or more countries and they control much of the trade in products (e.g., food, oil, electronics, pharmaceuticals); they are the main actors moving goods, services, and funds across borders; also known as multinational corporations (MNCs).

Tribe. A type of political unit that is usually associated with food-producing societies that is characterized by links that are both kinship based and non–kinship based (e.g., sodalities or associations that cross-cut societies on the basis of age, gender, occupation, or interest).

United Nations. The world body established in 1945 in which the world's states are members; an intergovernmental organization (IGO) that deliberates on international policy issues ranging from economics to politics and from humanitarian to conflict resolution issues.

Warfare. A state of usually open and declared hostile conflict between two independent political units in the pursuit of national, state, or group policy; armed conflict between two groups or nations.

World Bank. Also known as the International Bank for Reconstruction and Development (IBRD), the World Bank is a multilateral development bank and international finance institution (IF) based in Washington, D.C., that provides technical assistance, development aid, and loans to developing countries; it also monitors and evaluates development projects and programs.

World Trade Organization (WTO). The world body established in January 1995 that oversees international trade and that is the principal forum that negotiates rules and settles disputes in the global trade of goods.

Index

Index

Tuareg man in typical rural dress with his camel near an oasis in the Air Massif, Niger. (Courtesy Susan J. Rasmussen)

still live in rural areas. Rural communities now range from clusters of six to ten nomadic tents, enclosed by fences to keep out goats and temporarily camped to follow herds in search of pasture, to semisedentary hamlets with compounds of tents and adobe houses, to fully sedentarized or settled farming hamlets with mostly walled compounds of adobe houses. These settlements reflect their flexible cultural adaptation to their harsh, unpredictable physical environment and climate.

Traditional Subsistence Strategies

These physical settlement patterns also reflect socioeconomic features of Tuareg culture—namely, mixed occupations of herding and oasis gardening, the caravan trade across the desert, and nowadays, especially for many men, migrant labor. Even today, some men in the Air Mountains of northern Niger still participate in the caravan trade for approximately five months each year, going east first to trade millet cereal for salt and dates in the Saharan

Tenere region of Niger, and then south to Nigeria, for more cereals and household utensils, spices, and clothing. Both men and women inherit, own, and manage animal herds; more generally, this reflects the traditionally high social status and prestige, and economic independence, of many Tuareg women, particularly in nomadic society. Upon recent sedentarization, however, there have been some disadvantages for women. For example, in oasis gardening households, women tend to have more work in processing cereal grains by hand. Food processing restricts them more to the home than does pastoral nomadic herding of animals. There is more specialized artisan (arts/ crafts) work done by smiths, and Islamic scholarship done by Koranic scholars, many of whom inherit their occupations within clans and undergo long apprenticeships in order to acquire necessary skills.

Traditionally, most occupations corresponded to social stratum. Nobles controlled the caravan trade, owned most camels, and remained more nomadic. They came to oases and towns only to collect a proportion of the harvest from their tributary and servile peoples. Tributary, "vassal"-like groups raided and traded for nobles and also herded smaller animals, and tributaries could keep the animals' milk products and some offspring. Peoples of varying degrees of subservient status performed domestic, herding, and caravanning labor for nobles. Yet nobles depended on these peoples, and their statuses and work responsibilities were often flexible, involving mutual rights and obligations that could be negotiated. For example, during slavery, slaves could change owners. Tributaries, while officially subservient to the noble groups who had subjugated them in battles, could gradually acquire some valuable trade items, weapons, and animals they kept for nobles. Many slaves were freed even before official emancipation and abolition of slavery at mid-twentieth century, and they sheltered nobles in their homes farther south during nobles' caravan travel and migration away from disasters such as droughts. Artisans and smiths made jewelry, weapons, and household tools for noble families. But in exchange for all these economic rights and duties, nobles had specific obligations toward these people. For example, nobles provided military protection from outsiders and had a code of honor that made it shameful for them to mistreat tributaries, smiths, and slaves. Nobles were supposed to arrange marriages and assist with former slaves' marriage expenses, were obliged to pay smith/ artisans for their work, give them presents upon demand, and bring them back trade items from caravans. Many of these relationships continue in the countryside, although in modified form because of many social and political changes.

Social and Political Organization

Today, the Tuareg social strata remain important in rural areas, although they are undergoing many changes and are declining in importance in the towns. Formerly, membership in these social strata was based upon descent, that is, handed down from parent to child, and corresponded to specialized occupations of livestock herding, oasis gardening, caravan trade, Koranic scholarship, and black smithing (metal- and stonework, woodwork, and leather work and also including, among rural smiths, additional roles as musicians and oral historians). Nowadays, there is less rigid correspondence between social origin and occupation. Only smith/artisans continue to inherit their occupations and marry most closely within their own group.

Many other Tuareg, despite official rules of marrying only within one's own social category, have recently tended to intermarry with other social strata and practice mixed occupations. For example, while nobles in the past were more nomadic, owned most large animals, controlled the caravan trade, and disdained oasis gardening, many persons of noble descent have recently taken up gardening. Development agencies encourage the Tuareg to settle down and practice gardening, and many Tuareg themselves now believe that gardens bring greater prosperity if there is adequate rainfall. They say that if there is drought, gardens are more easily restored than animal herds.

Tuareg of diverse social origins have also begun tailoring and have opened shops. Recently, migrant labor in Nigeria, Libya, France, and Belgium and tourism work as guides in local travel agencies have become important occupations. Yet many rural nobles, even if impoverished, still claim prestigious social origins and attempt to arrange marriages for their children with partners of similar social background and sometimes between very close relatives who claim a common female ancestor in the same clan. Women, in particular, tend to prefer that their children marry close cousins. Traditionally, the purposes of such marriages were for political alliances and also to keep the property within the family. Property among Tuareg was "bilateral," inherited from both sides of the family, from the male as well as female relatives' sides. But such marriages are increasingly difficult to arrange, and property inheritance is increasingly disputed. There are several reasons for this. In Islam, the Koran decrees that most (two-thirds) of all property left by deceased parents must be inherited by sons; whereas in Tuareg cultural traditions before conversion to Islam in the seventh century, women's property and inheritance through female relatives were strong legal customs. While the latter coexist alongside Koranic inheritance today, nonetheless, Islamic scholars, who serve as lawyers in rural areas, encourage more male-centered inheritance rules. They also tend to encourage marriages favored by men, who sometimes have interests that differ from women in politics and property.

There are additional factors complicating Tuareg marriage and property institutions. Today many persons of noble origins are now poor, and many persons of nonnoble social origins are now wealthier than nobles. The reasons for this are complex and have to do with both the recent droughts and also certain historical influences affecting Tuareg social and political organization. Traditionally, the largest Tuareg political unit is the confederation, a regional group under the leadership of a supreme chief, known as the *amenukal* or sultan. He is also the traditional leader of several clans (each called a *tawsit*) who claim common ancestry from a female founder/culture heroine, grouped together into a unit called a "drum-group." These drum-groups are grouped together in this larger political confederation, under the sultan.

Before French colonialism, the sultan's authority was not absolute or based on coercion; rather, it was based on respect and his role of settling disputes among the warring drum-groups. Beginning with French colonialism, which began in the early twentieth century, his role began to change. The sultan became much more powerful, backed by the military forces of the central states, independent from France since 1960. He became in effect, a liaison or intermediary between the central government and the local Tuareg. His responsibilities included taxation and school registration. Until recently, many noble families tended to avoid sending their children to schools established first by the French and later by the Niger government, viewing these schools as threatening to their culture and livelihood. They felt intimidated when armed soldiers arrived in their homes and demanded a quota of children for school registration. So instead, they sent mostly children of lower-status slaves, smiths, and tributaries to these schools, as a way of resisting what they viewed as outside control. As a result, the children of lower-status persons tended to predominate in secular (non-Koranic) education and more easily found modern jobs.

Another reason for these current social upheavals is in the traditional pattern of occupational specialty. Smith/artisans have always had a special trade skill: the manufacture of jewelry, which is now in much demand among African townspeople and European tourists, most of whom can more easily afford this than many now impoverished Tuareg nobles, who formerly were the smiths' main customers.

Religion and World View

The local belief system, with its own world view and ritual, overlaps with official Islam, rather than standing in rigid opposition to it. That is, many Tuareg practice a combination of pre-Islamic and Islamic beliefs throughout their legal, ritual, symbolic-folkloric, and medical systems. Islam came to the Tuareg from the western Sahara and spread with the migration of holy men belonging to the mystic Sufi order in the seventh century. Various traditions credit Muslim clerics Sidi Okba and Ibn Yacin and an Islamic scholar of the Moroccan Almoravid religious order as proselytizers. The Tuareg initially resisted Islam and earned a reputation among early North African Arab travelers for being lax about some Islamic prac-

About the Editors and Contributors

DEE AKER is director of the WorldLink program and a staff member of the Joan B. Kroc Institute for Peace and Justice at the University of San Diego, San Diego, California.

LEMA BASHIR is a law student at the University of Nebraska at Lincoln.

LOIS BECK is a professor of anthropology in the Department of Anthropology of Washington University, St. Louis, Missouri.

JOHN BOCK is an assistant professor of anthropology in the Department of Anthropology at California State University at Fullerton.

M. CATHERINE DALY is a fellow of the Center for Afghan Studies at the University of Nebraska at Omaha and a development consultant in St. Paul, Minnesota.

LAUREL ERICKSON is the cultural orientation coordinator of the Refugee Resettlement Program at Catholic Social Services in Lincoln, Nebraska.

MARGARET FISHER is a graduate student in the Department of Anthropology and Geography at the University of Nebraska at Lincoln.

RALPH J. HARTLEY is an archaeologist with the National Park Service, Lincoln, Nebraska.

ROBERT K. HITCHCOCK is a professor of anthropology in the Department of Anthropology and Geography of the University of Nebraska at Lincoln.

DAVID HOMA is a high school social science teacher in Fremont, California.

SARA E. JOHNSON is an assistant professor of anthropology in the Department of Anthropology at California State University at Fullerton.

CLEA MSINDO KOFF is a forensic anthropologist for the United Nations.

VIRGINIA LULING is the Africa Campaigns officer of Survival International, London, United Kingdom.

STUART A. MARKS is an adjunct professor of anthropology in the Department of Anthropology at the University of North Carolina at Chapel Hill.

LUCIA ANN McSPADDEN is a senior research fellow of the Life and Peace Research Institute in Uppsala, Sweden.

MONA A. MOHAMED is a development consultant based in Dumfries, Virginia.

ALAN J. OSBORN is an adjunct professor of anthropology in the Department of Anthropology and Geography of the University of Nebraska at Lincoln.

A. OLU OYINLADE is an assistant professor of sociology in the Department of Sociology and Anthropology, University of Nebraska at Omaha.

SUSAN J. RASMUSSEN is a professor of anthropology in the Department of Anthropology of the University of Houston, Houston, Texas.

JEFFREY M. VINCENT is a doctoral student in the Department of City and Regional Planning at the University of California, Berkeley.

Recent Titles in
The Greenwood Press "Endangered Peoples of the World" Series

Endangered Peoples of Southeast and East Asia: Struggles to Survive and Thrive
Leslie E. Sponsel, editor

Endangered Peoples of the Arctic: Struggles to Survive and Thrive
Milton M. R. Freeman, editor

Endangered Peoples of Oceania: Struggles to Survive and Thrive
Judith M. Ftizpatrick, editor

Endangered Peoples of Latin America: Struggles to Survive and Thrive
Susan C. Stonich, editor

Endangered Peoples of Europe: Struggles to Survive and Thrive
Jean S. Forward, editor

Endangered Peoples of North America: Struggles to Survive and Thrive
Tom Greaves, editor